THE LIFE & LETTERS
SERIES, VOLUME 13

CATHERINE THE
GREAT

¶ The *Life and Letters Series* is a selection of non-fiction books previously published at a higher price and now re-issued in a uniform format and at a uniform price.

¶ A list of other titles in the series will be found at the end of this book

CATHERINE THE GREAT
from a lithograph by Motte drawn by Grévedon
photo Mansell

THE LIFE AND LETTERS SERIES NO. 13

KATHERINE   ANTHONY

CATHERINE THE GREAT

With a frontispiece

London - JONATHAN CAPE - Toronto

First published 1926
Re-issued in
The Life and Letters Series
1930

1444

PRINTED IN GREAT BRITAIN BY
LOWE AND BRYDONE (PRINTERS)
LTD. LONDON, :: :: N.W.I

Contents

1 FIKE OF ZERBST IS BORN   11

2 SHE IS EDUCATED   29

3 RUSSIA   44

4 SHE GOES TO RUSSIA   63

5 FIKE BECOMES CATHERINE   84

6 CATHERINE BECOMES A MOTHER   103

7 PONIATOVSKY   123

8 ORLOV   151

9 CATHERINE THE GREAT   185

10 POTIOMKIN   218

11 CATHERINE BECOMES A GRANDMOTHER   256

12 SHE GROWS OLD   287

INDEX   311

Fike of Zerbst is Born

EARLY in the eighteenth century, the north German town of Stettin had all the grim and rigid characteristics of a frontier post. It was a border town and had long been a centre of warfare. The broad rich lands of Pomerania, bursting with fertility, had been repeatedly devastated by the march and countermarch of Russian and Prussian soldiers. High on a strip of barren coast, the grey stone walls of Stettin overlooked a bleak northern sea over which the boats of the great Russian Peter had come sailing to batter and destroy the town. But if Stettin had trembled before Peter, who was six and a half feet tall, it had trembled even more before Frederick William, who was so short that his children called him Stumpy behind his back. Ceded finally to Stumpy by treaty in 1720, Stettin settled down to the dull routine of garrison life.

It was not a place in which the refinements of society flourished. A reviving commercial life brought no relief to the rigid military atmosphere which prevailed. Ships moved out of the harbour laden with guildsmen's stuff from the interior of Germany. A chamber of commerce came into existence, and a new class of prosperous tradespeople appeared on the scene. But the hereditary aristocracy of Stettin was not prosperous. Stumpy's officers were usually hard-up; they were under-paid and over-regimented. Their wives led a dull life in the Prussian garrison where society was neither gay nor gracious. Stettin had no style.

Its military and religious grandees understood each other perfectly. In those days the Prussian warrior was so pious and the Lutheran believer so militant that they faded imperceptibly into each other. Frederick William and Martin Luther worshipped an identical God.

'Ein' feste Burg ist unser Gott,
Ein' gute Wehr und Waffen.'

The Lutheran idol was an armoured hero whom a Prussian soldier could fear and respect. He dominated the spiritual climate of Stettin without a rival, except for the unimportant claims of a Calvinist deity worshipped by the French governesses and emigrant schoolmasters of the place. Luther had elected to throw in his lot with the German nobles, and they in turn had embraced his religion with the puritanical devotion of recent converts. In military circles bigotry was the fashion.

Such was Stettin in 1727, after seven years of regimentation by the Prussian king. In that year there stood at Number One in the Grosse Domstrasse a substantial grey stone house owned by the president of the Handelskammer. A newly-married pair took up their residence there in early winter. They were rather ill-matched as to age, the husband being thirty-seven and the wife fifteen. They were poor but pretentious, the kind of gilded paupers that heralded the decline of feudalism. Prince Christian August of Zerbst-Dornburg was the commander of a regiment of infantry quartered in Stettin. He was one of Frederick William's generals, who had reached this degree of promotion after many years of campaigning in the Prussian service. The business of soldiering had given him little taste or opportunity for home, and the family which he was to found in Stettin was not to see a great deal of him. His wife seemed to manage just as well without him.

The general was a cousin of the reigning Prince of Anhalt-Zerbst who was growing old without an heir. Christian August and his brother, Johann Ludwig, of the Dornburg branch, both had an eye on the little principal-

ity and its petty emoluments which loomed large to them.
The brothers were both pious and unmarried and were on
excellent terms with each other. It was clearly the duty of
one of them to perpetuate the family. But Johann Ludwig, the elder and the natural successor, lived in Jever with
a spinster sister and did not wish to change his state. It
therefore fell to Christian August to go forth and seek a
wife. The history of his wooing is unfortunately not
known to us. Whether he saw it as a duty or an opportunity we cannot say. At any rate, he was successful.

Promoted to the status of a married man and the father
of a family, he was regarded by the elder but childless
brother Ludwig as co-heir. When the reigning duke
finally died the two brothers inherited Zerbst together, and
ruled the principality as co-Regents. They were peace-
loving men who lived in harmony with each other, except
for occasional strife, stimulated, it is said, by sister Sophie
Christine. At any rate, the loyal pair did not live long to
rule in Zerbst. After three years Johann Ludwig died, and
five months later Christian August followed him. Two
months afterward Sophie Christine was buried beside her
brothers. They died as they had lived in the narrow bonds
of mediæval clannishness. It was an unaggressive and
obscure strain. Not all the efforts of German historical
research have availed to discover any brilliance or heroism
in the race.

In the meantime, the marriage of Christian August had
yielded, after some disappointments, the desired heir.
This son lived to become the last reigning Prince of Zerbst
and followed in the undistinguished steps of his ancestors.
Only because he turned out to be the brother of Catherine
of Russia did he become more famous than the rest.
Catherine's memoirs refer with vague sarcasm to the 'peculiar exploits' of his career, and Schlözer speaks of him as a

gentleman of 'unstable temperament.' Although married in his youth for a few brief years, he left no heirs behind. With his death in 1793 the house of Anhalt-Zerbst came to an end. The heroic attempt of his father to perpetuate the family had only resulted in prolonging it by one generation. In the personality of this sterile princeling, however, the general commonplaceness of the Zerbst family was touched with eccentricity. This proceeded without doubt from his mother, who was a clever, energetic and hysterical woman.

Johanna Elizabeth of Holstein-Gottorp was not yet sixteen when she married her Prussian general, yet she ruled the family from the first. The portraits of this lady and her spouse which hang in the Potsdam palace reveal, even through the conventional art of Pesne, marked differences of temperament. The general has the dreamy eye that betrays the extreme idealist, while his wife looks out with the peculiar verve and readiness of a real woman of action. 'Apparently they got on excellently with each other,' says their daughter in her memoirs, 'in spite of the great difference in age and although their inclinations were so different. My father, for instance, was very saving; my mother, on the other hand, was quite extravagant and openhanded. My mother loved pleasure and fashionable society exceedingly; my father valued retirement. She was cheerful and wilful; he serious and austere in his morality. . . . My mother passed as more clever and intellectual than my father; but he was a man of earnest and sterling character and well-stocked knowledge. He liked to read, as did my mother, but all that she knew was very superficial. Her spirit and beauty had won for her a great reputation; moreover, she understood the ways of the fashionable world better than my father.'

Christian August had married his wife at the Court of

the Duchess of Brunswick, her godmother, who had brought her up as if she were her own child. Johanna Elizabeth was the daughter of the Bishop of Lübeck, who had twelve children. Having lost Schleswig to the Danes, and finding himself therefore in reduced circumstances, he willingly gave away one of his children to the kind godmother who offered to bring her up. The Court of Brunswick, which thus became the home of the keen little Princess of Holstein-Gottorp, was one of the most showy in Germany. It was far more elegant than the Court of the parsimonious King of Prussia. Here Johanna Elizabeth seems to have grown up partly as a much-spoiled favourite and partly as a poor relation. She brought nothing to her marriage but the bridal chest given her by her godmother. The newly-married pair started housekeeping in the Domstrasse house in the most frugal circumstances. Garrison life must have seemed sordid to her after the refinements of Brunswick. One hope at least she had. If she produced an heir she might one day become the reigning Princess of Anhalt-Zerbst instead of being merely the wife of a Prussian general in a garrison town.

In the meantime she made the most of being a Holstein-Gottorp, a clan whose members had married royalty and were related to thrones. Johanna Elizabeth's brother had been affianced to the youngest daughter of Peter the Great and, but for his death by the smallpox, would have become the great Czar's son-in-law. Johanna Elizabeth's first cousin, who was a nephew of Charles XII of Sweden, had married another daughter of Peter the Great, and had left a son who had claims upon the thrones of both Sweden and Russia.

These alliances with Holstein-Gottorps were supposed to bring to Russia a strip of sea-coast, and sea-coast was Peter's passion. No doubt he regretted that he had only two daughters to sell for a bit of strand. But he never realized on these schemes, and the young ladies themselves fared badly. Elizabeth, who lost her betrothed through smallpox, remained unmarried all her life, while Anne, who went to live in Kiel, was scandalously neglected by her husband. 'I have to tell you,' she wrote to her sister, 'that the Duke and Mavrushka [her best friend] are quite loose. He stays not a single day at home, rides out with her in the same carriage, or goes visiting or to the theatre.' Poor jealous Anne was obliged to stay at home because she expected a child. Three months after its birth, she gave up her spiritless existence and died of 'tuberculosis and homesickness.' Her son, who was called Karl Peter Ulrich, was handed over to nurses and developed into a sickly, unpromising boy.

But no tragedy could dim the lustre of the Russian connection in the eyes of the romantic Johanna Elizabeth of Holstein-Gottorp. She felt that her husband should announce their marriage to the Russian Court. The Prince of Zerbst therefore wrote: 'Imperial Highness: May you, in your world-renowned magnanimity, not take it ill that I venture to inform you with the most humble respect that on the eighth of November, after previous betrothal, I married the youngest sister of the Bishop of Lübeck recently deceased in Petersburg, the Princess Johanna Elizabeth of Holstein-Gottorp, in the country seat of Weheln in Brunswick-Wolfenbüttel.' This humble composition bears all the marks of being the Prince's own.

Soon after her marriage, the Princess made a round of visits accompanied by her husband in order to present the general to his numerous Holstein relatives. 'In this week,' says a family letter, 'comes the Princess Elizabeth and her husband.' The Holsteiners were not especially impressed by the Prince of Zerbst and took him rather casually from the first. As time went on the Princess managed to escape from the dullness of her Stettin home as much and as often as possible by making long visits to Holstein relatives in Hamburg and Brunswick. After the first formalities of introduction were over she left her husband at home. But she was always accompanied by her daughter on these restless flights from the tedium of small town life.

§ 2

The ambitious Lady of Zerbst had encountered several discouragements in the matter of producing an heir. Her first child, born May 2, 1729, in the Domstrasse house, was a girl. 'It has been told me,' wrote this girl, looking back after forty years, 'that I was not so very joyfully welcomed when I first appeared because a son was expected. My father, however, showed more satisfaction than did his suite.' Perhaps his natural reserve and a certain philosophy which he undoubtedly possessed helped him to conceal his disappointment. The Princess's chagrin can easily be imagined. The child had nearly cost the sixteen-year-old mother her life. We can picture the ordeal of her confinement in the small bedroom one flight above the noisy Domstrasse: the long Lutheran Sunday which happened also to be May Day; the morning and evening chiming of the church bells; the religious atmosphere of a prayerfully expectant household; the crude methods of the midwife; the waiting cradle and the charcoal pan beside which the first-born son was presently to be swaddled. Finally in the grey dawn of Monday morning, at the chill hour of half-past two, a daughter was born instead of the expected son.

As the new-born infant lay in her cradle, the charcoal pan set fire to the floor. The board was almost burned through before anyone noticed it, so preoccupied was everybody with the condition of the mother. The new baby was further overlooked in several ways. Neither her birth nor her baptism was registered in any Stettin church, an extraordinary omission on the part of such a pious family. The only birth record in existence is the letter which Christian August wrote to Cousin Johann August who was waiting with his childless wife at Anhalt-Zerbst to hear the outcome of events at Stettin. The general announced that his consort had been delivered that morning of a Princess-daughter who would be baptized on the next day but one, and would receive the name of Sophie Auguste Friedrike. The little girl was always called Fike.

Of Fike's relation to her parents, she says, 'My father, whom I saw less frequently, regarded me as an angel; my mother did not trouble much about me. A year and a half later she bore a son whom she loved idolatrously. I was merely endured and was often harshly and vehemently scolded, and not always with justice. I felt this without being, however, quite clear in my knowledge.'

This son, Wilhelm Christian, at first an object of so much pride, soon became a source of deep concern and even of humiliation. From an unknown cause, which was discovered after his death to have been a dislocated hip, he was from infancy a cripple unable to walk without a crutch. He died at the age of twelve. Johanna Elizabeth's talent for the enhancement of life's experiences is shown again in her exaggerated grief at her son's death. 'My mother was inconsolable,' writes Fike, 'and the presence of the entire family was necessary to help her bear her grief.' Even Fike's old grandmother journeyed all the way down from Hamburg to Dornburg to comfort the bereaved Princess. But a second son, Friedrich August, born in 1734, came to take his brother's place, and eventually to become the last Prince of Anhalt-Zerbst. Two more daughters were added to the family but both died in infancy. Of the five children, only two, Fike and Fritz, lived to grow up.

Fike was oldest sister. She played teacher to her brothers, training them in the art of penmanship as she had learned it from Monsieur Laurent and Pastor Wagner. This doubtless meant a saving for the general's purse, which was always too slender for the requirements of Fike's mother. When, at the age of fifteen, she held in her hands the first money which she had ever owned and which had been given her by the Russian Empress for card-playing, she wrote to her father at once, 'I have heard that your Highness has sent my brother to Homburg; I know that this occasions a rather heavy expense. I beg your Highness to allow my brother to remain there as long as necessary for his recovery, requesting for myself the privilege of paying all his expenses; and beg your Highness to mention a banker to whom I may send whatever is necessary.' Her maternal attitude towards Fritz survived for many years. As an Empress she played with the idea of making him an Elector, but nothing came of it. The best that she could ever do for him, after she had become an influence in the international politics of Europe, was to restore him to his modest inheritance of Anhalt-Zerbst, which through his own and his mother's folly had been temporarily lost.

§ 3

Born a girl, Fike's only prospect for a career was to become the wife of some German princeling whose rank was at least equal to that of brother Fritz. Her chances of marriage were often discussed in her presence. They were not brilliant. In the first place, the girl was not beautiful.

Catherine the Great

'I do not know for sure,' she says in her memoirs, 'whether as a child I was really ugly, but I remember well this was often said of me, and that I must therefore strive to show inward excellence and intelligence. Up to the age of fourteen or fifteen years, I was firmly convinced of my ugliness, and was therefore more concerned with acquiring inward accomplishments and was less mindful of my looks. I have seen a portrait of myself painted when I was ten years old, and that is certainly very ugly. If it really resembled me, they told me nothing false.' While this confession tells us little of Fike's real looks as a young girl, it tells us a great deal about her private hopes of getting a husband.

It was not as if her parents could dower her with influence or riches. There was, for instance, her third cousin in Eutin, the son of the dead Anna Petrovna, a peevish boy for whom no one had a good word. Sophie's mother dangled the sickly Duke of Holstein before her daughter's eyes from time to time, only to withdraw him again with the remark, 'Not him; he needs a wife who can support his rights and claims by the power and prestige of her family. My daughter will not be suitable for him.' More hopeful was old Bolhagen, a faithful henchman of Fike's father, who visited the nursery every afternoon and there spun yarns about his travels. One afternoon when Fike was seven, the old man brought with him a newspaper from which he read the report of the marriage of the Princess Augusta of Saxe-Gotha with the Prince of Wales. 'Do you know,' said the old soldier to the governess, 'this Princess is not really so well educated as ours, and nevertheless, she is now destined to become Queen of England. Who knows what ours may yet become?' 'He then began,' says Fike, 'to preach to me wisdom and Christian virtues, and stern morality, to the end that I might be worthy to wear a crown, should one ever be allotted to me. This

crown never again went out of my head and has since given
me much to do.'

This story indicates that the girl began to think of marriage at the age of seven. By the time she was fifteen she
had had a long time to occupy herself with hopes and fears.
In her memoirs there is no mention of the latter. Perhaps
the passage of years erased these unhappy recollections.
On the other hand, her memory for episodes in which this
Prince or that sued for her hand and was turned away by
her high-minded father is very good. Her account of how
Prince Henry of Prussia almost became a suitor does
not quite ring true, although one's imagination likes to
dwell on the possible consequences of such a union. What
would the aggressive Sophie of Zerbst have done had she
been immured like those other women who were married
to the Princes of Prussia, the wives of Prince Henry and
Great Frederick himself? It is hardly conceivable that
she would have succumbed without adding a dramatic
chapter to the annals of the Prussian house.

As a portionless Princess, she had probably considered
before she was fifteen the alternative to marriage. The
alternative was vivid enough. Both sides of her family
bristled with old maids. Two hundred years of Lutheran-
ism had failed to abolish celibacy among the daughters of
the German nobility. For, while Luther preached against
celibacy, he also preached in favour of monogamy. The
combination, however, was better adapted to the stable
bourgeois class which was just beginning to dominate
society than to the restless aristocracy which has flourished
in the Middle Ages. The feudal families who went over to
the Reformation and the Lutheran idea of marriage were
still obliged to dedicate as many surplus daughters as ever
to the convents and priories.

Little Princess Fike had several aunts who lived in convents. There was great-aunt Marie Elizabeth who was Abbess of Quedlinburg; and Aunt Hedwig Sophie who was Provost in the same abbey. There was also Aunt Sophie Christine who was Canoness of Gandersheim. Fike often went with her mother to visit the aunts at Quedlinburg. 'These two Holstein princesses,' she says, 'who remained unmarried and had to live in one and the same house, quarrelled incessantly and often refused to see each other for years at a time. My mother often tried to mediate between them, and sometimes she was successful.'

Fike's memories of her aunts remained ever vivid. Her portraits of them, penned after thirty years of life in Russia, have a clearness of detail like that of a Dürer drawing. 'The Princess-Provost Hedwig Sophie Augusta was a great friend of dogs and especially loved the so-called pugs. As a child, I have been amazed to see at one time in her chamber, which measured in size at most four cords of wood, as many as sixteen pugs. Many of the curs had young, which also lived in the same room with my aunt. They slept and ate there and attended to their necessities. A maid was employed to keep them clean and this took her the whole day. A large number of parrots besides lived in the same room; one can imagine the fragrance which reigned there! When the Princess drove out, she had always in her carriage at least one parrot and a half a dozen dogs; the latter even accompanied her to church. I have never seen anyone who loved animals as much as she; she was wholly occupied with them the livelong day and only bestirred herself for their sakes. She had consequently grown quite stout, which, with her short stature, made her very ugly and even deformed. The Princess might have had her talents had she taken any trouble. She wrote German and French in the most beautiful hand that I have ever seen written by a woman.'

22

This dumpy old lady was **an** elder sister of Fike's mother, who was by contrast in her daughter's eyes the perfect pattern of beauty, grace, and fashion. Fike herself, who was not beautiful and had only her fine handwriting and good conduct to recommend her, might easily end her days at Quedlinburg in a room no bigger than four cords of wood, with a family of dogs. To be sure Aunt Hedwig might have had a bigger room and a much better thing of it altogether if she were appointed, as Fike's great-aunt had been, Abbess of Quedlinburg. Fike's mother tried to bring this about by using her influence, which she over-estimated, with the Prussian King. But Frederick had a sister of his own who needed this refuge and who eventually got it. Even to become a prioress, there was competition. Everywhere there was competition in life. This was one of the earliest lessons that Fike absorbed from her worldly-wise mother.

Another aunt, an elder sister of her father's, is also portrayed in her memoirs. Tante Sophie Christine, Canoness of Gandersheim, is the same spinster lady who is said to have fomented quarrels between her brothers, the Princes of Zerbst. 'She was more than fifty,' writes her niece, 'very tall and so thin that I had at eleven years old a bigger waist than hers; she was, however, very proud of her figure. At six o'clock when she arose she carefully laced herself in, and only took off her stays when she went to bed. She used to maintain that she had once been beautiful but that an accident had damaged her beauty. When she was ten years old her powder-mantle had caught fire and thereby the lower part of her face had been seriously hurt; the chin and the lower part of the cheeks were shrivelled up, and the parchment skin really looked ghastly. She was kind and good, but when she wanted anything, very hard-headed too. Upon the various German Princes who had passed under her inspection, she had made serious demands, and but for lack of willingness on their part she might have been well married.

'She made wonderful embroidery and loved birds very much. Her kind heart mostly went out to those who had suffered a misfortune. I have seen in her chamber a thrush that had only one foot, a lark with a broken wing, a one-eyed goldfinch, a hen whose head was halfway pecked off by the cock, a cock whose tail-feathers had been torn out by the cat, a lame and lop-sided nightingale, a parrot that could not use its feet and lay flat on its belly, and many other birds of different kinds that ran and flew about her room. I was a very lively and right wilful child, and I re-member how once I offended this Princess by doing some-thing for which she never forgave me. I was left alone in her room for a few moments and the idea of opening the window occurred to me. Naturally half of the menagerie flew out! I shut the window and ran away. When my aunt returned she found only her little cripples left. She could guess how this had happened and her room was in the future closed to me.'

Fike's gallery of portraits includes another spinster, Fräulein Khayn, who always accompanied her mother and herself on their travels. In the depths of the bitterly cold winter of 1740, the restless Johanna and her daughter, together with the companion, went to visit the old Duchess of Brunswick. 'I slept in the same room with Fräulein Khayn, a companion of my mother's,' says Fike. 'My bed stood against the wall and hers not far from mine, with only a small passage between. Another passage remained open between the windows and the bed of Fräulein Khayn. On a table between the windows stood a water-pitcher, a silver basin, and a night-light. The only door of the room was at the foot of the bed and was closed. Towards mid-

night, I was suddenly awakened by some one who lay down
beside me in bed; I opened my eyes and saw that it was
Fräulein Khayn. I asked her why she wanted to come into
my bed. She answered, "For God's sake let me be and go
to sleep quietly." I wanted to know what had caused her
to leave her bed and come to mine, for I saw that she was
trembling from fright and was almost speechless. When
I pressed her she said, "Don't you see what is going on in
the room and what is there on the table?" and drew the
cover over her face. I got on my knees, and reached over
her to draw away the curtain and see what was going on.
But I heard and saw absolutely nothing. The door was
closed; candles, basin, and silver pitcher were on the table.
I told her what I saw and she became somewhat quieter.
A few minutes later she arose to shove the bolt on the door,
but it was already locked. I went to sleep again, but the
next morning she looked wretched and quite distracted.
I wanted now to know why and what she thought she
had seen in the night; but she answered that she could not
say. I knew that she believed in ghosts and visions and
that she often claimed to have seen apparitions. She often
said that she was a Sunday child and that those who were
born on other days did not have the clear sight that she
had. I related the occurrence to my mother who was
already accustomed to Fräulein Khayn's experiences.
Often she had frightened and disturbed my mother. I
have often wondered why this adventure did not make me
fearful.'

Fike must have been deeply interested in the eccentricities of all these spinster ladies since she remembered and
described them so vividly so many years afterwards. Her
mother, the Princess Johanna Elizabeth, towered above
other women and also above her honest and pious consort,
undoubtedly a superior being. The Princess had a way of

absorbing the whole environment within herself and becoming its embodiment. Fike writes, for instance, 'My mother had that year an extraordinary adventure on the return journey to Stettin.' As the story develops, one learns that Fike herself, the ever-present Khayn, another attendant, and several postilions, shared along with Fike's mother the adventure of being lost in a terrible snowstorm. On another occasion, when Frederick the Great ascended the throne, Fike says, 'When my father had received in the name of the King of Prussia the allegiance of Pomerania, my mother journeyed to Berlin.' There several events took place at Court in the account of which the General is not mentioned. Presumably as the Governor of Stettin, he accompanied the party and had his day at Court as well. In the eyes of his little daughter, moving in her accustomed place in her mother's entourage, the General appears to have played a minor part even when he was officially the centre of the picture.

Princess Johanna Elizabeth was a clever woman but also a bit of a fool; that is to say, she was romantic and proud. As the wife of the Governor of Stettin, she tried to introduce in her dull town some semblance of Court etiquette. For instance, she required Fike to kiss the hem of the garments of distinguished ladies who visited the house. When the old King of Prussia died, she strove to induce the ladies of Stettin to wear mourning as the Court at Berlin was doing. But so cordially was the old King hated that not a lady would wear black for him. The Princess and her daughter and the faithful Khayn went bravely forth for a couple of Sundays in solemn weeds, but all the other Stettin dames united against them and the Princess was at last obliged to give up the fight.

While little Fike lived in a chronic state of filial bedazzlement, she had occasional glimpses of fact that left

26

their mark. When her mother visited the Court at Berlin, she was questioned there about the mourning episode at Stettin. 'She denied the fact,' says Fike. 'I was present and wondered greatly at this. It was the first time I had ever heard anyone deny a fact. I thought to myself, is it possible that my mother has forgotten something which happened so recently? I was near to reminding her; but I restrained myself, and that was surely my good fortune.'

The Princess was not always truthful. Deliberate falsehoods of the kind that her daughter noted at Berlin were probably not usual. But she was a fluent weaver of inward and outward deceptions, and she usually wore her rose-coloured glasses when she sat down to her correspondence. In this respect Fike was quite different from her mother. Although she could lie brazenly, for reasons, she had a clear sense of reality, and her letters and memoirs are remarkable for the small amount of romancing they contain.

Perhaps she had from her father, the Prince of Anhalt, a saving sense of moderation. He occupies so little space in his daughter's memoirs that no clear picture of his character is possible. But certain traits come through in his correspondence. In spite of his stiff pedantic style he reports the facts more reliably than does his wife in her more eloquent epistles. His ambition was tempered with philosophy. At one time in his life, after his daughter had gone to Russia, he tried unsuccessfully to become the Duke of Courland. 'I am, thank God,' he wrote, 'well satisfied with what I possess, yet I should like to hear no reproaches later that we had slept away our luck at such a favourable moment.'

This is the only time in his history that he shows himself in a covetous light. Perhaps his motive in grasping at

Courland was to be nearer to his daughter in Russia. He seemed to realize, as his wife did not, that German Princesses who married into the Czar's family had a way of being neglected and mislaid in that vast uncharted country.

2

She is Educated

WHILE Fike was still quite small, her father received an unexciting promotion. Already Commander of the garrison, he was made Governor of Stettin. This change did not bring the family any nearer to the goal of the Princess's hopes, a residence in Berlin. But it did rescue them from the commonplace house in the Domstrasse which Fike afterwards in the days of her grandeur referred to as 'Greifenheim's house.' As Governor of Stettin, her father was given quarters in the ancestral castle of the Duke of Pomerania. It was a gloomy rectangular structure surrounding a roughly-paved courtyard, and including as a corner building a church with a bell-tower. Fike's bedroom adjoined the bell-tower.

The family occupied the third storey of the left wing, the Princess's apartments being next to the entrance and her daughter's next to the church. Two or three times a day the little girl was allowed to visit her mother. In her memoirs she describes how she ran through the long corridor, but does not describe the visits. The supervision over her daughter's education with which the Princess is credited was apparently of the slightest. She was preoccupied with other things; an unambitious husband and an invalid son gave her plenty to think about. Besides, the family finances were not improved by the general's promotion. He still clung to his parsimonious habits and was backed up by his second in command, old Bolhagen, who as under-governor lived also in the Pomeranian castle and was always close at hand to help him. 'My father did almost nothing without at least asking him about it,' says Fike. It was certainly a situation which any wife would need philosophy to bear. The harassed lady was often driven to extremes. She railed at old Bolhagen that he 'did not love her,' and she boxed her daughter's ears from sheer irritation.

The two Princesses came to be familiar figures at several North German Courts, for Fike after the age of eight always accompanied her mother on her travels. Had the search for a husband already begun? Probably so; the conversation at home seems to indicate as much. The Princess neglected her daughter abroad, as well as at home. This did not escape notice, and Fike occasionally had the satisfaction of hearing strangers, with whom she early discovered how to get on, rebuke the Princess for her maternal indifference. In this way, the Swedish Count Gyllenborg incurred the lifelong gratitude of the proud, sensitive child. 'When he saw,' says Fike, 'how little or rather how not at all my mother occupied herself with me, he said to her that she was not right in giving me so little attention; that I was for my age a very well-developed child.'

Still another partisan was unexpectedly raised up in the person of a Catholic monk by the name of Mengden, whom Fike and her mother met at the Court of Brunswick. The monk occupied himself with palmistry and prophecy, which were, by the way, forbidden by his Church. The Princess gravitated towards the sorcerer, leading by the hand the little Princess Marianna of Brunswick-Bevern, to whom she had taken a great fancy. She praised the beauty of Marianna and demanded that the monk should prophesy a crown for her. 'He heard,' says Fike, 'how my mother praised the Princess and what she prophesied; he said to her that he saw not a single crown in the features of the Princess but that he saw at least three above my forehead.'

Fike never forgot this episode and related it more than once. She also thought it sufficiently important to mention in her memoirs thirty years later that the petted and beautiful Brunswick Princess eventually died unmarried. The plain little Fike, who was to become the apostle of enlightenment, continued always to believe in that fortune-telling monk.

Fike really owed her education to her French governess, Elizabeth Cardel, and her German tutor, Pastor Wagner. With Mademoiselle Cardel she spent her days and nights in the three small rooms beneath the bell-tower. They were Fike and Babet to each other. Babet must be the key to much that afterwards astonished the world in the Empress of Russia. But what the French governess was like it would be difficult to say. She has vanished into the limbo which is reserved for the domestic servants of the famous. Our history books do not consider these people important. But almost any child takes her nurse or governess quite seriously, and is influenced by her character regardless of the difference in their social station. The personality of the servant who cares for genius in its helpless infancy and during its stumbling childhood is a factor for biography to reckon with.

Certainly Babet Cardel was no ordinary servant; perhaps no ordinary individual. She may have been an extraordinary person. All we know of her is contained in the letters and memoirs of the pupil on whom she left her impress. She was another genteel spinster, but was of a tougher-minded variety than the German aunts and lady companions who otherwise figured in Fike's life. She never saw ghosts and she worshipped neither animals nor God too much. Without using flattery or caresses she knew how to gain and keep the affections of her pupil. Fike was a secretive child, yet she had no secrets from Babet, and this was partly because Babet was clever. **Her**

31

pupil had a lifelong habit of ready, off-hand scorn for stupidity.

The Cardel family were French emigrants; the father was a professor in Frankfort. Two daughters, Madeleine and Elizabeth, made their way to Stettin, where Madeleine was employed as Fike's governess. When her pupil was nearly four Madeleine was married to an advocate named Colhard. The child made a scene at parting. 'At Madame Colhard's wedding,' say her memoirs, 'I drank too much and would not go to bed without her. I bawled so loudly that they had to take me out and put me to bed with my parents.' Fike passed into the hands of Elizabeth Cardel. The two sisters were opposites: Madeleine was showy and insincere while Elizabeth was just and consistent. Madeleine 'took great pains,' says her pupil, 'to have me always appear before my parents in such a way that I, and she also, should please them. So it came about that I was for my years rather "deep." '

Babet laid less stress on appearances and strove to counteract the superficial methods of her sister. But Fike had acquired once for all the knack of making an impression. She was a canny child, precocious in her criticism of her environment and precocious in her ability to keep her own counsel. Babet, who was something of a phrase-maker, called her an 'esprit gauche.' In mature years, Fike still delighted in the title. 'Mademoiselle Cardel and Herr Wagner had to deal with a perverse spirit who took all that was said to her in the opposite sense.' Oppressed by moralities and preachments, her eager, curious nature took refuge behind a smiling but critical silence. 'One does not always know what children are thinking,' she says. 'Children are hard to understand, especially when careful training has accustomed them to obedience, and experience has made them cautious in conversations with their elders.'

Next to Elizabeth Cardel, Pastor Wagner was second in command. Fike called herself, 'half Mademoiselle Cardel's, half Pastor Wagner's pupil.' With Pastor Wagner she studied religion, history, and geography. He also taught her to write German, while Monsieur Laurent, a Calvinist schoolmaster, taught her French 'calligraphy.' A French dancing-master came to the little room beside the bell-tower, placed the four-year-old child on a table and trained her in positions and steps. 'This was money thrown away,' remarked the affluent Empress of Russia many years later; doubtless an echo of dear Papa's views, hardly of dear Mamma's. For seven long years Babet, who was musical herself, struggled to teach her pupil the rudiments of singing, but gave it up at last as hopeless. A music-master by the name of Roellig was called in at Zerbst, but his efforts also were fruitless. A drawing-teacher she never had; but somewhere along in her career she learned both carving and engraving, arts which she cultivated later in Russia. Her skill at embroidery is evidenced by rich ecclesiastical robes still preserved in Russian museums.

Fike afterwards described her teachers, always excepting Mademoiselle Cardel, as a rather poor set. Monsieur Laurent was 'an old weak-head who in his youth was but a dunce,' a Frenchman who spoke German 'like a Spanish cow.' The music-master was preserved in a burlesque sketch addressed to Grimm. 'About the poor devil Roellig I have never told you yet, because you know what success his lessons had. He always brought with him a creature who roared bass. He had him sing in my room; I listened to him and said to myself, "he roars like a bull," but Herr Roellig was beside himself with delight whenever this bass throat was in action.' Concerning Wagner and Cardel, she offered as her mature judgment: 'I cherish absolutely no grudge against Herr Wagner, but I am convinced in my inmost soul that he was a blockhead and that Mademoiselle Cardel was a clever girl.'

Fike scoffed at her education as she scoffed at her teachers. 'Very early it was noticed that I had a good memory; therefore I was incessantly tormented with learning by rote. They called it training the memory; but I believe it to have been rather a weakening. At first it was Bible verses; then specially-prepared pieces on the fables of La Fontaine which I had to commit to memory and repeat. If I forgot anything, I was scolded; I believe, however, it was not humanly possible to retain all that I had to memorize; also I do not think it worth the trouble. I still possess a German Bible in which all the verses which I had to learn are underlined with red ink.'

The most valuable part of her education was incidental to her association with Babet, 'who knew everything without having learned anything; she knew all the comedies and tragedies like her five fingers and was very amusing.' Babet's vocabulary and phrases were drawn from her reading. Often she reminded her pupil that the word 'Monsieur' 'never broke anyone's jaw-bone,' a phrase which Fike assumed had been drawn from some old comedy. She read Corneille and Racine and was saturated with Molière, who consequently became the daily bread of her pupil. Her favourite authority was 'common sense,' which she evoked habitually. 'That is not common sense,' represented a final judgment with the governess as it eventually did with the Empress. Everybody else in Fike's early environment dealt in moral principles and religious dogmas; Babet seems to have been a realist.

The governess had friends, French emigrants like herself, intellectuals, who are to be distinguished from the simple-minded Laurent, master of calligraphy. Babet received on Sundays in the nursery a certain Monsieur de Mauclerc, a clergyman, who was remembered by Fike chiefly as the editor of a History of England written by his father-in-law, Rapin Thoiras. The Mauclerc-Thoiras circle was pro-English, which meant in those days that they were philosophers and liberals. With these fellow-exiles of hers Babet was intimate, and her pupil was adopted by the group. In their circle Fike had her first experience of good conversation, which she afterwards passionately pursued as one of the main interests of her life. Here she learned to know as clever and delightful people those whom Pastor Wagner regarded as heretics. 'So far as Wagner was concerned, he had nothing in common with these arch-heretics who did not understand his language; nor he, theirs.' But Fike felt herself able through language and imagination to bridge the mental chasm which yawned between her French governess and her German tutor.

§ 2

The Princes of Anhalt-Zerbst were a pious line. Before the Reformation, one of them had been a celebrated saint. The sight of him wearing a monastic garb, emaciated by fasting and begging through the streets, had so impressed Martin Luther as a boy that it had helped to send him into a monastery. Zerbst had been close to the war with Tetzel about indulgences and the contemporary Prince of Anhalt had early ranged himself on the side of the reformer. Two hundred years before Fike was born, Luther had been intimate with the head of the house of Anhalt and had played chess with him. The passage of six generations had dimmed the worldly glory of these Princes, but the heritage of piety had persisted undiminished.

Prince Christian August followed in the footsteps of his forbears. He was a rigid Protestant, one of those puritanical Lutherans, who, according to Frederick the Great, were still numerous in that day. Frederick seemed to think that the cult had declined during his reign. But the free-thinking King exaggerated the extent of his own influence, which did not reach far beyond his own round table. The pious Princes of Germany, the special creation of Dr. Martin Luther, were destined to survive many centuries. Long after Frederick was dead and buried, they continued to impress their sombre personalities upon the history of Europe by marrying into all its royal families. Fike's father was one of these sombre personalities.

It was a matter of course that the daughter of Christian August should be educated by an evangelical pastor. In her little room against the church, so close that the sound of the organ came through, the parson instructed her and put her through her so-called *Prüfungen*. These examinations were high lights in a monotonous childhood. The reverend, black-robed gentleman did not scamp his duty like the music-master Roellig. He built himself into the very foundation of his pupil's character. Although she ultimately decided that he was a pedant and a block-head, she never forgot his teachings. The spirit of her old teacher accompanied her to Russia where he frequently walked and talked, and never out of character. As a middle-aged Empress, she would often quote him thus: 'The joys of this world, according to Herr Wagner, are not worth its pains'; or, 'The world is not good for much, said the blessed Herr Wagner, because of original sin.' Or, 'You say to me that the evils for which there is no remedy, can be met with peace and resignation. You learned that from your father; it is exactly the same thing that the blessed Herr Wagner, of ancient memory, used to say.' The pastor often discoursed to his pupil on the Last Judgment. Fike was so impressed with the difficulty of being saved that she began to have fits of weeping at twilight. Babet found her hiding behind the window curtains to indulge these melancholy thoughts, and induced the child to tell her the reason. Herr Wagner was forbidden to frighten Fike in the future with his sermons on the Last Judgment.

The pastor was the faithful representative of the Princess's father. He was dear Papa's man. The Prince of Anhalt, always on the march, could rest easy in the thought that his daughter was being firmly grounded in the doctrine of her fathers. In addition to her daily lessons with Herr Wagner, who was after all merely an army chaplain, she had higher religious education from the Lutheran pastor at Brunswick. By the time she was fourteen, the Prince could well afford to congratulate himself, as he did, on the thoroughness of his daughter's religious foundation.

Yet Fike did not swallow Wagner whole; she argued with him. She declared it unjust that Marcus Aurelius and others of antiquity should be damned because they had not known salvation. The pastor proved by chapter and verse that they were damned, but his pupil stubbornly defended her point. Babet Cardel was called in by the irate pedagogue and the governess patched up a peace between them. A second argument arose on the subject of chaos. Chaos, said the teacher, is what went before

37

the world. 'But what is Chaos?' demanded the pupil. And again Babet had to intervene and make peace. It was the same way with circumcision, which the pastor refused to explain. Babet's tact was once more called into service and order restored. It appears that Babet was not allowed to use the rod. Only dear Mamma could do that. But a quick box on the ears was more in Mamma's manner.

Fike was conscious of solid obstacles in her world. If she had been a boy her life would have been different. She would one day have ruled over Anhalt-Zerbst instead of Fritz. But girls do not reign. In Fike's home, however, everything was ruled by women. The Princess Johanna Elizabeth managed her husband and smacked her daughter. As between Babet Cardel and Pastor Wagner, it was always Babet who decided things and gave orders to the pastor. If Mamma had been a Prussian General, even under the close-fisted Frederick William, who wore a short coat because he was too stingy to buy cloth for a long one, she would not have been content with the small pay and inferior post of the Prince, her husband. The Princess was proud and ambitious. But she had obvious faults as a tactician; her nerves and quick temper sometimes betrayed her. Babet, who ruled by common sense and reason, was a better diplomatist. Fike had to admire Babet since she herself invariably succumbed to Babet's methods.

An old German Baroness who lived in the Stettin household says this of Fike's childhood: 'Princess Sophie was born, grew up, and was educated under my eyes. I witnessed her school instruction and her progress and I helped her to pack her trunks before her departure [for Russia]. I enjoyed her confidence to a degree that entitled me to believe that I knew her better than anybody else. Yet I had no idea that she was destined to attain so much fame. In her youth I noticed in her a serious, calculating and cold personality, which was as far removed from anything distinguished or brilliant as it was from error, eccentricity and frivolity. In a word, I thought her just an ordinary person.'

If the Princess of Zerbst did not make much of her daughter, it is not likely that one of her women would have held a different opinion. Probably the young girl was sufficiently commonplace. It remained for circumstances to make her into the unique and powerful personality that she came to be. For the rest, it is true that at all stages of her life she was more cool and calculating than she was eccentric and frivolous. To this extent the Baroness was right.

§ 3

Fike grew up in an atmosphere of illness. The first misfortune of the kind which befell the family was when her mother lay nineteen weeks in bed after her birth. The Princess had a delicate constitution. In letters which are still preserved in the archives at Moscow in a binding of pink plush lined with blue silk, she complains of the 'vapours' and the 'crampe d'estomac' as afflictions from which she habitually suffered. She could not endure blood-letting either for herself or her children, and since this was the only resource of the doctors of those days she was not a good patient.

Two daughters of the house died in infancy and two sons developed into invalids. The elder had a genuine affliction, a dislocated hip, which obliged him to walk with a crutch. The poor boy was dosed incessantly and sent to the baths at Teplitz and Karlsbad, but all in vain. The best physicians in Germany were consulted but were never able to diagnose his case until after his death, when he was 'dissected.' His invalidism made a profound impression on his sister. It was an expense which the family could ill afford, and it made the mother over-anxious concerning her second son, who, although he was not really delicate, was also sent to baths in search of health. The strain of the expense was long remembered by Fike, who, as we have seen, sent the first money she ever owned to pay for her brother's sojourn at the Homburg baths.

With her governess, Fike read Molière's plays in which various forms of hypocrisy and hysteria are exposed and satirized. Through Babet's eyes, which had been opened by Molière, she viewed the cases of illness about her. 'You must know,' she afterwards wrote in a letter to Grimm, 'that Mademoiselle Cardel made me mistrustful towards all physicians and medicine in general.' It remained a pet lifelong prejudice. Whenever, as Empress, she summoned a physician for a post, she usually prefaced her appointment with the remark that she had no confidence in his profession. She never lost a chance to criticize its pretensions. 'Tell me now,' she wrote, 'why does the most Christian King assemble all the charlatans to talk of their charlatanry? Does he believe in the physicians?'

Her prejudice was of course not consistent. Babet Cardel, the scorner of physicians, had never been able to cure her pupil of tone-deafness. The Empress was sometimes plaintive about her lack and wondered wistfully whether the physicians might not succeed where the teachers had failed. 'All that depends on the organization, does it not? Mine is faulty. I long to hear and enjoy music, but in vain do I try. It is noise and that is all. I long to send to your society of medicine a prize for him

who will invent an effective remedy against insensibility
to the sounds of harmony.'

Fike was herself a healthy child. She remembered only
one attack of illness in her Stettin years. Her recollec-
tion of this experience gives us a picture of her home,
its gloomy pieties and its crude superstitions; above
all, its wounded family pride due to the lameness of
the one bright hope of the house, the future Prince of
Anhalt.

'It was the custom,' says Fike, 'to kneel down every
evening and morning to say our morning and evening
prayer. One evening, as I was praying on my knees, I
fell to coughing so violently, that the strain caused me to
fall upon my left side, while sharp pains almost took
away my breath. Some one sprang to me and I was put
to bed where I remained three weeks. I lay always on
the left side and had a cough, stitches and fever. There
was no proper doctor in the neighbourhood. They gave
me remedies, but Heaven knows of what they consisted.
Finally, after much suffering, I was able to get up. When
I was dressed it was seen that I had taken on the form of
a Z: my right shoulder was higher than the left, the back-
bone had a zigzag line, and the left shoulder was hollow.
My women and those of my mother who were taken
into consultation, decided to call my parents' attention
to it.

'The first thing done in the emergency was to command the strictest silence about my condition. My parents were unhappy that one of their children should be
lame, the other deformed. Finally, after several experts
had been consulted with the greatest secrecy, it was
decided to seek out a skilful man who knew how to cure
dislocations. The search was vain, for they had a horror
of calling in the only person who had this kind of skill,

41

because he was the executioner of the place. They hesitated a long while, but finally decided to fetch him secretly. Only Babet and a chamber-maid were taken into confidence. The man examined me and ordered that every morning a girl, before she had eaten, should rub with spittle first the shoulder and then the spine. Then he himself prepared a kind of jacket which I was never to remove by day or night except to change my linen. He came every other day early in the morning to examine me further. Besides this he had me wear a large black ribbon which went around my neck, passed over the shoulder and the right arm, and was fastened in the back. In short, I know not whether I had no tendency to become crooked or whether these methods were effective. In any case, after a year and a half of such treatment, hope for my health was restored. I did not lay aside the uncomfortable jacket until I was ten or eleven years old.'

Fike's inflammation of the lungs befell her at the age of seven. It coincided with her period of deepest piety, her melancholy absorption in the Last Judgment. She had been saturated with bigotry by the conscientious long-faced Wagner. On her knees in prayer she was struck down with a prolonged and serious illness. It was not an experience which the seven-year-old sinner could ever forget, especially when as a consequence she was obliged to wear for four long years an uncomfortable strait-jacket designed by the local hangman. Pneumonia and the Day of Judgment were welded in her mind. Having recovered from this illness, she resumed her position as the healthy child of the family. Not until she was fifteen years old did she fall ill again. This was on the threshold of her Russian career when an attack of pneumonia almost killed her while she was preparing to leave

She is Educated

the Lutheran church and adopt the Greek faith. It was not easy for the daughter of Christian August and a descendant of the Anhalt Princes to become a turncoat in the matter of religion.

43

3

Russia

The long line of Russian monarchs have belonged to three houses: the house of Rurik, the house of Romanov, and the house which was founded by the Princess of Zerbst, half German and half Russian. The house of Rurik and the house of Romanov culminated respectively in the titanic figures of Ivan the Terrible and Peter the Great. After them, the Ruriks and the Romanovs seemed to fall away as if exhausted by the effort into a swift decline. The super-Czars were followed by a twilight of feeble heirs who opened the way for usurpers and women. Interlopers like Boris Gudunov and Sophie of Zerbst found it easy to dispose of the descendants of these Great and Terrible fathers.

It appears that tyrants are usually under somebody's thumb. They are given to having favourites and to being ruled by them. Ivan was influenced by the monk Sylvester and Peter by the pastry-cook Menshikov. Neither was engaged in what is usually regarded as a red-blooded masculine occupation, but they were powerful men through their influence on their protectors who were autocrats. It is commonly said of Peter that he sacrificed his son for the sake of the new Russia which he had created, because Alexis was inimical to his father's work. Menshikov played a large objective part and no doubt a larger psychological one in the torture and death of the miserable Czarevich. Similarly, Ivan the Terrible followed the advice of his favourites in browbeating the son whom he finally slew. 'Give the son in his youth no power,' said the monk Sylvester. 'Break him with the rod; he will not die but only grow stronger.'

Of all the murders which have disfigured the family

life of Russian rulers, these two are perhaps the most revolting and at the same time the most romantic. As themes they have intrigued the imaginations of painters and dramatists. Ivan and Peter were primitive fathers who recalled an age in which their deed would have been regarded as blood-sacrifice and not as crime. They brought the practice of ritual murder down into modern history. The inheritors of a dark tradition, they helped to carry on a bad example for the future. Homicide in one form or another, in family quarrels and palace revolutions, was never far away from the royal family of Russia. In all the struggles around the dynasties and against them, violence has survived into modern times as a Russian folk-way.

Peter the Great was a miracle of energy. He was a madman, who built and destroyed with demonic power. If we knew the source of his phenomenal energy, we should know one of the profoundest secrets of human nature. Whence came his amazing drive, his mysterious complexities, his staggering contradictions, his power nevertheless of being always at one with himself in the supreme act of authority? We are forced to believe that his enormous stature played some part in his psychological complexity. He was six feet and seven inches tall, with the flashing eyes of a magician and the soft lips of a woman. Memories of the Norsemen and of Rurik the Viking who was the first ruler of Russia, were dear to him. They urged him to the sea and to a lifelong struggle to procure for Russia adventurous outlets to the sea. He dreamed of a campaign to India; as Rurik the Norseman had come to rule over Russia, so Peter the Russian would one day come to rule over India. Through his work, Europe and Asia would be united. He died without realizing this magnificent dream, but left it as a heritage for the greatest of the women autocrats who came after him.

As the youngest son of old Alexis Michaelovich and his girl-wife, Natalie Narishkin, Peter had at first little prospect of inheriting the crown. But the death of his stepbrother Feoder elevated Peter and his half-brother Ivan to a double throne. The throne, which was literally a double one built for two Czars, is still to be seen in the Kremlin. Behind the seat of Ivan is a concealed opening through which Sophie Alexeievna, who was Regent for six years, was accustomed to whisper responses to the weak-witted Ivan. The high-spirited Peter soon tired of a situation which enabled his sister to rule Russia from behind the scenes. At the age of seventeen, already a physical giant, he secured from his brother a voluntary abdication and forced his domineering sister into a convent. His hatred for Sophie was as intense as was his love for his mother, the beautiful young widow who spent her life among the coloured shadows of the Kremlin. His victory over Sophie gave Peter his first taste of violence. Then came the revolt of the Streltsi, in which the ambitious Sophie shared. Hastening home from Europe, Peter executed the conspirators before his sister's convent window. With his own hands, he severed their heads from their bodies. This was his first actual taste of blood.

After his return home, Peter found his first wife, Eudoxia, too dull and too orthodox. She was sent with shorn locks to languish in a convent, while Peter began a new life with his good-natured concubine, later Catherine I, who had been a camp-follower but was soon to become an Empress and deign to let Princes kiss her hand. Peter shared her favours with his best friend Menshikov, a practice not uncommon in mediæval friendships. To

Catherine and Menshikov Peter remained loyal for
the rest of his life. All his aberrations were in the
nature of orgies from which he always returned to his
permanent favourites. 'He was a real artist in lust,'
said Admiral Villebois; 'and, though hard-working,
he abandoned himself from time to time to attacks of
amorous frenzy in which age and sex mattered little to
him.'

§ 2

The history of morals in Russia differs from the history
of morals in the rest of Europe. This was once pointed
out by Catherine the Great in a letter to Senac de Meilhan: 'Every stranger who writes of Russia ignores the
ancient cast of its manners and morals and by this he
misleads himself many and many a time.' The woman
who made this comment on Russian life was born and
brought up under the concentrated influence of the German Reformation. Her early education taught her to
appreciate the difference.

The religious, political, and economic development of
Russia has been unique, and the development of morals
has been equally so. The introduction of Christianity in
the eleventh century was accompanied by no great revolu-
tionary upheaval. The Greek Church with its bejewelled
priests was assimilated by the Russians with suspicious
ease. Religious persecution, notwithstanding the Raskol-
nik burnings, never went so far in Russia as it did in
Western Europe. The Russian did not tremble before an
awful God but made a household pet of him, hanging
the icon in the corner of the best room and surrounding
it with family portraits. As late as the seventeenth
century, a serious European scholar published a work on
the subject: Are the Russians Christians? They had

accepted the Christian symbols and imbued them with the pagan spirit.

In Russia religion remained a passion play. The people slumbered on in their mediæval idolatry while the rest of Europe struggled through an age of passionate Protestantism. The rise of the rights of private property in the west, which was logically bound up with the monogamous inheriting family, had nothing to correspond with it in Russia. The break-up of communism which came with the growth of private property in Western Europe, did not exist among the Russians. The peasants continued to hold their land in common and pagan habits survived even within the church.

Standards of conduct which derived from the Greeks were in good odour all the way down through the eighteenth century. This is especially true with regard to sexual relationships. That curious and fascinating chapter in the history of European morals which deals with the rise of romantic love had no counterpart in the history of Russia. There was never a Russian Sir Galahad. The Byzantine Madonna never attained the prestige achieved in Rome. She had an oriental cast of features slightly suggestive of the queen of the playing cards. Her dark beauty betrayed her Greek and perhaps pagan origin. Besides, she belonged to a cloistered sex which spent its life in terems, those semi-oriental apartments in which women and children were secluded and which differed from harems only in that the Russians were not polygamous.

The seclusion of women continued to exist after the acceptance of Christianity and Madonna-worship. It explains why romantic love did not flower in Russia with the introduction of Christianity. While the Russians raised altars to the wonder-working virgin they continued to build churches to saints who reigned in pairs. Saint Peter and Saint Paul were enshrined together; Saint Boris and Saint Gleb, Saint Cyril and Saint Method were their Russian counterparts, just as the two Czars Peter and Ivan were enthroned together. The romantic value which the Russians attached to brotherly love is seen in the way in which large families of brothers clung together after marriage with the same degree of loyalty and dependence. It colours the myths and legends of the country. Masson relates the following: 'It is singular enough that in the same countries that were said to have been inhabited by a society of women [Amazons] who proscribed all men, a society of Zaporogue Cossacks have dwelt, who would not suffer a single woman among them, recruiting their forces solely by carrying away youths from the neighbouring lands. This barbarous republic was destroyed by Potiomkin, and they who composed it were distributed in the different armies and among the other Cossacks.' That such a myth could still persist and be believed in the Russia of the eighteenth century is not surprising when we remember that, prior to that century, all the visible political and social life of the country was, as in ancient Greece, carried on exclusively by men.

It was Peter the Great who changed all this. With his usual way of regimenting everybody, he commanded the women to come out of their terems and take part in society. But just as the Russian men clung to their be-loved beards when Peter commanded them to shave, so the women clung to their precious seclusion. Peter brooked no nonsense: he shaved the men by force and sent the military officers to fetch the women to balls and dinner-parties. The ladies, however, showed courage. They resisted emancipation bravely all through Peter's reign and for a long time afterwards. It was not until a generation later, during the reign of the Empress Elizabeth, that the Russian women assimilated the idea and began to enjoy the free life which Peter's ukase had unlocked for them.

§ 3

After the death of the great Czar a woman sat for the first time on the throne of Russia. The autocrat who had killed his son because he was incompetent to rule left his country to a woman who could neither read nor write. Good-natured, tawdry, and illiterate, the second wife of Peter the Great became Catherine I, autocrat of all the Russias. She ushered in a regiment of women. For three-quarters of a century Russia was ruled by women monarchs. Except for the brief reigns of Peter II and Peter III, the eighteenth century was dominated by three women autocrats, Anna Ivanovna, Elizabeth Petrovna, and Catherine Alexeievna. Russians, priests and peasants alike, who had been brought up to believe such proverbs as: 'A chicken is not a bird, nor is a woman human' and 'The more you beat the wife the better tastes the borstch,' were obliged to bow the knee three times in succession to autocrats in skirts. Among the Raskolniks were consistent fanatics who had to be knouted because they refused to take the oath of allegiance to women.

Catherine I, who had eleven children, was survived by only two of them: the melancholy Anne, married for a strip of sea-coast, and the frivolous Elizabeth, who remained unwed. The Empress left a will bequeathing the crown to the twelve-year-old son of the murdered Alexis. But the boy died of the smallpox after a brief reign of two years, and another Empress ascended the throne. His successor was Anna Ivanovna, daughter of the weak-witted Ivan, who had 'of his own free will' surrendered the crown to Peter the Great. Ivan's daughter, who had been considerably Germanized since leaving her Russian terem to become a Duchess of Courland, was now enthroned as supreme autocrat. She was the first of the two Annas, both unbeautiful and unpopular.

Having no children, she adopted a niece, Anna Leopoldovna, the daughter of a favourite sister. This niece was married to Prince Anthony Ulrich of Brunswick, a poor shadow of a man whom she much disliked and by whom she was much disliked in return. Nevertheless, they had a large family of children, the first of whom was destined to become the infant Czar, Ivan VI. Scarcely was this child born when Empress Anna died, leaving the Regency for the infant Czar in the hands of Bühren, her favourite. The mother of Ivanushka did not long submit to this arrangement. She contrived to send Bühren to Siberia and had herself made Regent in his place.

Anna Leopoldovna was a recluse and a sloven. She left the government to her minister, and reverted to the old terem life, spending her days in deshabille with her favourite, Julie von Mengden and Julie's numerous female relations. Her neglected husband was more neglected than ever. The Regent became more and more invisible; her retirement, more and more obsessional. She went forth only on moonlit nights to take the air. Ivanushka was shown to the public from a balcony on state occasions, for instance when the Persian Ambassadors brought the first elephants to Moscow. As the Imperial family withdrew from sight, gossip about them ran faster and faster. The Regent was only living as women had formerly always lived in the Russian terems, but her way of life was now regarded as reprehensible and scandalous. Julie von Mengden, her favourite, was after all a harmless, unambitious person, but she became a bogy in popular estimation. Anna Leopoldovna was unable to reign because she was too shy to show herself. One of the duties of her office was what Catherine the Great called 'representation' and she neglected it. Consequently her power lasted only one year.

§ 4

In the meantime Elizabeth Petrovna had been living her own life in her own way. Having signed her dying mother's will, for Catherine I could not read or write, she retired to private life apparently without regret and left the crown to her half-brother, Peter II. The Empress Anna who followed Peter was as ugly as Elizabeth was beau.iful. From jealousy she drove the debonair Princess away from the capital. Elizabeth lived in the country and shared the life of the peasants. She had a profound liking for low company and could not avoid being picturesque. In the company of her lover Shubin, she took part in all the peasant festivals. She loved to wear men's clothes and for years wore nothing else. Her tall figure and radiant beauty were at their best in male attire. When she was obliged as Empress to return to skirts again, she introduced a fashion at Court of balls called 'metamorphoses,' where all the women were obliged to dress as men and all the men as women. The metamorphoses were not popular with the diplomats who tangled themselves hopelessly in their skirts while the Empress marched about gracefully and happily in her velvet breeches.

Elizabeth was born under the most auspicious circum-

stances. Her birthday coincided with the victory of
Pultava. When Peter came swaggering back to Moscow
he was met by the announcement of the birth of a daughter
at Kolomenskoe. The great Czar cut short the victory
celebration in the Kremlin in order to post away to see
his babe. It was his eighth child and a girl, but Peter
was never blasé.

Elizabeth was a pampered darling. Even as an infant
she was a show child and a prize beauty. Her portrait in
the nude, suggesting the babyhood of Venus, is one of
the art treasures of the Petersburg collection. This much
admired work of art may have contributed to that lack of
modesty for which she was celebrated afterwards. Her
father's exotic taste expressed itself in the rich Spanish
costumes which formed her everyday wear, and in the
pets such as monkeys and parrots which he gave her.
The child was affectionate but not intellectual. She liked
to sing and dance and amuse herself. The only book she
ever read was the Bible. Her gaiety was tempered by a
melancholy which grew on her as she advanced in years.
The approach of these attacks was marked by an excess
of piety to which she completely abandoned herself. She
prayed for hours at a time, fasted with enthusiasm, and
made long pilgrimages on foot to the shrines of miracle-
working saints. Her religious orgies alternated with
periods of abandonment to frivolity and self-indulgence.
She astonished the world by these apparent contradictions. It seemed paradoxical that she should in
turn be so immoral and so religious. As she revelled in
the follies and gaieties of Butter Week, so she revelled
in the ritual of the Greek Church. She was fully as
religious as her brother Alexis, whose orthodoxy had so
much infuriated Peter the Great that he put him to the
torture.

Elizabeth was, also like Alexis, intensely Russian. Although her mother had been a foreigner and a Lutheran, and her father had been as much of a Dutchman as he could make himself, Lisanka was pure Slav. It is true that she preferred Petersburg to Moscow as a residence, and that she built the great Winter Palace there in the style of Versailles and not of Kolomenskoe. In this respect and in her politics she followed in the footsteps of her father. But her personal way of life was exceedingly Russian and somewhat provincial. She loved luxury and show as much as did Peter himself, but she was at heart a home-keeping body with a fondness for the simple ways of her country. Her life among the peasants had helped to make her so. Among her lovers were no foreigners. Shubin, Voshinsky, Buturlin, Razumovsky, and Shuvalov —there were only five in fact though tradition makes them three hundred—were all Russians. The two Annas were given to German favourites who were inclined to be ambitious and efficient. Elizabeth's lovers were an easy-going set of men who did not exploit their position. She, on her side, loved them for their *beaux yeux* and not for their ability or distinction. She kept a sergeant, a hostler, a page, and a chorister in turn. Perhaps the French Duke who once refused her hand felt more than ever justified in his decision when he heard that the beautiful daughter of Peter the Great had consoled herself with such simple and lowly persons.

Elizabeth adored her family. The child who was painted in the nude and paraded in Spanish finery before an admiring world was her father's pet and plaything. For her sake Peter decided to make her mother his legal wife and to crown her as Empress. The girl was still in her teens when her father and mother died and her sister Anne married and went to a foreign country. Attachment

54

to the memory of her family never left her; it was the mainspring of her life.

Elizabeth's mother had a German physician whose name was Lestocq. He was born in Hanover and was one of the many German doctors whom Peter the Great brought to Russia. From the year 1713 he was attached to Catherine's family. Elizabeth therefore inherited him from her mother and allowed herself to be led by him. He liked to pull the strings of political intrigue and to gratify his sense of power. It was he who finally persuaded Elizabeth to dispossess the Regent and her infant son and seize the crown for herself. The Grand Duchess was now thirty-two years old. She had no more real desire to be Empress than her mother had had before her, but Lestocq was an energetic manager. He induced her at last to act by telling her stories about the torture and the convent that awaited her at the hands of Regent Anna. He also offered her sound French money that Versailles was ready to invest in a Petersburg revolution.

Elizabeth's imagination was no doubt stimulated by recent events in Austria. In October, 1740, Charles VI died and named his daughter as his successor. If Maria Theresa had become an Empress, why should not Elizabeth Petrovna? No Pragmatic Sanction was needed in Russia where two Empresses had already occupied the throne. If Europe was going to ask questions, Elizabeth could produce her mother's will which she herself had signed. The testament read: 'If the Grand Duke [Peter II] should die without heirs, the right to ascend the throne shall pass after him to the Czarevna with her descendants, after her to the Czarevna Elizabeth with her descendants, after her to the Grand Duchess; whereby male heirs shall have at all times preference over female. But never at any time shall anyone rule over the

Russian Empire who does not belong to the Greek Church or who wears already another crown.' The Czarevna Anna had left a son in Kiel, but he was a Lutheran. The will in question had been declared illegal by Empress Anna, but was now restored to legality by Empress Elizabeth who thought it best to have a document to justify her intentions.

The revolution was not as costly as a modern theatrical revue, with which the old palace revolutions in Russia had much in common. Elizabeth Petrovna came to the city for the winter and kept open house in a little palace on the Field of Mars. While the Regent remained concealed in the Winter Palace, Elizabeth went abroad early and late and smiled upon the population. She visited the guards in the barracks, stood godmother to their children and gambled away her French money to them. On fine days she sped through the snowy streets of Petersburg, a shining Snegurotchka, with guardsmen perched on the rear of her sledge. The apathetic Regent bestirred herself sufficiently to reprove Elizabeth for her improprieties. But Elizabeth knew that her mother had not become Empress by observing the proprieties, nor had Peter the Great had much regard for formalities. Her mother's own daughter, Elizabeth, had a way with soldiers which she now used for political ends. The guardsmen adored her.

Though Peter the Great had been feared and hated in his lifetime, he had now been dead long enough to become a popular idol. His youngest and favourite daughter had only to stretch out her hand to collect the interest on his popularity. Elizabeth's revolution was easy, so easy that the foreign diplomats were shocked. They reported to their home ministries that a purse of money, a cask of wine, and a handful of soldiers had done it all.

Elizabeth's revolution was regarded as an illustration of the political indifference and supineness of the Russian people; but, as Bilbassov has touchily but convincingly pointed out, the revolution of 1741 was easy because it fulfilled the popular wish. The unlovely Annas had had their day and the turn of the gracious Elizabeth had come. Thirty-two, unmarried, and childless – she prolonged her beloved dynasty through a kind of political Indian summer.

On the 5th of December, 1741, Lestocq decided that the time for action had come. Elizabeth left her palace at midnight, and, accompanied by Lestocq and Vorontsov, was whirled away in her sledge to midnight Mass. After the litany, she again entered her sledge and sped to the barracks of the Preobrazhensky regiment. While three hundred guardsmen were silently getting into line, she disappeared into her dressing-room and arrayed herself as if for a première. Presently she appeared before the soldiers in full military regalia, a shirt of mail over her shoulders and a spontoon in her hand. If Peter the Great had fancied himself a Viking, his daughter fancied herself a Brunnhilde. Russia had had Empresses before Elizabeth, but she was the first to seize the throne in male attire. She set the fashion for the Empress who came after her.

In the dense black cold of a December night in Petersburg, the soldiers took the oath of allegiance under their breaths. Elizabeth in her coat of mail placed herself at the head of her warriors and marched to the Winter Palace, where the sleepy Anna, though scarcely more sleepy than usual, and the shivering Anthony Ulrich were hurried into their clothes at the point of the sword. One hopes at least that the von Mengden sisters bore themselves with spirit during the invasion; nothing of the kind was to be expected of the feeble Brunswick pair. The Regent and her household were removed by the guards to the palace on the Field of Mars which Elizabeth had just abandoned, while Elizabeth remained in the imperial chambers.

§ 5

Almost the first act of the new Empress was to select her successor. Her choice was hastily made and precipitately executed. The indolent woman, who usually had to be prodded into action by her advisers, showed great energy and decision in this matter. She dispatched a messenger secretly to Kiel and brought her nephew, Karl Peter Ulrich, to Petersburg. She told her intentions to nobody until she had the boy safe in her keeping. He was inducted into the Greek Church, and hastily proclaimed heir to the throne. The determined Empress spared no efforts to bring this about. To make the step irrevocable and cut off all possibility of retreat for the boy, she destroyed any claim he might make to the Swedish throne. She made it a condition of the Russian-Swedish treaty that the former guardian of her nephew, Adolph Friedrich of Holstein, should be nominated in her nephew's place as heir-apparent of the Swedish crown. By these measures, his Swedish expectations were cut off, and Karl Peter Ulrich became Grand Duke Peter Feodorovich, a good Romanov name that was supposed to wipe out the taint of his Lutheran past.

Elizabeth had proclaimed her nephew heir without consulting the Privy Council or the Senate. She did not even ask advice of the nobles who had led her party and supported her revolution. The gentlemen thus overlooked were irritated and everybody was mystified by her

driving haste. The diplomats were obliged to find reasons
for her behaviour, and there were many near at hand.
Her sister's son was her competitor for the throne and
if his claims were backed by France and Sweden they
might prove dangerous. As Grand Duke of Russia he
was in the hands of his aunt. It was also seriously suggested that the pious Empress wished to bring another
soul into the Greek Church and that she wished to find a
good excuse for not marrying.

Her devotion to the memory of Anushka was a real
factor, but there was something more. Her behaviour
was a good deal like that of a pathological kidnapper.
She may have cried over little Ivan in his cradle but she
had let him go. Peter was never to escape. In her several
kidnappings, for this was only the first, she always maintained an appearance of reasonableness. The considera-
tions of state which she invented to justify her abduction
of her nephew and her nephew's heir were merely convenient excuses for the satisfaction of her desire for
children.

In spite of Elizabeth's reputation as a voluptuary, it
is impossible to find any authentic traces of her children's
existence. Her mother's illegitimate offspring and that
of Catherine the Great are matters of history. Did she
actually have no children or did she dispose of them so
completely that not even a rumour of their existence
has come down to us? It seems hardly consistent with
her character as we know it that she should have been
so sensitive to public opinion as to have drowned them.
In any case she had all the symptoms of a woman who
had been disappointed in maternity. Romantic and sentimental as to all family ties, she had mourned her lost
lover for twenty-five years and cherished a feeling of
widowhood. When the Grand Duke was confirmed in

the palace chapel, Elizabeth threw herself upon the
ground and burst into a flood of tears.

§ 6

Three years after the Empress had adopted Peter, she
sent an envoy to Kiel to find out something about the boy.
The results of the investigation were not encouraging.

His mother had died three months after his birth. The
boy's father, a cruel, sickly little man, had neglected his
son as he had neglected his wife. He died early, leaving
Peter fully orphaned at the age of ten. The child was
brought up by a Swedish governor named Brümmer who
achieved such bad results that he was accused of having
intentionally destroyed the boy's character. The Russians,
Bestushev and Panin, believed that Brümmer, after discovering that Peter was to be the heir to the Russian
throne and not the Swedish, took pains to corrupt his
mind and disposition. 'But I have always doubted this
abomination,' says Catherine, 'my opinion is that the
unsuccessful education of Peter III is to be traced to a
combination of unfortunate circumstances.'

The boy's mental endowment was poor; but there had
been stupid Romanovs before him. Many excuses have
been suggested for his inability to learn. He was taught
Russian and Swedish alternately because he had pretensions to both crowns, and as a result he learned
neither. But many children learn two languages whether
alternately or simultaneously. Another excuse for his
shortcomings relates that the Rector of the Kiel Grammar
School who undertook to teach him Latin employed
such tactless methods that Peter learned only to hate
all study. When he arrived in Moscow at the age of
fourteen he knew nothing at all. The Empress, whose
standards were certainly not very high, was much

disturbed by his ignorance and hastened to give him a tutor.

Stehlin was a forerunner of the best modern teachers of the feeble-minded. He used concrete materials as much as possible, borrowing from the art gallery coins and medals, picture-books, globes and models. As the Grand Duke was literally unable to sit still, Stehlin walked up and down the room with him. For three years the patient man kept it up, although his unconventional teaching was often ridiculed. The scholars thought him a jester instead of a teacher. Nevertheless Stehlin seems to have been the only one in the Grand Duke's environment who made any attempt to handle the boy intelligently and sympathetically. Peter learned little or nothing, it is true, but he remained on friendly terms with his preceptor.

The mischief had been done long before Stehlin had a chance with him. Spoilt by his nurses, Peter had been handed over at seven to brutal Holstein officers who subjected him to a military régime. At fourteen he was passionately fond of military drill but had no more endurance than a baby. To play with toy soldiers was his one idea of manœuvres.

Brümmer, his Swedish governor, was a typically well-seasoned cavalry officer. Stehlin said of Brümmer that he might be fit to train horses but he was not fit to educate a human being. In order to harden his pupil, he tortured him. His favourite punishments were to deprive the boy of his meals, to beat him with a riding-whip, to make him kneel with naked skin upon dry peas. The victim responded as might be expected. He was timid and antagonistic, cowardly and boastful. He made friends only with the meanest of the servants, those whom he was allowed to strike, and he tortured his pet animals. By the time he was brought to Russia to become its future Czar he was hopelessly degenerate.

Life had been made too hard for Peter. His instinct of survival had been undermined. He frequently fell ill and with every attack it was thought that he was going to die. The grandson of Peter the Great, that miracle of human energy, had no energy at all. He was just a stupid little boy who was destined never to grow up.

4

She goes to Russia

THE Princess Johanna Elizabeth of Anhalt-Zerbst wrote with gilt ink and many flourishes. Like King Frederick and every other educated person in the Germany of her times she carried on her correspondence in French. Her style was as ornate as her penmanship, for she never lacked the courage of her enthusiasms. As a finished letter-writer she lost no opportunity to display her art. When the news came that Elizabeth Petrovna had ascended the Russian throne, she at once wrote to congratulate the new Empress who might have been her sister-in-law. It was an exciting moment when the reply came back, penned by the hand of the glorious autocrat herself. Direct communication had been established between the obscure Stettin family and the imperial court of Petersburg. The enterprising Princess walked on air.

Luck favoured her. She had in her possession a precious relic which the Empress wanted, a portrait of Elizabeth's dead sister Anna. It had been painted many years before by Axel von Mardefeld, the Prussian minister to Russia. Mardefeld was a seasoned diplomat who had survived twenty years of service at the Russian court and expected to survive many more. He spared no pains to ingratiate himself with the new Empress. The portrait which he had painted of Anushka gave him his opportunity. He knew that this work of art, which had strayed out of Russia, was now in the hands of a trustworthy person, the Princess of Anhalt-Zerbst. Elizabeth was as eager to secure the return of this family relic as her father would have been to import a priceless Italian Venus. At the suggestion of Mardefeld, she wrote to her 'dear niece,' the Princess of Anhalt-Zerbst, and begged for the return of the picture promising to reward the sender at the earliest opportunity.

The Princess of Anhalt-Zerbst was naturally delighted to do a favour for the Empress of Russia. The portrait was sent at once: soon a messenger came posting back to Berlin bearing a return gift from the Empress. It was a miniature of Elizabeth set in diamonds worth eighteen thousand roubles. The Princess did not allow the grass to grow under her feet. She had her daughter's portrait painted by Pesne, and the following spring Uncle August of Holstein made a journey to Petersburg to bear this offering to the Empress. Stehlin thought the workmanship was poor; he said the elderly artist had lost his skill. But Elizabeth was no connoisseur as Peter the Great had been. It was the portrait of a pleasant-looking, well-grown young woman. Her Imperial Highness did not ask for more; her feelings could supply the rest.

In the meantime Petersburg buzzed with speculation concerning the Grand Duke's marriage. The diplomats had been taken by surprise when the Empress had produced her nephew as her heir, and they were resolved to be more alert in the matter of his marriage. Gossip spoke of several Princesses, not all of whom were real. The French Princess who figured in the rumours absolutely did not exist. In Saxony, however, there lived a real Princess who was sponsored by a strong party headed by Bestushev the Vice-Chancellor. The Princess Marianna was the daughter of August the Strong who, having altogether more than a hundred children, did not consider them as precious as if he had been the father of only five or six. He was willing to send Marianna to Russia. Besides, as King of Poland he had strong political reasons for wanting an alliance with that country. He would be delighted to marry his daughter to the Grand Duke.

Frederick of Prussia wished at all costs to prevent this alliance. It was a trying situation for him. He had two . marriageable sisters with either of whom he might have filled the breach. But as a brother Frederick was too chivalrous. He belonged to one of those families whose members hate each other cordially yet cling inseparably together against all the rest of the world. The idea of sending Ulrica or Amelia to Russia filled their brother's soul with consternation. 'In order to destroy the Saxon's project,' he wrote to Mardefeld, 'propose a Princess from some old ducal house of Germany. With regard to my sisters, you know my opinion. I shall send neither of them to Russia. I wonder that the Empress does not hold to her choice of the Princess of Zerbst, since she is of the Holstein family that the Empress loves so much. Besides there are still two Princesses in Hesse-Darm-stadt, one of whom is twenty and the other eighteen years of age.' Commenting on his conflict at this crisis, Frederick afterwards wrote, 'Nothing was more contrary to the welfare of the state than to permit this alliance; nothing was more unnatural than to send the Princess Ulrica there. Woe to those politicians who sacrifice even their own blood to their interests and ambition.' Thus Frederick agonized while the Russian Empress kept her counsel. It appears that she never wanted Ulrica for the Grand Duke, having destined her for another rôle, the rôle that she later came to fill as Queen of Sweden.

The Empress's choice was made. Her hesitation sprang from other causes. An obstacle had to be removed; it was the near relationship existing between the Grand Duke Peter and the Princess Fike of Zerbst. The

65   E

point was referred to the Archbishop of Novgorod and the Synod, the facts of the relationship being given and the young lady's name withheld—such was Elizabeth's passion for secrecy. The Synod reported that the Church had no objection to the marriage; that the couple were cousins did not count since they were related on the maternal side only. Their relationship was therefore merely 'the shadow of a relationship'.

Still the impatient Empress hesitated. A second obstacle deterred her. This time it was a question for physicians not clergymen to settle. Lestocq was a physician and Lestocq had serious reservations regarding the immediate marriage of the Grand Duke. Stehlin says that Lestocq advised the Empress to wait at least another year while other memoirs say that the Hanover physician told the Empress to postpone the boy's marriage until he was twenty-one. It was plain to all observers that the boy was under-sized and under-developed for his age. The English ambassador said of him, 'He looks very puny and he is not taller at fourteen than the generality of children, not remarkably small, are at ten.' The worst of it was that he did not improve in his new environment.

The Grand Duke's vitality was low. Whenever anything went wrong, he fell ill and he recovered but slowly. The morbid relation between himself and his governor Brümmer continued unabated under the auspices of his adoring but ignorant aunt. Scenes of violence took place which made the amiable Stehlin's hair stand on end but which he concealed from the easy-going Empress. His pupil was terrorized and browbeaten by the Prussian officer and the foolish boy had no other idea of self-defence than to fight back with blustering impotent rage. He went so far as to threaten Brümmer with his

dagger. Undoubtedly the weak boy could be irritating.
Just before Christmas, 1743, Peter fell desperately ill.
His aunt was in a panic; death had robbed her so often.
Were all her plans to be brought to naught on the eve
of their bright fulfilment? She cast all caution to the
winds and decided to bring the German Princess to
Russia at once. Brümmer was sent to write a letter invit-
ing the mother and daughter for a visit. Scarcely was this
letter dispatched than Brümmer was sent to write another
bidding the ladies to make haste. Elizabeth's customary
indolence was laid aside, she summoned Brümmer again
after a few days had elapsed and demanded to know
whether the guests from Zerbst were not already on their
way. The officer played his part between the two ladies
well. To the Empress he said that the Princess of Zerbst
wished only for wings to come flying to her Majesty. To
the Princess of Zerbst he wrote that the invitation was due
to his devoted services on behalf of the House of Holstein.
He continued to bully the prospective bridegroom just
as much as ever.

§ 2

While Brümmer's letter was travelling from Petersburg
to Berlin, the Stettin family was spending Christmas in
Zerbst with Uncle Johann Ludwig. There were three
children at this time: Fike, Fritz and Lischen, the baby
who had been named after the glorious Russian kinswoman. Christmas at Zerbst was a sober Lutheran
Festival with much hymn singing in which Fike did
not shine, and gifts of handiwork in which she excelled.
New Year's Eve came, when a glimpse of the future can
be caught in candle-flames, in bits of molten lead, and
similarly strange messengers of fate. It was a night for
Fräulein Khayn to see ghosts if she ever saw them, for

a courier was riding from Berlin to Zerbst bearing destiny in the form of Brümmer's letter.

On the morning of New Year's Day the whole family went to church. When the bells began to ring the little procession emerged from the castle, two stiff old men and a frail little nine-year-old boy accompanied by their numerous women folk, among whom the youthful Sophie walked as tall as any of them. It was time that she should be married, but dowerless and plain how was she to find a husband? Fike's thoughts were at this time fixed on her Uncle George, a younger brother of her mother's who had been paying her court. Although the Princess of Zerbst had encouraged her brother's suit, viewing him favourably as a bird in the hand, the melancholy George had not really asked his niece to marry him. Still, on this New Year's Day Fike's thoughts were with her uncle as she sang out of tune with the others the long, chanting hymns of the Lutheran service.

While the family sat at dinner the courier arrived. A package of letters was handed to the General who tore off the outside covering and gave a thick missive to his wife. As the Princess read, her daughter sitting next to her caught sight of the words ' . . . with the Princess your eldest daughter.' From that moment Uncle George was forgotten. The shrewd girl guessed the contents of the twelve-page letter in her mother's hands although nothing was said to her. Her parents shut themselves up in the library for three days with ostentatious secrecy while the rest of the household buzzed with excitement. Behind the closed doors the old General was putting up a stubborn resistance. He did not wish to send his daughter to Russia for the same reason that Frederick did not wish to send his sister there.

'At the express and particular command of her Imperial Highness,' said Brümmer's letter, 'I have to inform you, Madame, that the Empress wishes that your High-ness accompanied by the Princess your eldest daughter, shall come hither as soon as possible and without loss of time and repair to whatever place the Imperial Court at the moment may be. Your Highness is too clever not to understand the true meaning of the impatience of the Empress to see you here as well as the Princess your daughter of whom report has said so much that is lovely. There are times when the voice of the world is not other than the voice of God.

'At the same time our incomparable Monarch has expressly charged me to inform your Highness that his Highness, your consort, shall under no circumstances come with you. Her Majesty has very important reasons for wishing it so. A word from your Highness will, I believe, be all that is necessary to fulfill the will of our divine Empress.' Brümmer enclosed an order for ten thousand roubles payable in Berlin and another credit for two thousand roubles payable in Petersburg.

A second courier arrived two hours later bringing a letter from King Frederick who, like Brümmer, took all the credit for the invitation, urged the need of secrecy, and repeated the injunction of the Empress about leaving the General at home. Elizabeth Petrovna guessed that Fike's father would be a hindrance to her plans. She had bought off the guardian of Karl Peter Ulrich by transferring to him the boy's own claim to the Swedish throne. In the same canny spirit, she limited her dealings to the mother of the bride whom she wanted for the Grand Duke and excluded the girl's father from any share in the negotiations. Having firmly put the General in his place she left it to his overlord, the King of Prussia, to keep him there. Even had the Prince been a man of aggressive character, which he certainly was not, his hands could not have been tied more effectively.

Three days sufficed to demolish the General's resistance. On the fourth of January, the Princess Johanna Elizabeth penned her replies to the letters. Her correspondence with Elizabeth has unfortunately been lost; the Empress was notoriously careless with letters. In her answer to Frederick the Princess declared her intention of bowing to the will of Providence and of following the instructions of the Empress to the last detail excepting one. 'I understand completely the necessity for secrecy which your Majesty has recommended. Yet for various reasons, which can be more easily understood than written, I have been obliged to initiate the Prince, whose discretion I will guarantee, into the secret. I hope thereby to have merited no reproach.' She had really considered the possibility of taking Fike off to Russia without her father's knowledge.

Preparations for the journey were simple. The trousseau of the German Princess consisted of little more than a travelling apprentice might have carried in his bundle. Three dresses, a dozen chemises, and as many handkerchiefs were all that Fike had to pack for that mid-winter journey. The Baroness von Prinzen who afterwards said in her memoirs that she had helped Catherine the Great to pack her trunks for Russia rather overstated the case. The packing of Fike's trunks must have been a simple matter. It was a source of life-long chagrin to her that she came to Russia without a bridal chest. Her mother at least had had that. She had no bed linen of her own and was obliged to use her mother's sheets. No deeper humiliation for a German bride can be imagined. Even as an old woman Fike could not forget it. It was something which she had always to

make up. Because she had come without sheets to
Russia she was obliged to effect the Partition of Poland.

On the 10th of January, 1744, Fike's mother set forth,
ostensibly for the Berlin Carnival. The party consisted
of the General, who was to accompany them as far as
Schwedt, the Princess and her daughter, two attendant
Fräuleins, an officer named Lattorf, and a cook. They
made their first stop in Berlin. The Princess hastened to
an audience with the King and Minister von Podewils
who invested her with the responsibility of furthering the
Prussian cause with the Empress.

In Berlin, the Princess continued as formerly to neglect
her daughter. Her tactlessness was illustrated by an
incident described in Fike's memoirs. 'When the King
of Prussia, who knew exactly the object of the journey,
learned that I had arrived in Berlin, he wished without
fail to see me. My mother said I was ill. Two days later
he caused her to be invited to dinner with the Queen,
his consort, and expressly requested her to bring me with
her. My mother promised but when the time came she
went alone to the court. When the King saw her he
inquired about me. She replied that I was ill. Whereupon he replied that he well knew that it was not true.
Then she said that I was not dressed for court, to which
he answered that he would postpone the dinner for me
until the next day. Finally, my mother said that I had
no court dress. He ordered that one of his sisters should
send me one. At last my mother saw there was no way
out of it and sent me word that I should dress myself
and come to the palace.'

It was late in the afternoon when Cinderella arrived.
During supper she sat at the right hand of the King, who
paid her elaborate eighteenth-century compliments. The
shy girl blushed furiously, but kept her head. It was the

one and only meeting of these two great monarchs. Between the Princess of fourteen and the King of thirty-one no vital contact was made; it was an official occasion. But his flattery lingered with her always like a pleasant dream. But she hated sister Ulrica, who was too precious to be sent to Russia and whose dress the King had offered to lend her.

In the middle of January, the Princess's coach rolled out of Berlin. Lumbering through the deep frozen ruts of the outer streets, it took a northerly direction as if homeward bound for Stettin. The snowless winter obliged the party to travel on wheels as far as Riga, while the bitter winds sweeping down from the Baltic waters made the journey a severe ordeal. They lost no time, however. Frederick had ordered fresh relays of horses at every post. No expense had been spared; were not the roubles of the Russian Empress to pay for everything? But real comfort was not procurable at any price. Few travellers, except the couriers, took the post road from Berlin to Petersburg at this time of the year. The quarters in which the party sought their night's lodging were just endurable. 'As the rooms in the stations were not heated,' the Princess wrote her husband, 'we were obliged to go into the common room which was not unlike a pig-sty; the master and mistress, the house dog, the cock and the children – children everywhere, in cradles, in beds, on the stove, on mattresses – everything was rolled together in disorder like weeds and roots. There was nothing else to be done; I ordered a bench to be brought and lay down in the middle of the room.'

In spite of the cold and discomfort, they hastened onward, through the short days and the long nights. The Princess wrote her husband about an encounter with

72

robbers, but her daughter's description of the journey contains no reference to any adventure of this kind. More exciting for Fike was the great comet of 1744 which they saw while crossing Courland. Against the background of the long black nights and the tedium of the never-ending journey accentuated by the hoof-beats of the flying horses, the comet lingered in the girl's memory as something awful and unforgettable. The cold grew worse and worse. The ladies wore woollen masks to keep their faces from freezing. Fike's feet succumbed to the frost and were so swollen that she had to be carried to and from the carriage. She also made herself ill drinking beer. 'In these last days I had a little indigestion,' she wrote to dear Papa, 'but it has had no further consequences. I was partly myself to blame because I had drunk all the beer I could find along the way. Dear Mamma has put a stop to that, and I am well again.' This was priggish Fike travelling to Russia in her fifteenth year. She obeyed her dear Mamma, but dear Papa could understand her better about the beer.

Having said good-bye at Schwedt, the General returned to Stettin with his secret. The town marked the disappearance of his wife and daughter and rumours began to circulate. They made the Prince uncomfortable. He wrote a letter which overtook the Princess at Köslin and asked permission to announce the journey in the newspapers. But the Princess said no. 'It seems to me essential that you should hold back the announcement in the newspapers of my journey until I have passed Memel. Likewise the prayers for a safe journey which you plan to have said in the churches of Zerbst must be postponed.' As far as Memel, she felt that she could manage the trip without any special aid from Providence. From Königsberg she wrote to Fike's grandmother, who drew a yearly pension of ten thousand roubles from Empress Elizabeth. The aged Duchess was the only one of Sophie's relatives who did not join in the protest against the marriage. The Abbess of Quedlinburg and the Duchess of Brunswick were outraged. They heaped reproaches on the head of the General whom, without regard to justice, they made the scapegoat for his wife's proceedings. They bombarded the Prince with long letters which reminded him of the tragic fate of Princess Charlotte who had married Alexis Petrovich and the sad plight of the Brunswick family imprisoned by Elizabeth. The Prince was harassed by Holstein and Anhalt relatives at the same time, since he had luckily remained where both sides of the family could get at him and relieve their feelings. The Princess Johanna Elizabeth was not surprised; she had not expected their support.

'I did not doubt,' she wrote to her husband, 'that our journey to Moscow would stir up a storm. Religion and rivalry give the best grounds for that. But the Tante [the Abbess] as little as we would have had the power to turn aside the wise decrees of Providence. We cannot ascribe my journey here and the entire circumstance to anything else and we can be assured that the All-Wise One fulfils thereby purposes for us inscrutable.' To arguments like this the pious General had no reply. But still disturbed by memories of the unhappy marriage of Princess Charlotte, he asked his wife to stiffen the terms on Sophie's behalf in the marriage contract. He wanted for his daughter the guarantee of a pension with a home if possible in Holstein if not in Livonia. Nothing of the kind was ever even discussed by his wife after her arrival in Russia.

Thanks to the foresight of the Princess, none of this

opposition was started until mother and daughter were safely beyond the Russian border. As far as Riga, the Princess travelled under the name of the Countess of Rheinbeck, the cognomen which Brümmer had suggested for the purpose. In Fike's memoirs, she says that her mother assumed a fictitious name for the journey but she could no longer remember it. At Riga the travellers were met by escorts, compliments and presents. 'At mid-day,' wrote the Princess, 'I met Chamberlain Narishkin, whom her Imperial Majesty had placed at the head of a guard of honour that came to meet me as a mark of distinction. He brought me letters and greetings from her Majesty who overwhelmed me with honours and compliments. A quarter of a mile from the city I was met by Vice-Governor Prince Dolgoruki. We drove across the ice of Dwina. As the carriage in which I was sitting was just beyond the end of the great bridge, the first salvo was fired from the great guns on the fortresses. I found ready to wrap us in the sledge two splendid sables covered with gold brocade for my daughter and myself, two collars of the same fur and a coverlet of another fur, quite as beautiful.'

Wrapped in their rich sables, the travellers climbed into the long Russian sledge, designed by Peter the Great, and flew over the snowy chaussées that led to Petersburg. On a frosty February day they arrived at the Winter Palace. The Empress and the Court had gone away to Moscow. Petersburg was empty, but a small group of couriers had remained to welcome the German guests. The Princess was more than bedazzled by the reception they gave her. 'It seems as if I were in the suite of her Imperial Majesty or of some great monarch. It does not seem real that all this can happen to poor me, for whom at only a few places a drum was ever stirred and at others not even that. Here everything goes on in such magnificent and respectful style that it seemed to me then and now at the sight of the luxury surrounding me as if it all were only a dream.'

§ 3

Fike's memories of her arrival in Petersburg are appropriate to a fourteen-year-old girl. She remembered the names of the four young ladies of honour who came forward to welcome her and the names of the men they subsequently married; the fourteen elephants which the Shah of Persia had given to the Empress and which actually performed tricks in the snowy palace court-yard; the carnival and the wonderful sledging expedition led by Semion Cyrilovich Narishkin; above all she remembered and described to the last knot and ringlet the extraordinary style of hair-dressing favoured by her new Russian friends. Once in the Petersburg palace, the girl promptly forgot all the hardships of the journey. Her mother, a little tired but ever busy with her pen, continued her stream of correspondence with Zerbst and Berlin. 'Fike bears the fatigue better than I, yet we are both well, praise be to God. May He continue to guide and direct us.' This to her husband, the General; to King Frederick, she wrote rather less piously: 'Considering the hardships of the season, the journey and the change of air, I should need to have an iron constitution to keep up my resistance. My daughter is more fortunate. Her youth supports her health and like young soldiers who scorn danger because they know nothing about it, she delights in the splendour by which she is surrounded.'

In some subtle way, the conquering spirit of the Princess of Zerbst began to fail her as soon as she arrived in Russia. It was equally evident that Fike, from the moment when Narishkin helped her with a jest into the sledge at Riga, was swimming with the current. Not that the Princess was aware of falling behind in the race. Courageous and confident, she attacked the great task before her, her diplomatic mission from King Frederick and von Podewils. She had found everything in Petersburg just as they had said. Things had to be changed. Bestushev, the enemy of Prussia, must go. While her mother pursued these political interests, Fike was learning to stand on her own feet in a strange environment. For the first time she allowed herself the luxury of a cold-blooded judgment of the Princess's character. It happened on the journey from Petersburg to Moscow.

'After the departure from Petersburg,' says Fike, 'the sledge in which my mother and I were travelling struck in turning against a house, whereby an iron hook became dislodged and fell, striking my mother on the head and shoulder. She insisted that she was severely hurt but outwardly there was nothing to be seen, not even a bruise. This incident delayed our journey by several hours.' In describing the accident, her mother says, 'I believed myself to be wounded but I was not. The blow had struck with full strength against the fur; otherwise, without doubt, my head, neck and arm would have been crushed.' Only the costly furs given by the Empress had saved her.

With this one interruption, the train of thirty sledges, each drawn by ten horses, dashed onward without pause. They intended to arrive in Moscow before the Grand Duke's birthday, on the 21st of February. The way was prepared. Bonfires burned at night along the snowy highway. Post-stations sprang up suddenly out of the snowdrifts, ready with hot coffee and fish soup, while fresh horses stood waiting in their dugas. The excitement was intense. At four o'clock on the third day, the flying train came suddenly to a halt within seventy versts of Moscow. An envoy from the Empress met the party here with the request that they should delay their entrance into Moscow until after darkness had fallen. While they waited, the travellers arrayed themselves with as much care as possible. Fike put on a close-fitting dress of rose-coloured moiré silk, trimmed with silver.

The horses were again put to the sledges, this time sixteen instead of ten to each, and the train leaped forward. Sievers, the Empress's envoy, seated himself beside the Princess of Zerbst, and urged the coachman forward at every breath in true Russian style. The procession drew up before the Golovin Palace at eight o'clock in the evening. It was just six weeks since the country cousins had driven with so much caution and secrecy out of the little Lutheran town of Zerbst.

They were received on the staircase by the Prince von Hesse-Homberg, Adjutant-General of the Empress, who conducted them to their chambers. Scarcely had they laid aside their heavy sables when the Grand Duke came running into their room, unable longer to control his impatience to see them. At ten o'clock Lestocq appeared with greetings and a summons from the Empress. Attended by the Prince von Hesse-Homberg and the Grand Duke, the two Princesses made their way to the Empress's reception room. As they passed from room to room, the Court ladies and gentlemen were presented and bowed low to them. 'It is impossible to say how all those present stared at these Germans from head to foot,' wrote the Princess to her husband. Yet those old aunts at Quedlinburg who opposed the journey would have wished the Princess of Zerbst to forgo this triumph.

The Empress advanced to the doorway to meet them. 'She allowed me,' exulted the Princess, ' scarcely time to take off my gloves and embraced me, I must say, with tenderness.' In rhetorical French, the Princess delivered an address of gratitude for all the Empress had done for the Holstein-Gottorp family. The Empress replied that her own blood was not more dear to her than that of the Princess and that all she had done was nothing in comparison with what she intended to do. It was a meeting of Greek with Greek. Fike was at last presented and embraced. The Empress invited the company to be seated, but, since she herself was too excited to sit down, nobody else could do so. The reception lasted for half an hour. At one point the Empress abruptly left the room to conceal the tears she was obliged to shed. They were called forth by the strong resemblance between the Princess Johanna Elizabeth and her deceased brother once betrothed to the Empress Elizabeth. Fike's memoirs say nothing of these tears, although her mother was much affected by them.

Fike preserved for us, however, the appearance of the Empress at this time: 'More than anything else, I was astonished at her great height,' she says. 'I must say one could not behold her for the first time without astonishment at her beauty and her majesty. She was tall and, though rather stout, no lack of freedom was noticeable in her movements. Her head was very beautiful. On this day she wore an enormous hoop-skirt, which she loved to do when she made a grand toilette and which she only did when she showed herself in public. Her dress was of shimmering silver taffeta trimmed with gold lace; she wore a black feather on her head standing upright a little to one side with many diamonds in a coiffure of her own hair.' The young girl in the rose-coloured moiré frock never forgot the picture.

The next morning, the Princess and her daughter were summoned to the audience chamber by the Empress. 'A few moments later, the Empress in grand attire came from her dressing-room. She wore a brown dress embroidered in silver and quite, that is as far as head, neck and waist were concerned, covered with jewels.' She presented the ribbon and star of Saint Catherine to her guests. Then she passed on to mass. When they next saw her, she was on her way to confession; the next time, to communion. A few days later, on her way to the Troitsky Monastery, she came to say farewell 'in a long-sleeved gown of black velvet adorned with all the Russian orders; that is, the order of Saint Andrew as a scarf, of Saint Alexander about the neck, and of Saint Catherine on the left side.' There seemed no possible limit to all this grandeur. Elizabeth had ten thousand dresses and five thousand pairs of shoes.

But Fike, her mother's ownc hild, was not overawed. She expanded in an atmosphere where ostentation was the rule. With precocious tact, which she owed either to her own intelligence or to Babet Cardel but scarcely to her mother, she established herself securely in this glittering and treacherous environment.

§ 4

Prince Christian August had given his daughter a book as a parting gift. It was a treatise by a professor at Halle which discussed at tedious length the differences between religious creeds. He had prepared to be used with this book a memorandum of instructions for his daughter's use.

Somewhere along the route, how attentively can be imagined, Fike had read this document, and had written one of her primmest letters to dear Papa thanking him for his 'gracious instructions.' The first half of the memorandum was taken up with religious counsel and the second half with her future marriage. The General's style is an awkward contrast to the fluent preciosity of his wife. He addressed his daughter in the third person and outlined her future duties thus:

'Next to the Empress, Her Majesty, she has to respect the Grand Duke above all as her Lord, Father, and Sovereign; and withal to win by care and tenderness at every opportunity his confidence and love. Her Lord and His will are to be preferred to all the pleasures and treasures of the world; and do nothing which he dislikes or which causes him only a little pain; and still less to insist on her own will.

'Never to enter into familiarity or badinage, but always have respect as much as possible.

'To regard the domestics and favourites of her Lord with a gracious mien; not to demand the services of her Lord but ever to respond to the favour and love of her Lord.

'To speak with no one alone in the audience chamber and to conduct herself always according to etiquette there.

'To detest and avoid playing cards for high stakes, which is a mark of avarice and self-interest.

'To take charge herself of the pocket money which may be given her, to guard it and to pay it out gradually to a servant on an account, in order that she may not submit herself to the trusteeship of a governess; to employ it for her use and pleasure, and with it to do good, in order that she may win for herself and not for others instead of her the love and inclination of her dependants.

'To intercede for no one, because one may not understand the laws and a one-sided report cannot be trusted, and the side discriminated against becomes an enemy; and he whom one helps with such intercessions forgets the good deed and goes and sins again.

'Especially to enter into no affairs of government in order not to irritate the Senate.'

At fifteen Fike was not and probably she never became mature enough to appreciate the irony of this document. The abject submissiveness which her father thought appropriate to her status as a wife had certainly never been exemplified by her vivacious mother. She must have been aware that her father played a minor part in the family life at Stettin and at Zerbst, but it was a condition in her little world which from sheer familiarity seemed only natural. What could be more normal than that the man of the family should be kept in leading strings? Few girls in her situation would have contrasted her father's theories with his actions and Fike certainly did not.

Frederick the Great always kept the delusion that he had played the chief rôle in this German-Russian marriage. But he over-estimated his actual part. If Elizabeth had found it necessary to spirit the young Princess away against his royal will she would have done so. Since it was not necessary she welcomed his timely and useful aid. At the right moment Frederick promoted Prince Christian August to the post of Field-Marshal, and after Fike had gone to Russia he helped to reconcile her father to her conversion. 'My good Prince of Zerbst was very restive on this point,' he wrote. 'I had a great deal of trouble in overcoming his religious scruples. He responded to all my representations with: "Meine Tochter soll nicht Griechisch werden!"' His struggles died away gradually under the tactful treatment of his free-thinking King who persuaded him that the Greek and Lutheran Churches were identical. 'Lutherisch-Griechisch, Griechisch-Lutherisch, das gehet an,' the submissive General repeated. If the King of Prussia said so what else could a Prussian officer reply?

82

She Goes to Russia

The marriage was made by three women. It was begun by the Princess of Zerbst and the Empress of Russia and carried through by the fifteen-year-old Fike who took charge of the campaign herself when her mother's tactics failed. Not one of the men who might have been expected to influence the situation did so. Those like Lestocq and the Prince of Zerbst who offered contrary advice were overridden. The others were permitted merely to play the part of bystanders.

5

Fike becomes Catherine

'MY daughter,' wrote Fike's father, 'is already so well grounded in her religion that she knows the principles of the true redeeming faith, and that no one can win or attain it by his own works, vows or the words of the saints, but that all must proceed alone from the merit of Christ, the Son of God. Whatever resembles this faith she can herself prove and accept; the other not. . . . To compel or persuade my daughter to accept a strange religion in which she herself finds errors is never to be advised. . . . And rather eventually to give up the regency than to suffer offence in her conscience.'

These solemn words made a deep impression on the girl. The admonitions which related to her marriage, the Empress, and the Senate were not so serious. She felt herself able to cope with these concrete forces, but the abstraction called conscience is a more terrifying thing. 'I beseech you,' she wrote, replying to her father in his own vein, 'to be assured that your admonitions and precepts will be forever implanted within my heart, as is the seed-corn of our holy religion in my soul. I pray God to give me the strength which I need to withstand the temptations to which I shall be subjected. Through the prayers of your Highness and of my dear mother, God will grant me this grace which my youth and weakness cannot give.'

Fike still believed when she penned these lines that she would be acceptable in Russia as an Evangelical Grand Duchess. In common with her God-fearing father she put her trust in the precedent supplied by the Grand Duchess Charlotte. Their trust was misplaced. Peter the Great was liberal in religious matters, but his daughter was orthodox. Peter did not himself go to church and took pleasure in exposing the sham miracles of the wonder-working

Virgins of Russia who were able to shed real tears before
their worshippers. His daughter did not inherit his scepti-
cal spirit. She was loyal to the Russian Church and a lover
of miracles. Her mother's will provided that no one should
occupy the Russian throne who did not profess the orthodox faith. Fike perceived the finality of this at once.
'From my entrance into the empire,' she said, 'I had been
firmly convinced that the heavenly crown could not be
separated from the earthly one.' On the threshold of her
new life she was plunged into a conflict with her conscience. She wrestled with temptation and the scars of her
struggle remained with her through life.

'The change of religion,' wrote Mardefeld to King
Frederick, 'gives the Princess infinite pain and her tears
flow abundantly when she is alone with persons of whom
she is not suspicious. Nevertheless ambition is gaining
finally the upper hand.' Remembering the religious conflict of his own youth, Frederick was alarmed. But he put
his faith in the Princess Johanna Elizabeth. 'It only remains, Madame, for me to beg you to overcome the repugnance of your daughter for the Greek Church, after which
you will have crowned your work.'

Fike was converted by Simon Todorsky. Having
studied four years at the University of Halle, at that time
a famous school of theology, he knew the language of
Luther well. What was more to the point in dealing with
the young person from Zerbst, Todorsky was familiar
with the subtleties which the intellectuals of Halle had
recently invented. These were things of which good Pastor Wagner, who, after all, was only an army chaplain,
had never even dreamed. With the assistance of Todorsky's hair-splitting arguments, Fike was able to see that
there was very little real difference between the Lutheran
and the Greek Church. If only her father had not con-

tinued to harry her conscience. 'Thou shouldst not take this trial frivolously,' he wrote, 'but must search thyself with care whether thou art really in thy heart inspired by inclination; or whether, perhaps, without thy being aware of it, the marks of favour shown thee by the Empress and other high-placed persons have influenced thee in that direction. We human beings often see only that which is before our eyes. But God in His infinite justice searches the heart and our secret motives, and manifests accordingly to us His mercy.'

As the awful shades of Judgment Day closed about her, Fike fell ill. Once before in childhood she had succumbed to an attack of religious terror complicated by pneumonia. In Russia the experience recurred. 'The physicians ascribe the disease,' wrote her mother, 'to the inflaming of the blood caused by the hard journey.' For twenty-seven days the child hovered between life and death. In unconsciousness and delirium she made the decision which her father had urged her to weigh so carefully. Believing that Fike might die, the Princess suggested that a Lutheran clergyman should be called to her bedside. But the sick girl said, coming for a moment to consciousness, 'Why? Call Simon Todorsky rather. I would like to speak with him.' It was a triumph of diplomacy, an instance of that superb presence of mind which was to carry Fike through every crisis of her life.

During her convalescence, Fike resumed her lessons with the Russian priest, a fact which her mother carefully concealed from the Prince of Zerbst. As soon as she was able to hold a pen, she wrote a stiff respectful letter to her father asking permission to change her religion. She sent her greetings to Uncle Johann Ludwig and promised to write to him by the next post. 'My hand is still very weak,' she said, 'so that I cannot do it to-day.' The two old Puritans at Zerbst with their white wigs and pious ways were vastly important to Fike although nobody else felt that they had to be conciliated.

In after years, when she had become Catherine the Great, Fike made light of the whole business of conversion. When her daughter-in-law had to go through the same experience, she spoke of it merely as a matter of routine. 'As soon as we have her here we shall go about the conversion. In order to convince her, we shall need about fourteen days. How much time will be needed to teach her to read the confession of faith correctly and distinctly in Russian, I do not know.' The fourteen days were taken from Fike's own experience; it was after two weeks of Todorsky's hair-splitting dogma that she had succumbed to pneumonia and the temptings of ambition. Though she could speak of her conversion so casually in after life it almost killed her at the time. The great crimes of which she was accused as Empress made less impression on her conscience. As Catherine the Great she identified her principles with those of Henri IV of France, that brilliant wayward monarch who changed his religion for the sake of a crown. It was only one of many ways in which she tried to justify her departure from her father's Church.

On the 28th of June, pale from a three days' fast, Fike was confirmed and re-christened. The Empress had a gown made for her exactly like her own, of red *gros de Tour* worked with silver. Her godmother was the aged Abbess of the Novodeviche Convent, bowed with years and steeped in sanctity. The Empress with her fondness for tableaux, had arranged all. Krazny, the gorgeous red so beloved by the Russians, dominated the scene. Kneeling on a large square cushion, the convert recited the creed in a clear unfaltering voice. She had learned it, she says, 'by heart, like a parrot.' Indeed she had learned it twice, for Simon Todorsky, the priest, had taught her the Ukrainian pronunciation, and Basil Adadurov, the tutor, had taught her the Russian. For the public ceremony she chose the Russian. As her clear young voice rang out in the first response, the tears of the assembled company gushed forth. Fike maintained her self-control, which gave an impression of deep sincerity and religious fervour and was much praised. 'Her bearing from the moment when she first entered the church,' wrote her mother, 'and throughout the entire ceremony was so full of nobility and dignity that I should have admired her had she not been to me that which she is.'

Standing before her in embroidered and bejewelled robes, the Archbishop of Novgorod intoned: 'Wherefore art thou come to the Holy Orthodox Church of God and what seekest thou from her?' And Fike recited in stereotyped phrases a long impressive creed, in which among other things she professed: 'I believe and confess that faith alone is not sufficient for our justification, but that good works also which proceed from faith and charity withal, as badges of Christ, are necessary to salvation; without the same, faith is dead according to the testimony of holy writ. . . .

'I believe and confess that the pictures of Christ and the mother of God, the Virgin Mary, as those of other saints should be preserved and should be duly venerated, but should not be worshipped.'

Fike's mother sent an enthusiastic but discreet description of the ceremony to her spouse. It was a trifle to her that her daughter's name had been changed, but the girl's father and her aunts would probably be hurt. The name Sophie was a good Russian name, none better, but it happened to be that of the rebellious sister whom Peter the

Great had locked up in a convent. Therefore Elizabeth hated it. So Fike was baptized Catherine Alexeievna for Elizabeth's mother and Sophie Auguste Friedrike ceased to exist. The Princess of Zerbst broke the news to her husband as tactfully as possible. 'In order to seal publicly such a confirmation,' she wrote, 'a name is added; our daughter will be Catherine and the Alexeievna follows the custom of the country and means daughter of August; for the name August, according to the dialect here, cannot be rendered other than Alexis.' The Princess of Zerbst had taken lessons in the Russian language to please the Empress but her progress had not been great. It is possible that she believed that August and Alexis were identical in Russian though probably she knew better. In any case her little fiction would scarcely be discovered by the German General. The rumblings from Zerbst and Stettin died down. The Prince was pleased because his daughter was a Grand Duchess and addressed her by this sonorous title. The Princess continued to call her daughter Fike and carped at her husband for adopting the title of Grand Duchess. 'Fike will think that you no longer love her,' she wrote. But the Prince continued to be respectful. As his daughter had once trusted him to understand her weakness for beer he now trusted her to understand his weakness for etiquette. He was swaggering for them both.

After her confirmation, Catherine Alexeievna followed the Empress from cloister to cloister, for Elizabeth had come to spend more and more of her time as a pious pilgrim. She had apartments in the Troitsky Monastery where she sometimes lived with her court. The Abbot of Troitsky and the Bishops of Moscow and Petersburg accompanied her everywhere. With her three priests, she appeared in the box at the opera and even at masquerade balls. The young Grand Duchess could not imagine good

Pastor Wagner in the rôle of polite escort and cavalier. Her new church had undreamed-of possibilities of romance. Kiev, which she visited with her aunt, seemed a kind of orthodox Arabian Nights. 'Here as in all cities which we had touched since Moscow,' she wrote, ' the clergy of Kiev came to meet us. As soon as the church banners were visible, we left the carriages and entered the city on foot behind the cross. The Empress betook herself to the Petchersky Cloister and entered the church containing the wonder-working portrait of the Holy Virgin said to have been painted by Saint Luke. Never in my whole life have I been so impressed as by the magnificent splendour of the church, in which all the saints' pictures were covered with gold, silver and jewels. . . .'

'Towards the end of our stay in Kiev, the Empress visited with us a monastery where a comedy was to be played. The performance began at seven in the evening. We had to go through the church to reach the theatre. The play consisted really of several plays: there were pro-logues, ballets, a piece in which Marcus Aurelius had his favourite hanged, a battle in which Cossacks fought with the Poles, a fishing scene on the Dnieper, and choruses without number. The Empress held out until about two o'clock in the morning; then she sent to ask whether it would not end soon. The answer came back that only half of the performance had been given but if her Majesty so ordered they would stop at once. She replied that they should finish soon; they begged only for permission to burn some fireworks. . . .'

Such was Christianity in Russia: images covered with gold and silver, plays about a pagan named Marcus Aure-lius, and displays of fireworks. As the pupil of Pastor Wagner, and the daughter of her father, Catherine could not fail to realize that these things proceeded from Satan and from Satan alone. She knew though she dared not admit it that they were idolatrous. And yet she revelled in them. Dr. Martin Luther had thrown an ink-stand at the Devil when he put his head through the window. Every true Christian recognized the Evil One at a glance, and made short shrift of him. The Prince of Zerbst, her father, had once encountered him. It was at Rome during a visit of the Prince that the Pope had tempted him to become a Catholic. But the Prince had not yielded to the blandishments of anti-Christ because, like the heroic Doctor Luther, he recognized the Wicked One in spite of his pompous disguise. The Prince of Zerbst returned to his army and his church unharmed. As a matter of fact it is doubtful whether he had ever seen Rome and still more doubtful whether the Pope would have paid any attention to an obscure German Protestant. But legend is as good as history if the legend is believed, and the Prince's daughter had been brought up to admire this heroic steadfastness of her father's. Of course the Russian Church was like the Lutheran and not the Roman, as Father Todorsky had explained to her and as she had explained to dear Papa. Catherine Alexeievna, however, re-baptized in the Greek faith, found it tactful to conceal a great deal from her father about her new faith and the things the Russians did in the name of their religion.

§ 2

The Empress's attachment to the young Princess had been strengthened by her illness, while the two elder women had been alienated from each other. When Catherine fell ill the Empress was sojourning in her Troitsky retreat. The Court Physician rushed to the sick girl's aid and prepared to bleed her. To their astonishment the Princess of Zerbst forbade the operation. She had always been alarmed about blood-letting, and she stubbornly refused to have her daughter bled. The doctors were outraged. They sent a messenger in haste to their Empress who could not believe her ears. She ordered her carriage and her favourite and posted to Moscow.

Arriving after candle-light, Elizabeth and Razumovsky entered the sick-room and found the patient unconscious. The Empress seated herself on the side of the bed, took the girl in her arms, and told the doctors to operate. The mother was summarily excluded from the room and Lestocq bolted the door. During her illness, Catherine was bled sixteen times, often as much as four times a day. Her mother's opposition was set down by the Court as showing a lack of natural maternal affection. The Empress praised the girl's courage and presented her with a pair of ear-rings and a necklace worth twenty-five thousand roubles. She removed the Princess of Zerbst as head nurse and put the Countess Rumiantsov in her place. The chasm between the mother and daughter was broadening.

Though hurt by all these slights, the Princess of Zerbst could not learn by experience. The climax of her tactlessness came at Easter. Catherine had a piece of blue and silver brocade which Uncle Johann Ludwig had given to her on parting, a rich fabric woven on one of the looms of Zerbst. Her mother coveted the piece and at last sent a messenger to ask for it outright. Catherine resigned her treasure reluctantly, which the Countess Rumiantsov, who acted as spy as well as nurse, observed and reported to the Empress. Elizabeth forthwith sent two gorgeous lengths of stuff to the convalescent girl and openly expressed her opinion of this thoughtless mother. Before they had been in Russia two months, Catherine had won an ally in the Empress while her mother had created in her a bitter enemy.

In the meantime the foreign offices of Prussia, France and Sweden were leaning hard on the Princess of Zerbst to whom they looked for aid in forming an alliance with Russia. The Princess was fascinated by her political mission and did not realize that her mismanagement of her daughter's affairs failed to help the cause of Prussia with the Empress. The Russian Minister of Foreign Affairs, Bestushev, favoured an alliance with Austria against Prussia. He called the King of Prussia 'predatory' and the King of Prussia called Bestushev 'corrupt.' History has shown that both gentlemen were correct.

Bestushev's influence with Elizabeth was supreme because he had been a protégé of her father's. At fifteen he had been sent abroad and educated by Peter the Great. He then entered the diplomatic service and lived for twenty years or more in western Europe. Bestushev was one of the most versatile and gifted Russians of his day. His name was known throughout Europe as the inventor of a medicine called Bestushev's Drops, which was popularly regarded both as an elixir of life and also as a curative dose for hysterical ladies. When Catherine the Great ascended the throne, she bought the formula for Bestushev's Drops and published it as a benefaction to the human race. With all her scorn of doctors she had great respect for Bestushev's Drops. She used them always in her own family.

Bestushev's researches in the black arts had other consequences. He employed in the department of foreign affairs a German by the name of Goldbach, who tampered scientifically with mail. In such matters the Russians supplied the will but they usually employed a German to do the deed. Goldbach opened the French Ambassador's letters and read there a great deal that was not intended for the eyes of the Empress of Russia. He therefore laid the correspondence before Elizabeth who read that she was frivolous and indolent and that her chief interest in life was in changing her costume four or five times a day. She furthermore learned of the secret correspondence going on between the King of Prussia and the Princess of Zerbst and of the strong influence which the Princess was supposed to wield upon herself. It would be mild to say that the Empress was angry. Bestushev's method of gaining his end was simple and successful.

The Empress struck at once. She ordered the French Ambassador to leave Moscow within twenty-four hours and to make for Riga without even touching Petersburg. It was the same Chétardie who had provided French money for her revolution, but he went at once. It was a famous exit. Bestushev continued quietly to shuffle the cards. He now aimed at the meddling Princess of Zerbst.

At Troitsky the Empress and her train occupied a suite of pleasant chambers with low ceilings, English clocks, and Dutch stoves. She had domestic tastes and warm affections and satisfied in this retreat her desire for a quiet family life. Here and at Montplaisir, where she had a summer kitchen in which she cooked with her own hands, she lived her happiest moments. The cosy family atmosphere was interrupted by a painful explosion which took place between the Empress and the Princess of Zerbst after Bestushev had pulled the strings quietly to this end.

The Empress and her guests had just arrived from Moscow. The Empress had made the journey on foot, leaving the others to overtake her in carriages. The entire party entered the gates in the form of a procession, which first turned into the Cathedral for mass and afterwards became a sort of English house-party in which affairs of state and sociability were indiscriminately mixed. 'After the mid-

day meal,' Catherine says, 'when the Grand Duke had
come to our chambers, the Empress entered unexpectedly
and commanded my mother to follow her into the next
room. Count Lestocq went in with them. Awaiting my
mother's return, I seated myself with the Grand Duke
upon the window ledge, and we chatted. The conversation in the closed room lasted a long time.'

The first to appear was Count Lestocq who, assuming
his best German manners, said to the young girl, 'There
is nothing left for you but to pack your things; you will
start at once on your homeward journey.' Lestocq did
not waste courtesy on fallen favourites, but he was not
always shrewd enough to know who had fallen and who
had not. Then the Empress appeared at the door. For a
moment her imposing figure towered beneath the low ceil-
ing, her blue eyes flashing with anger. Behind her appeared the culprit, the Princess of Zerbst, her eyes red
with weeping. The two young people hastily sprang down
from the high window-seat and stood in attitudes of respect. The impulsive Elizabeth laughed, kissed the boy
and girl who were to make up to her for the romantic
marriage she had missed, and passed quickly out of the
room. Lestocq's prophecy was not fulfilled. The Princess and her daughter were not sent home.

Frederick the Great was to feel the effects of this family
quarrel in the Seven Years' War. Elizabeth's dislike of
the Prussian King was greatly strengthened by the explosion at Troitsky. The Princess of Zerbst she never forgave.
Mardefeld, the Prussian minister, was allowed to linger
for a time, but when the Princess of Zerbst returned to
Germany, the Empress demanded Mardefeld's recall.
She hit upon the humiliating device of requiring the
Princess herself to go to the King of Prussia and deliver
the message requesting his minister's recall. The Prussian

Ambassador, who had survived twenty years at the Russian court and had landed on his feet after two palace revolutions, was finally wrecked by his alliance with the Princess of Zerbst. Frederick the Great lost substantially then and afterwards by enlisting the diplomacy of Catherine's mother. He did not forget it.

§ 3

In all her difficulties, Catherine could look for no support from her natural protector and future consort. If she had been an average girl, the defective Peter would still have been a child beside her. But she was far from being an ordinary girl. The fifteen-year-old Princess was more than a match for the two adult women who fancied they were leading her. To steer her course between the Empress and her mother took all her attention at first. For a time she disregarded the Grand Duke as a factor in the situation.

Her account of their relationship shows that they met like children, without any thought of a more mature relationship. 'The Grand Duke appeared to rejoice at my arrival. In the first days he was very complaisant towards me.' During her illness, his goodwill continued. 'During my sickness the Grand Duke had shown me much attention. When I became better he continued this. I seemed to please him; but I cannot say that he either pleased me or displeased me. I only knew how to obey and my mother had to marry me.' The boy gave her his confidence, chattering like a child about everything that came into his head. He confided to her his former love for Princess Lapukin whom the Empress had banished from the Court and whose place had been taken by Catherine herself. The girl, who was passionately proud, could not understand that these were the outpourings of a fragile sexless boy.

She only saw that her lover was indifferent and then pretended to the others that she did not see it.

'When the fair weather came we moved over into the Summer Palace. Here the visits of the Grand Duke grew less frequent. I must say this lack of attention and his coldness so to speak on the eve of our wedding did not exactly incline me in his favour. The nearer the time came, the less could I hide from myself the possibility that my marriage might be very unhappy. But I had too much pride and too much self-respect to allow the world to suspect that I thought myself unloved. I regarded myself too highly to believe that I was contemptible. The Grand Duke had a somewhat free manner with the ladies-in-waiting of the Empress which did not exactly please me, but I restrained myself from speaking about it and no one knew my deepest feelings. I tried to distract myself by romping in my chamber with my maidens.'

The Grand Duchess did not understand that the Grand Duke's attachments to other ladies was as childish and unvirile as his attachment to herself. She says in her memoirs that at this time she scarcely knew the difference between the sexes. But jealousy was an old familiar feeling. Far back among the dim memories of her Stettin childhood was the shadow of a dreadful day when a baby brother had upset her world. She did not like those memories. 'I should have been the most unhappy creature in the world if I had allowed myself to be carried away by feelings of tenderness for him,' she says of the Grand Duke. 'He would have ill-repaid me and I should have died of jealousy, which would have done nobody any good. So I tried to control myself in order that I might not be jealous of a man that did not love me. But in order not to be jealous there was only one means: not to love him.'

The Grand Duchess grew high-strung and nervous. It

97   G

was not the first time that she had failed to meet the requirements of an important situation. Born a girl, she had disappointed her parents' hopes of the succession at Anhalt-Zerbst. Lacking beauty, she had not been attractive to suitors. And now that her future husband did not love her, she had to reassure herself that she was not 'contemptible.' Under the stress of bruised self-feeling, she became capricious and masterful with her maidens. Covering the floor of her room with mattresses, she had all eight of them to sleep in her room. Another time she led the damsels out for a midnight walk through the gardens of Peterhof for which they were all roundly scolded. Like a Sultana she divided the custody of her possessions among them, entrusting her jewels to one, her laces to another, her linen to another and so on. She cut her front hair short, wore it in a kind of frizzled bang and ordered her girls to do the same. Some of them wept and pleaded, but the Grand Duchess had issued a ukase. She would not be moved. Peter the Great had not relented when old men wept and begged to be allowed to keep their beards. Let Maria Petrovna, the Skorodov sisters; and the two dwarfs dry their tears and order in the barber at once to cut off their hair exactly like the Grand Duchess. . . . In addition to her elaborate hair-dressing, Catherine had taken up the habit of painting her face.

§ 4

The Empress arranged the marriage for her two adopted children as if they had been puppets or ballet dancers. No such marriage had ever been seen in Russia except perhaps the famous ice festival in the reign of Anna Ivanovna, when Prince Galitsin married his Lilliputian bride. To satisfy a whim of their Empress the couple had been escorted to an illuminated ice-palace on the Neva and put upon a bed made of ice. Fortunately for Catherine and Peter they were to be married in midsummer. The date was originally set for July 1st, but was postponed twice. Not until late in August was everything finally ready. The whole summer the Empress was so taken up with preparations that she suspended all affairs of state. Her own ministers and the foreign ambassadors had nothing to do but play cards and drive in the Nevsky Prospect.

For months in advance the fashionable world was busy providing itself with 'the richest clothes possible,' since nothing less was specified by the ukase issued by the Empress. Bales of silk, velvet, and brocade were constantly arriving from England and Germany, for the Russians were no weavers. The English ambassador wrote home complaining of the Empress's neglect of official business when he might have better congratulated his country on the increased importation of English goods in Russia. From German looms came the heavy cloth-of-silver from which Catherine's wedding gown was made. It was a rigid structure with a bodice shaped over a wooden form, to which was suspended a train more than three yards long. The fabric was spun silver and the whole thing weighed upon her like a suit of armour.

Clad in this unyielding garment and bearing on her head a ponderous crown of jewels the Grand Duchess spent a miserable day. She held out bravely during the wedding ceremony in the church of Our Lady of Kazan and throughout the state repast in the Winter Palace afterwards. But just before the ball began, she humbled her pride and begged to have the crown removed for a few minutes. The Empress, who thought this might bring bad luck, reluctantly consented.

The wedding was a triumph for Elizabeth's maternal

pride. She ordered every detail of the ceremony with
jealous tyranny, not omitting to command the bride to
take a bath the evening before. Early next morning she
sent for Catherine to come to her chamber to be robed in
state. There ensued a heated argument between the Empress and the barber concerning the bride's style of hair-
dressing. Catherine sat before the mirror and seemed to
take no part. There was not a rift on this day in her good
relations with the Empress. A supreme satisfaction in the
great event united them completely.

Although it was also the wedding-day of the Grand
Duke, he played a rather minor part. The ill-starred boy
had managed to contract the smallpox recently and appeared at his nuptials with a dreadfully pockmarked face.
His august aunt always dreaded his public appearances
lest some piece of childish misbehaviour on his part should
disgrace the Romanov family. Peter bore himself sufficiently well on his wedding-day, however, to cause no
comment among the on-lookers. His only caprice was to
offend his bride. While the young couple were still kneeling opposite to each other, waiting the final words of the
priest, one of the court ladies whispered in the Grand
Duke's ear. 'I heard him say to her,' says Catherine,
' "Clear out! Such nonsense!" ' Then he turned to me and
told me that she had advised him not to turn his head
while he stood before the priest, for whoever of us first
turned our head would die first and she did not wish him
to be that one. I thought this compliment not very
friendly on our wedding-day but I did not allow myself to
notice it. She saw, however, that he had repeated to me
her good advice. She grew red and made reproaches,
which he again repeated to me.'

At ten o'clock, the Empress herself conducted the
young people to their apartments and left the Grand

Duchess with her maidens. She was relieved of her burdensome wedding garments and put to bed beneath a velvet coverlet. 'All of them went away,' Catherine's narrative relates. 'I remained alone more than two hours and did not know what I should do. Should I get up again? Should I remain in bed? I knew nothing. Finally my new lady of honour, Madame Kruse, came and informed me with great merriment that the Grand Duke was waiting for his supper which was about to be carried up to him. After his Imperial Highness had supped well, he came to bed; and as he laid himself down, he began to talk of how it would amuse his servant in the morning to see us both in bed. Then he fell asleep and slept soundly until the next morning. The cloths of fine linen on which I lay were very uncomfortable owing to the summer weather and consequently I slept badly; all the more as the morning grey of the daylight disturbed me considerably, for the bed had no curtains, although otherwise furnished magnificently in red velvet with silver embroidery. Madame Kruse attempted the next morning to question us young married people. Her hopes however proved unfounded. And in this condition our affairs remained during the next nine years without the least change.'

The Empress was not satisfied with one day's celebration of the marriage. The festivities were prolonged for ten days. The streets were given over to merry-making; heralds on horseback, fountains spouting wine, fire-works and white nights, and all the bells and cannon of Petersburg made a continuous carnival. An unbroken succession of dinners, operas, masquerades, and quadrilles crowded upon each other.

The Princess of Zerbst was hard put to it to describe these festivities adequately to her spouse. For he was not present. Somehow the invitation which should have

brought the Prince of Zerbst to his daughter's wedding
had never been sent. He had expected it from week to
week, since Frederick had told them that it would surely
come. In the end, the old Prince was overlooked and had
to console himself with his wife's description of his daughter's wedding. The exuberant Princess wrote, 'The Grand
Duchess sends you her respects, but has no time to write,
since it is still so new for her to be with her husband. They
can scarcely be separated for a quarter of an hour.'

The Little Grand Duchess moved through everything
like an automaton. She stepped through the white and
gold quadrilles with tears in her eyes. 'Never in my life,'
said she afterwards, 'have I seen a more woeful and stupid
amusement than were those quadrilles.' The beginning of
her honeymoon was just as woeful. 'After my wedding,'
she said, 'I felt best when I was with my mother. I strove
all the more eagerly to stay with her as my household could
scarcely be called pleasant. The Grand Duke had nothing
but child's play in his head; he gave himself up to playing
at soldiers, surrounded by his menials in whom alone he
showed any interest.'

6

Catherine becomes a Mother

Two weeks after the wedding, the Empress sent the young married pair with the Princess of Zerbst to Czarskoe Selo. It was the month of September and the birches were turning to gold. But the bride had suddenly lost her enthusiasm for the Russian scene. For the first time she was homesick for Germany and dreaded the moment of her mother's departure. 'At that time I would have given much if I could have left the country with her.'

She was sustained, however, by a new sense of power and importance which came from having money in her pocket. This enabled her to patronize her mother by assuming her debts, for the extravagant Princess had obligations amounting to seventy thousand roubles and no idea how she was ever going to meet them. Catherine promised to pay in her mother's stead a sum which was absurdly beyond her means, for the Empress allowed her only thirty thousand roubles a year. Lifted so suddenly from the meagre circumstances of her Stettin life, the Grand Duchess had no measure for her newly-acquired riches. They seemed to her limitless. Of course she was in a position to come to her mother's assistance and she came. Even if her new husband did not love her she was a rich woman now and could afford to be generous. This was the beginning of a labyrinth of debt in which she progressively involved herself until it brought her within a few years to the verge of bankruptcy.

At the end of September the Princess of Zerbst and Fräulein Khayn set forth on their homeward journey. They were laden with presents from the Empress. Two chests filled with Chinese and Damascene stuffs accompanied the travellers; and to console the long-neglected Prince of Zerbst, his wife carried with her as gifts from the Grand Duke diamond shoe-buckles, diamond coat-buttons, and a diamond-studded dagger. The party was escorted by Catherine and Peter as far as Krasnoe-Selo, the old Red Village of the Czars, where the Princess and her daughter saw each other for the last time. 'I wept a great deal,' says Catherine, 'and in order not to make me still more sad my mother went away without taking leave of me.'

As soon as she arrived home, the Grand Duchess went to find her favourite maiden, Maria Petrovna Shukov, to comfort her in her loneliness. But the girl had disappeared during Catherine's absence. It happened that she had been sent away at the suggestion of the Princess of Zerbst. The Princess and the Empress had put their heads together over the unpromising status of the newly-made marriage and the banishment of Maria was the result. They remembered the part which Julie von Mengden had played in alienating the former regent, Anna Leopoldovna, from her husband, and they feared that Maria Shukov might play a similar part by increasing the estrangement between Catherine and Peter. The Grand Duchess learned then that she could never have a confidante in the future.

Anything which reminded Elizabeth of Anna Leopold-ovna's family was hateful to her. She wished to forget the deposed Regent if possible, but the wretched woman, as if to revenge herself on the Empress, had continued to increase her family. Four children had been born to her at Kolmogory, two of whom were sons. The Major in charge sent a faithful report of each birth to the Empress, who tore his reports into pieces. At last he sent a report which she did not tear into pieces. Anna had died in childbed. The Empress gave orders that the body of the deceased Regent should be dissected, and brought to

Petersburg for burial. Accompanied by the Grand Duchess, both draped in heavy black, she attended the funeral ceremonies in the Alexander Nevsky Cathedral where the ill-starred Anna was laid to rest between her grandmother and her mother. Her grandmother was the old Czarina Prascovia Feodorovna, who had laid a curse on her daughter, and her mother was the daughter who had been cursed. The unlucky Anna weighed on Catherine's conscience not a little.

The death of Anna occurred about nine months after the marriage of the Grand Ducal pair. The Empress gave them another month of grace while she repaired with her favourite to spend May at Czarskoe Selo. Presently she returned, advancing upon the sterile couple like a threatening Juno. She had apparently expected that the Grand Duchess would, without preliminary warning or symptoms, present her with a Romanov heir in the ninth month after marriage. Disappointed in her hopes, she took drastic measures to remedy the situation.

This time it was Bestushev and the Empress who put their heads together. Bestushev, it will be remembered, had not favoured this marriage and Elizabeth's discontent with its results directed her thoughts towards him. At her wits' end, she asked him to devise a régime, a programme, for the young people, which he did with spirit and enthusiasm. He gave the Empress an elaborate memorandum concerning the behaviour of the Grand Duchess and a still more elaborate memorandum concerning the behaviour of the Grand Duke. The instructions were for the use of the guardians who were to take charge of the pair. Bestushev's document rehearsed at length the faults of the Grand Duke: his disrespectful behaviour in church; his weakness for toys and tin soldiers; his familiarity with pages and lackeys; his low language, his grimaces, his indecencies at table. In short, the Vice-Chancellor drew a picture of the Russian heir-apparent that might have been mistaken for the portrait of a child in bibs. All of its statements are confirmed by Catherine in her memoirs. The rules which he prepared for the Grand Duchess consisted entirely of prohibitions, chief of which was a ban on all private correspondence with her mother, the Princess of Zerbst. This drove the girl to clandestine communications in which she became at last very skilful and which she learned to use later on for political ends.

The keystone of the new régime was the appointment of a married couple as guardians. The Choglokovs were chosen for special reasons. Maria Choglokov had married her husband for love and was known to all the court as the pattern of a faithful and devoted wife. Bestushev brought the young matron to the Grand Duchess's apartment and introduced her as the new governess or duenna. 'Imme-diately,' says Catherine, 'I began to weep violently.' This did not help to ingratiate her governess. The atmosphere became hysterical. Catherine went to bed for a whole day and had to be bled the next morning. The Empress came and scolded angrily. Young wives who did not love their husbands always wept; Catherine's mother had assured her that Catherine had no objection to marrying the Grand Duke; she, the Empress, had not forced her to marry him; and, finally, now that they were already married there was no use in crying about it. Thoroughly frightened at the Empress's display of temper, Catherine murmured, 'Little mother, forgive me, I am in the wrong.' She feared that the Empress would actually beat her as she did sometimes beat the ladies and gentlemen of the court.

The new duenna performed her duties well, setting the good example which the Empress had expected of her.

Catherine Becomes a Mother

'From 1746 until the death of her husband,' says Catherine, 'who died in the year 1754, we really never saw her except pregnant or in childbed.' The Grand Duchess hated the prolific Maria, and no wonder. Scarcely was the wretched Anna Leopoldovna well underground than this new and vivid reproach sprang up before her very eyes. The Kolmogory family had been at least out of sight, but Maria's babies were born under her own eyes and the birth of each was heralded as an important public event. Bestushev wrote to Count Vorontsov in London: 'In these days it has pleased her Imperial Majesty to commission Nicolai Naumovich Choglokov to journey to the Roman Emperor to congratulate him on the attainment of his high distinction; he will not, however, depart before his wife has been delivered; that is, the middle of March.' On the 14th of March Bestushev added: 'In these days Maria Semionovna . . . has given birth to an infant daughter. And Nicolai Naumovich will depart soon from here to Vienna.'

The Empress hoped apparently that Maria's fertility was something which the Grand Duchess might acquire by association and imitation. Yet year after year passed by and the miracle did not happen. Catherine remained childless while Maria bore a child every year. In writing her memoirs drops of gall fall from her pen whenever she speaks of the Choglokovs. 'Although he was loved so much he was not at all lovable. Of all the people in the world, he was the most puffed up and conceited; he thought himself extraordinarily beautiful and clever. He was a stupid coxcomb, arrogant and spiteful, and at the least quite as malicious as his wife, who was so not a little.' The Grand Duchess indulged in petty revenge, such as the following story shows. One of her maidens had a trick of imitating with a pillow the walk of the pregnant Maria. Catherine encouraged her in this performance by peals of appreciative laughter. Her spitefulness extended itself to Maria's sister Martha. 'How far the stupidity of this woman went is shown by the following pretty story: she was quite astonished at the cleverness of the midwife who prophesied that she would bring either a boy or a girl into the world. She could not understand whence the midwife had this knowledge.'

Madame Choglokov and her sister were Skavronskys, nieces of the Empress. They represented the stock from which Elizabeth had sprung on her mother's side. The Skavronskys were more prominent in the Empress's environment than the Romanov side of her family, and Catherine liked to remember that the Empress was a Skavronsky. The houses of Zerbst and Holstein, although impoverished, did not produce women as weak-witted as the Empress's nieces. Catherine found in that reflection a satisfaction for her resentment and jealousy.

§ 2

Her memoirs describe a nine-years' purgatory of mental and physical suffering. She says but little of her attitude towards the Grand Duke, but that little is significant. When the Empress accused her of not loving him, she spoke the truth, for Catherine says herself that, as a protection against jealousy, she schooled herself to be indifferent towards her husband.

Peter, who had all the pride which goes with a weak personality, tried to console himself in the usual way. He became a good deal of a ladies' man. In tender glances and in compliments he was not at all backward; he could give an excellent imitation of a young man in love. His pose was so good that it deceived his aunt and humiliated his wife. He became better and better at it. Finally he entered into a relationship with Elizabeth Vorontsov who came to be regarded as a real mistress. Catherine knew that Peter was incompetent to have a physical relationship, but she realized that others did not know it. As Peter's affectations grew his actual condition became worse. Nor did the stony indifference of his wife help to make matters any better. On the contrary, it helped to make them worse. The Grand Duke crystallized into a little manikin incapable of feelings of any kind.

Catherine's life was full of illness and hypochondria. A catalogue of her ailments can be made up from her reminiscences. She fills up pages with stories of headaches, toothaches, insomnia, influenza and measles. She describes these afflictions with a serious attention to detail which she scarcely achieved in describing the Turkish Wars of her later years. She says impressively that her colds were so severe that she used twelve pocket-handkerchiefs a day. At one time her physician thought she had tuberculosis. He ordered her to bed and put her on a diet of ass's milk. She suffered from a consuming fear of smallpox and every time anything went wrong with her she believed herself stricken. Once it turned out to be only measles, but her spots, she assures us, were as large as roubles. All of her illnesses and afflictions during those years were the worst that could be suffered and survived.

The story of her skull-bones has a dramatic climax and a happy ending. 'During this entire year,' says the heroine, 'I suffered continually from headache and sleeplessness. Madame Kruse brought me as a so-called medicine a glass of Hungarian wine after I lay in bed, which I was supposed to drink regularly every evening. I refused this remedy for sleeplessness and Madame Kruse drank it in my stead and to my health. After I had returned to the city, I complained to Dr. Boerhaave of my sufferings. He was a very sympathetic man; he also knew the kind of life I lived and knew my relation to my husband as well as to my environment. He bade me show him my head some morning before my hair was dressed and carefully he went over the skull. Finally he said that, although I was seventeen years old, my head had the formation of that of a six-year-old child; that I must be very careful and never allow the upper part of my skull to get cold; in short, the bones of my head had never yet closed up. He believed that the bones would only close up when I had reached the age of twenty-five or twenty-six and that this was the cause of my headaches. I followed his advice and it was a fact that the separation between the skull-bones disappeared only when I was twenty-five or twenty-six years old as he had prophesied.'

This happy cure of Catherine's skull coincided with the birth of her first child which occurred when she was half-way between twenty-five and twenty-six. Apparently her physician was also something of a fortune-teller who could read the future, predict events, and give accurate dates.

Catherine pictures her experience with toothache and tooth-pulling with more than Russian realism. Twenty-five years after she had lost a tooth, she could seat herself at her writing table and recall in fancy the painful moment when her physician and her surgeon and a male assistant had removed it. After the operation was completed it was discovered that the Grand Duchess had lost a piece of jawbone 'as large as a ten-sous piece.' The surgeon wished to examine the wound but the patient would not allow him to touch her. 'I learned then,' she says, 'that the pain which one suffers often creates hatred towards the one who causes it.' In the midst of her absorption in her tragedies, Catherine was capable of flashes of psychological insight.

'My situation was really not to be laughed at,' she says. 'I stood completely isolated among all the people there.

Meantime I had accustomed myself to it; the reading of good books and my cheerful turn of temperament helped me easily over the situation. Besides I had a presentiment of future destiny which gave me courage to bear all that I had to bear and to endure daily unpleasantness from more than one side. Already I wept much less when I was alone than in the first years.'

The Empress had given Oranienbaum to Peter for a summer residence. Here the young people led a comparatively free life. Catherine used her freedom to go duck-hunting, rising at three o'clock in the morning to pursue her sport. With one old man for an attendant, she sometimes took a boat and followed her game far out into the open waters of the Finnish gulf. As she roamed about alone in the white light of the summer dawn, her romantic musings were mingled with ambitious thoughts. 'At that time I read only romances which heated my imagination, of which verily I had no need.' She wore men's clothes on her shooting expeditions, as Elizabeth had done before she became Empress. But her thoughts were occupied far more than Elizabeth's had ever been with thoughts of the crown and the succession.

Sometimes for as much as thirteen hours a day she rode on horseback. It was an exercise which she passionately loved. Whenever she touches on the subject of her skill as a rider, her vanity gets entirely out of hand. Her prowess was such that her riding-master wept tears of enthusiasm and, speechless with joy, could only run to kiss her riding-boot. The actress in blue velvet whom little Fike had seen at the age of three could hardly have expected more! Catherine's riding soon became another source of conflict between herself and the Empress. She preferred to ride astride and the Empress feared that this might be the reason why she had no children. The Empress forbade the practice and Catherine did not dare to disobey her openly. But she had an English saddle made with a movable pommel, so that she could ride either sidesaddle or astride. When safely out of sight of the Empress and her nasty Skavronsky relations, she rode as she pleased.

§ 3

In Bestushev and his drastic Instructions, Elizabeth had exhausted her last resource of discipline. But her disappointment and chagrin caused her to continue in a thousand petty ways to harass the Grand Ducal pair. They were kept on a nursery régime of restrictions. Neither of them was allowed to leave the house even for a drive without the express permission of the Empress. She regulated their slightest movements, ordering them from the Winter Palace to the Summer Palace or from Petersburg to Oranienbaum without a moment's notice. Sometimes she allowed them to form a part of her entourage when she took a journey. Catherine complains, however, that the Empress always omitted her from her hunting parties, although she knew how passionately the Grand Duchess loved to ride and shoot. On the other hand, the Empress always remembered to include her in her religious pilgrimages.

Catherine describes Elizabeth's excursions in a rather critical spirit. There was, for instance, a trip to Reval when she had to sleep in a kitchen where bread was being baked and where the ovens sent out a terrible heat. Sometimes the Empress's party spent the night in tents and Catherine recalls rather scornfully those forlorn occasions when storms came on and the wind blew out the torches and the rain soaked the finery of the courtiers. Once they went to visit a wonder-working Virgin in a holy cloister, but she could not possibly be seen because the boards on which she was painted were covered with black filth. In this carping spirit Catherine described the best the Empress had to show her, and yet she felt surprised and injured because the Empress did not like her. 'Her dislike of me,' she said, 'has increased from year to year, although my entire aim has been to please her in everything. The Grand Duke is a witness that I have done everything to persuade him also to do this. My respect, my obedience in all that she has wished, has been carried to the uttermost limit to which a human being can carry it.' Yet the Empress called her 'Ochen upriany,' very stubborn, and refused to see her for weeks and months at a time.

During the second spring following her marriage, Catherine received the news of her father's death. The Prince had died of a stroke of apoplexy. Catherine wept so violently and long that the doctors came and bled her. Still she wept on. The Empress grew impatient and finally sent word through Madame Choglokov that Catherine should dry her tears. 'My father had been no King, and the loss was not so great. . . . But to the credit of her Majesty, I cannot believe that the woman said to me what she had been commanded to say, for that did not exactly show goodness of heart!' Catherine was allowed to wear mourning for only six weeks and was limited to mere black silk instead of crêpe. 'I must confess,' writes Catherine, 'that to-day (twenty-five years later) I cannot think of it without rebellion in my heart.'

The Empress's irritation made her variable temper more variable than ever. She grew more restless and eccentric. Every day she had the furniture shifted in her apartments. Her people were left waiting hours and days for orders which she delayed for mere whims. Once the Grand Duchess remained sitting upright on a chair, fully dressed for early mass, while the hands of the clock slowly passed from four o'clock in the morning to three o'clock in the afternoon. The Empress had summoned her to go to church but had changed her mind at the last moment and gone to the bath instead.

The wishes of the young Court were never consulted, even formally, about anything. A favourite attendant would vanish overnight and be heard of next in Astrakhan, Orenburg or Kazan, whither he had been banished. Always, Catherine says, the exiles passed first through the court called the Secret Chancellary, a form of inquisition which was the terror and horror of Russia at the time. One day the Grand Duke's Holstein servants were suddenly sent back to Germany without warning, and he was left alone with Russians whom he detested. Another day Catherine's attendant, Madame Kruse, who happened also to be a Holsteiner, was suddenly dismissed and replaced by Madame Vladislav, who was a Russian. The Empress had apparently hit upon the forlorn hope that it might be German influence which kept the young couple sterile.

Catherine's new woman, Prascovia Nikitichna Vladislav, made an important contribution to her education. Prascovia was about fifty and her gossip about the Russian grandees and their families went back to the time of Peter the Great. Catherine was fascinated by these histories which gave her the orientation in Russia that she needed. Peter would not listen to Prascovia. He was homesick for Holstein, and as the German group which once surrounded him grew less and less and finally disappeared completely, his heimweh increased. The last to go was Baron Lestocq, who was imprisoned for five years in the Fortress of Saint Peter and Saint Paul and finally banished to Uglitch. The Empress was done with Germans for all time.

Catherine seemed to forget very easily the old friends of

her mother's party and to pass on quickly to an alliance with the Russians. In time she found herself and Bestushev, the official enemy of that party, on the same side and even united in their political schemes. She had an elasticity of temperament which was her one salvation in her trying circumstances. For there is no denying they were intensely trying. 'For eighteen years,' she writes, 'I have led a life from which ten others would have gone insane and twenty in my place would have died of melancholy.'

The petty persecutions of the Empress were the only thing that drew the young couple together. When Catherine was scolded by her duenna, Peter flared up in her defence. In return, Catherine gave Peter advice and comfort when he fled to her in terror at the threats of the Empress and his governors. But Catherine found his fears excessive; with a certain detachment and objectivity she recognized that they were beyond the ordinary and uncontrollable. She wondered at this trait at first and yet sympathized with him; but later on when other things had come between them, her wonder changed to scorn. Her story of the Grand Duke and his abhorrence of the Russian bath shows that she early appreciated the dangers into which the young man's stubbornness was leading him.

During the first week of Lent, the Empress ordered Catherine and Peter to go to the steam bath, as a part of the regular preparation for communion. The Grand Duke excitedly refused. He would not enter the bath; he had never been there before and it was a ridiculous ceremony anyhow to which he attached no significance. Besides, the bath was harmful and would make him ill. 'He did not wish to die; his life was his most precious possession. The Empress could never force him to the point of going there.' To all this Madame Choglokov replied with equal heat. She threatened the young man with the fortress of

Saint Peter and Saint Paul and reminded him that the son of Peter the Great had perished as the result of disobedience. 'Much of this,' Catherine reflected, watching Madame Choglokov, 'comes from herself but much is from the Empress. I came to the conclusion that the threat of the fortress must have come from the monarch and I saw in it a sign of her strong resentment against the Grand Duke.'

The mischief-making Maria reported all this back to the Empress, whose wrath flared out in her usual strong language: 'Very good; if he is so disobedient towards me, I will not kiss his accursed hand any more.' This was faithfully carried back to the Grand Duke, who said, 'That depends on herself. But I will never go into the bath. I cannot bear the heat.' The Empress kept her word and her nephew kept his. Yet she never gave up the attempt to force him into the bath. He was not again threatened with the fortress, but he always felt the threat lurking in the background. The quarrel made a great impression on the Grand Duchess who tells of it at length in her memoirs. She regarded it correctly as a symptom of something extreme in his character, but she could not understand it. Her common-sense was baffled by the behaviour of a youth who feared the Russian bath more than he feared imprisonment in a fortress. In his obstinacy and excitement, Peter gave various reasons for refusing to obey the Empress but he scarcely gave the real one. The Russian bath was a social affair, participated in by naked men and women. The custom, a mere everyday affair in Russia, was regarded with horror in Germany and the rest of Europe. The young Grand Duke was still a German and, without being clearly aware of the reason, he dreaded the exposure and found the idea of it unendurable. Imprisonment was a trifle by comparison. The Grand Duchess faced this problem as she did others in her new life. She had been brought up a puritan and a protestant. But she no longer lived in Zerbst; she lived in Russia and did as the Russians did. The Grand Duke continued to dwell in an imaginary Holstein of his own which was as different as possible from the Russia which lay around him.

§ 4

Elizabeth's capriciousness increased. Having changed her furniture and everything else at hand that could be changed, at last she changed her favourite. The easy-going Razumovsky was displaced and relegated with honours and riches to private life. There is a tradition that the Count had been secretly married to Elizabeth. Whether this be true or not does not matter much. The time had come for him to go. The discarded lover retired to the Anitchkov Palace which the Empress had built for him and where he dreamed away his life for another twenty years. Razumovsky was a charming decoration on the early reign of Elizabeth Petrovna. He was wholly impracticable and without ambition of any kind, a poetic indolent Ukrainian. He was loyal to his mistress to the end and devoted to her successor, Catherine the Great.

Ivan Ivanovich Shuvalov, the new favourite, was a cousin. As the Empress grew older she suffered increasingly from melancholy which she strove to lighten by drawing the circle of relatives closer around her. Ivan Ivanovich was ably supported in his new duties by his family. He had a sister, a cheerful person whom the Empress relied upon to rescue her from low spirits. He had besides two brothers who guarded him on both flanks and reaped a rich harvest of monopolies. The Shuvalov brothers were ambitious and grasping as the Razumovskys had never been. Their advent made a great difference at court, for the Empress, who became more indolent and fanciful every day, gave more and more power to the Shuvalovs. She had failed in her dearest scheme: her nephew and successor, the Grand Duke Peter, had no heir.

With the year 1750 the problem of an heir seemed to grow desperate. In the Grand Duke's court a matter of urgent necessity had to be faced. It was represented chiefly by Madame Vladislav, Catherine's lady-in-waiting, and by the mother of young Sergei Saltikov, a young chamberlain of the Grand Duke. Slowly the idea took shape without anybody's expressing it that the Grand Duchess might, by merely transgressing her marriage vows, redeem the situation. By some means this idea was insinuated into the heads of the stupid Choglokovs who afterwards thought they had invented it. Maria Choglokov suggested it to Catherine; put it to her, so to speak, as her patriotic duty. It seems rather odd that all of them had been so slow in coming to this plan. Apparently Catherine would have gone on indefinitely in the dilemma if the older married women had not finally suggested a way out.

Catherine wrote two accounts of her affair with Sergei Saltikov. One was set down only three or four years after it was over, and the other she wrote in her old age. The old lady's story is a lively romance, portraying an ardent courtship, a horseback ride, a lonely island, and an importunate lover. The young woman's story is less romantic and more political. She says in this version: 'Madame Choglokov used all possible arts of persuasion to seduce me. This and the attractiveness and talents of him for whom she spoke would have found less resistance in another than in me. It is really true that I was distinguished by discretion and exemplary innocence.'

Sergei Saltikov was a merry and irresponsible youth without ulterior ambitions. His relations with the Grand

Duchess began in the year 1752. In December of that year the Grand Duchess reported miscarriage. The following July the same misfortune befell her. She seemed doomed to bad luck and delay. Not until the 20th of September, 1754, did she actually become a mother. On that date she bore a son. 'There was inexpressible joy over it,' is her laconic comment. It was about this time, according to her memoirs, that her skull-bones closed up.

Whether the Empress was aware of the intrigue between Catherine and Sergei Saltikov we do not know. We do know, however, that with the year 1754 her attitude towards the young Count underwent a decided change. Choglokov and his wife saw great possibilities for the future, hoping to reap the credit for the new and gratifying turn of events. When the Empress began to turn a friendly gaze upon the young Count, Choglokov lost his head and tried to woo her. Catherine admits that she and her mischievous Sergei encouraged this indiscretion which invited dangers unforeseen by their inexperience and youth. The brothers Shuvalov were strongly intrenched and were ready to make short shrift of any rival. At a masquerade ball, the softened Empress encouraged Choglokov with tender glances. Ivan Ivanovich, the favourite, saw them, and his clan closed in around her, at once, and insidiously. In the end Choglokov was insulted by the Empress in public. 'She called him,' says Catherine, 'in a public conversation at dinner a blockhead and a traitor, which he so took to heart that he fell into the jaundice. Kandoidi, the Shuvalov's man, was called in, and, as he had long known that the patient was an enemy of theirs, believed that he would do them a favour by murdering him. At least all the doctors who were called in during his last days maintained that he had been treated as a creature whom one wished to kill. Four days after his death his wife was told that she

could remain in Moscow. . . . I believe that Saltikov
would have been banished at that time too if I had not been
pregnant and they had not feared to afflict me with this
grief.'

At last the midwife declared that the moment was at
hand. The Empress, who occupied adjoining chambers,
was summoned from her bed at two o'clock in the morning. She swept upon the scene in a mantle of blue satin,
for the room was cold with the chill of a late September
dawn. At noon the child was born. The Empress waited
only for the midwife to bathe and swaddle the infant.
Then she called the priest and had him christened Paul.
This was the name of the first child born to her mother
and Peter the Great, a bastard son who had died at the age
of three. Commanding the midwife to carry the child in
front of her, the Empress retired to her own apartments
where she arranged a nursery and cared for him with her
own hands. If he whimpered she ran to him at once; her
devotion became the subject of wide comment and general
praise. It gave rise to the rumour that the child was actually Elizabeth's own and not Catherine's at all. The Empress was not displeased with the rumour; there were
moments in her last years, years given over to vapours and
moods, when she almost believed the myth herself. That
she had done violence to the young mother in kidnapping
her child never entered her head. She asked Maria Theresa of Austria to be godmother to her child. Austria
should now realize that Russia also had an heir.

§ 5

Very little is known of the father of Paul. The unhappy life of Catherine's son and his final insanity have set
many writers and historians at work discussing his heredity. But they always have assumed that his father was

Peter III and that his grandfather was Peter the Great. If this were true, the deficiencies of Catherine's son would be easy to explain, for heredity on the Romanov side left much to be desired. Peter the Great had a feeble-minded brother and Peter III had a mental twist. But all this has nothing to do with Paul, who was not a Romanov but a Saltikov.

We must rely upon Catherine's memoirs for the little that we know about the Saltikovs. Sergei and Peter were brothers in the service of the Grand Duke. Their father was the General Saltikov who had welcomed Catherine and her mother in Riga on their way to Russia. The mother of the Saltikov brothers had been a Princess Galitsin and a loyal helper of the Empress Elizabeth when Elizabeth seized the throne. The tradition is that Maria Saltikov had squandered her virtue in Elizabeth's cause. However this may have been, the Empress was devoted to this lady and attached her two sons to the Court of the Grand Duke. Sergei was a great favourite of Peter's and often slept with him. At the time when Maria Saltikov promoted the affair between her son and the Grand Duchess she was a confirmed invalid, but she seems to have kept her initiative and energy to the last. As she had helped her Empress gain a throne she now stood ready to help her gain an heir for it.

Sergei Saltikov was a typical ne'er-do-well. Catherine tried to make the most of her lover in her memoirs, but not a great deal could be made of him. He was a merry fellow, a brunet, who said of himself when he was once attired in a silver costume that he looked 'like a fly in the milk.' Catherine says of him that he 'was beautiful as the day; no one could compare with him, even in the great Court, still less in our own. He was not without spirit and possessed those charming manners which one acquires from living in the world of fashion and especially at the Court. In the year 1752 he was twenty-six years old. His birth and other qualities made him an outstanding personality. He had his faults, which he knew how to conceal; his greatest faults were a tendency to intrigue and a lack of strong principles. This however was unknown to me at that time.'

She then passes on to his brother Peter, whom she presents in a quite different light. Peter 'was a fool in the fullest sense of the word, and had the most stupid physiognomy that I have ever seen in my life: great leaden eyes, a turned-up nose, a mouth always half open. Besides, he was a terrible tattle-tale.' Evidently Peter was no credit to the Saltikov family. Yet he happened to be the uncle of her son.

It was afterwards said of Paul, when he became Paul I of Russia, that his portrait with its turned-up nose was considered even by himself too ugly to be imprinted on his coins; and that when the crowds of Paris gathered to look at him they cried out, 'My God, how ugly he is!' His looks, we might fairly conclude, were a gift which the bad fairies of heredity had borrowed from Uncle Peter. There were other disadvantages which the bad fairies doubtless took from the Saltikov family, for Paul was afflicted in several ways which always remained a puzzle to his mother.

AFTER the birth of her son, the Grand Duchess recuperated but slowly. The icy winds from the Neva penetrated her apartment and she suffered continually from colds. She was querulous. Her chamber, in which she was obliged to pass all her time as a convalescent, was too small. Eight archins in one direction and four in the other, it measured but little more than the humble room in Stettin in which Catherine herself had been born. As a Grand Duchess, she resented these narrow walls; she resented the badly-drawn pictures on the tiles of her Dutch stove; she resented the Grand Duke's tobacco smoke which invaded her premises; and she resented the 'wretched pieces of jewellery' which the Empress had been pleased to give her. The present of a hundred thousand roubles which accompanied the jewels was the sole bright lining of her cloud. Catherine always needed money.

But even this joy was tarnished by the fact that the Empress immediately borrowed the whole sum and did not repay her until the following January. The Empress recalled the money because the Grand Duke, on hearing that his wife had received it, raised a great outcry on his own behalf. As there was no money in the treasury with which to silence him, the Empress hastily sent to the Grand Duchess and asked for the loan of her treasure. Obviously Catherine was in no position to refuse; besides she eventually got it back again. It was not so with her baby, which the Empress had taken away without once saying by your leave and which was never restored to her. Here also, apparently, the young mother believed herself in no position to refuse, for she allowed the Empress to rob her without a single protest. Her acquiescence was complete.

She was permitted to see the child but rarely, and when she did consoled herself with criticisms of the way his foster-mother took care of him. 'From sheer over-carefulness, he was literally smothered. He lay in a very hot room entirely wrapped in flannel, in a crib made of black fox-fur and covered with a wadded satin coverlet. Above this was a red velvet coverlet lined with black fox-fur. . . . The sweat ran down his face and down his whole body.' Yet she made no attempt to rescue him. To try it would have been useless, for the autocrat of all the Russias was easily supreme in her own household. Catherine also probably had too little confidence in her own rights of possession.

Three weeks after the child's birth, Saltikov was sent to Sweden to announce the event. 'That depressed me greatly,' says Catherine, 'because I was thereby exposed to the talk of the whole world.' She must have felt even at that early date that her secret was pretty widely known. It could have been no comfort to her, sitting alone in her little draughty, smoke-filled room, to hear, as she soon did, that the frivolous Saltikov was continuing his Don Juan career in the Swedish capital. 'I held fast to what I had begun,' she writes, 'less from inclination than from steadfastness, and worked for his return, tirelessly conquering obstacles and battling with all my strength against every hindrance.' Through her new alliance with Bestushev success was achieved. Sergei Saltikov returned to Petersburg during the Carnival season.

With great difficulty the Grand Duchess arranged a rendezvous and waited until three o'clock in the morning for a lover who never came. There was an elaborate explanation, how he had been dragged into a Freemason lodge by one of the Dolgorukis, and could not escape. But the Grand Duchess was not deceived. She no longer opposed the plan which had been suggested of sending Saltikov to Hamburg as resident envoy. His departure was delayed from week to week, but Catherine's influence was not causing the delay. The Empress did not get around to signing his official papers, and this was what kept the young man waiting. Elizabeth Petrovna was growing more and more dilatory every day in the performance of her duties, more and more irregular in her habits, more and more uncertain in her health. Her passionate attachment to the baby in the fox-fur cradle had not given her the new lease on life which might have been expected.

The effect of Saltikov's neglect on the feelings of the Grand Duchess was soon apparent. She says in her memoirs that, brooding in her winter of solitude, she decided definitely to assert herself, to let the Count know that she would not suffer insult without retaliation. Had she not after all risen to her supreme obligation? Had she not given to Russia an heir? She was entitled to consideration and was determined to have it. Looking about for a scapegoat, she did not have far to seek. Saltikov was safely out of reach in Hamburg and the Empress was rapt in her phantasy-cloud. But the brothers Shuvalov remained within reach, and she found to her joy that they were vulnerable. Neither of the brothers was clever and Alexander was disfigured by a grimace – an ugly facial *tic*. It was easy to make people laugh at the Shuvalovs and her *bons-mots* at their expense ran through the town like wildfire. She says that her attack was supported by Count Razumovsky, ex-favourite of the Empress, and his brother, Cyril. But their support must have been weak, however willing. The two Razumovskys were artists and dreamers and feeble fighters even for their own cause.

Catherine throve on her new aggressiveness. Soon another enemy was added to her list. A mysterious Herr Brockdorf had come up from Holstein and had quietly established himself in the retinue of the Grand Duke. The Grand Duchess did not like Herr Brockdorf and pursued him with her mockery. She gave him a nickname, 'Babaptitza' (a pelican for ugliness!), and wherever the sombre Holsteiner went he heard it whispered after him.

§ 2

Following the birth of Paul, the breach between the Grand Duke and the Grand Duchess widened. 'After my confinement,' says Catherine in her memoirs, 'he usually slept in his own chamber.' The change of habit broke the only tie which existed between them. For nine years he had slept in chastity beside his wife. But something disturbing, incomprehensible had come between them, and he was no longer at ease in his wife's bed. He made futile efforts to attach himself to other ladies of the Court, but his enthusiasm wandered and failed to strike root anywhere. His interest in military occupations began to absorb all others.

More and more he occupied himself with his favourite toys, soldiers made of lead, wood, starch, or wax. Whole regiments were set up on tables and operated by means of ingenious mechanical devices, in making which the youth, who had never been able to learn anything from his tutors, showed a high degree of skill. Entering his room one day, the Grand Duchess found a dead rat on a gallows and was informed that a military execution had just taken place following a court-martial of the culprit. On another occasion when the Grand Duke was expecting a visit from a lady to whom he was paying court, he called his wife to survey the bower which he had prepared for her. 'He showed me,' says Catherine, 'how, in order to please the lady, he had fitted it out with muskets, military caps, shoulder-belts, so that it looked like a corner in an arsenal.'

The year which followed the birth of Catherine's child and the retreat of the Grand Duke from her bed saw a marked increase in the preoccupation of the latter with his military toys. By the time her second child was born, which was three years later, his preoccupation had grown abnormal and he was capable of the following extraordinary display. He had been called by the midwife, says Catherine in her description of that night, and after some delay put in an appearance. 'He entered my chamber in his Holstein uniform, booted and spurred, with a scarf around his body and a great dagger at his side; that is, in complete regalia. Astonished at this pomp I asked him the reason for this elaborate costume. Whereupon he replied that only in time of need could one know one's true friends; in this costume he was prepared to do his duty. And the duty of a Holstei. officer was to be true to his oath and defend the Ducal House against all enemies. Because I was not well he had come to my aid.'

Catherine decided that her husband was drunk and sent him back to bed. Although she was an accurate observer of the Grand Duke's behaviour, she had no real comprehension of the nature of his affliction. His old tutor, Stehlin, who had once made such heroic efforts to teach him, was apparently the only person in the young man's environment who perceived the morbid element in his behaviour. Stehlin called it his 'marotte militaire,' that is to say, a kind of 'folie militaire,' something which surpasses the limits of normal youthful folly. The Empress was merely angered at every eccentricity and hurled punishments and penalties upon the offender's head. 'That accursed nephew of mine has angered me unspeakably,' she would say. 'He is a monster; may the devil fly away with him.'

The crux of the Grand Duke's military obsession was his devotion to Frederick of Prussia, the greatest military general of his age. It was clearly not the thing for the heir to the throne of Russia to bestow his heart thus unreservedly on a foreign potentate and especially on one with whom Russia was actually at war. Peter's strange devotion is reasonably explained in Poniatovsky's memoirs: 'One must assume that his nurse and his earliest teachers in his fatherland had been Prussian and devoted to the King of Prussia. For from childhood on he nourished such a strong and at the same time such a comical feeling of veneration and love for this Prince that the King of Prussia once said about this passion [for it was really a passion]: "I am his Dulcinea. He has never seen me and has fallen in love with me like Don Quixote."'

§ 3

The military madness of the Grand Duke found a congenial ally in the person of the mysterious man from Holstein, Herr Brockdorf, whom Catherine so cordially detested and nicknamed 'the pelican.' The red-haired Holsteiner, who wore a 'miserable, discontented look because the corners of his mouth hung down to his chin,' hated the Grand Duchess cordially in return. He repaid her compliment about the pelican by announcing that he had come to Russia to 'tread upon the serpent,' meaning thereby no other than Catherine herself.

Brockdorf was apparently a nondescript visitor of no real political importance, but his influence over Peter at this crucial period has given him a place in history. Exactly what this oddly-assorted pair had in common is hard to say. Perhaps it was the Protestant complex which united them. We know that Peter's only reading was the Lutheran prayer book, which he imported from Germany by the hundred, and we suspect that Herr Brockdorf's references to 'the snake' in Catherine was his metaphorical way of saying that she had gained the reputation of being an immoral woman. At any rate the contest between Catherine and Brockdorf was intense and their feud a bitter one. They competed for influence over the Grand Duke who wavered back and forth between them as guides and advisers in the management of the affairs of his beloved Holstein.

It was shortly after the entrance of Brockdorf on the scene that the first real quarrel took place between Catherine Alexeievna and Peter Feodorovich. The encounter assumed a significant form. 'His Imperial Highness came to my room one evening after dinner,' says Catherine, 'and declared to me that I really was becoming too unbearably proud, but he would soon bring me to reason. I asked him wherein this pride consisted and he replied that I carried myself too upright. Thereupon I asked him whether I should bend my back to please him, like the slaves of the Sultan! At this he grew angry and repeated he would soon bring me to reason. I asked him how he would do this. Thereupon he placed himself with his back against the wall, half-way drew his dagger and showed it to me. I asked him what that meant, whether he would fight me. Then I also must have one. He thrust his half-drawn dagger again into its sheath and said my malice had grown to be something quite amazing. . . .'

It was through the kind offices of Brockdorf that a regiment of Holstein soldiers appeared at Oranienbaum in the early summer of 1775. The Grand Duke's military play had suddenly become a dangerous reality. Soldiers of lead and wax no longer satisfied him. He was obliged to have flesh-and-blood toys, strong burly fellows who had to be housed and fed and who quarrelled with the Russian guard already stationed at Oranienbaum. 'These accursed Germans are all sold to the King of Prussia,' said the Russians. 'They are traitors brought to Russia.'

The Grand Duchess realized the danger of this new development. She decided to eliminate herself from the situation as completely as possible and devoted her summer to reclaiming waste land and planning a large English garden. The Empress's advisers, the Shuvalovs, also realized that the presence of the Holstein soldiers at Oranienbaum was undesirable and yet they found it curiously impossible to make Peter see the point or to persuade him to remove this very disturbing element. Like parents trying to get a child to exchange a dangerous toy for a safe one, the Shuvalovs decided to present the Grand Duke with real Russian soldiers for his games. In the spring of 1756, they sent a detachment of one hundred cadets to Oranienbaum for Peter to command. But the Grand Duke was not so easily duped. The Russian cadets might remain but the number of his beloved Holsteiners continued to increase. The accommodations of the little village were strained, giving rise to more friction and more rumours. . . .

While the Grand Duke delighted in playing with his Holstein soldiers, he found the administration of the government, for which he had been responsible since the age of nineteen, tedious and burdensome. He relied much on the Grand Duchess whom he called Madame la Ressource. While Brockdorf contested her influence in Holstein affairs, she nevertheless retained first place in the long run. It was a great relief to Peter to hand the seal over to

her along with all important and difficult documents and
to forget the government of Holstein while he paraded his
fascinating soldiers. In time it came about that the diplomats who had anything to say about Holstein consulted
Catherine direct and accepted her decision. Things went
on in this way for a number of years until the Empress,
suddenly discovering that Holstein was being ruled by the
Grand Duchess, issued a ukase that the Grand Duke
should take care of these political matters himself. It was
a ukase, however, which commanded the impossible.

§ 4

In the autumn of 1755 an Englishman came to Petersburg. He was a man just past middle age, a Whig, and an
aristocrat. He had been for nine years in the diplomatic
service and was known for his caustic wit and elegant
manners. His satirical poetry was much admired. These
talents, however, were not always an asset. Six years previously he had been sent to Berlin as Ambassador at the
Court of Frederick the Great. But Frederick had not liked
the biting tongue of the man and had asked for his removal. The Englishman was sent back to his old post at
Dresden where August the Strong was apparently obliv-
ious of his satire. Not being a satirist himself, as was
Frederick the Great, perhaps he could more comfortably
endure the presence of a rival. Transferred to the Court
of Petersburg, the sophisticated Englishman found himself in a still less intellectual atmosphere than that of the
Saxon Court. Catherine says that the art of conversation was unknown among the Russian courtiers of that
time. The arrival of a polished diplomat who dealt in
brilliant talk and repartee could not fail to make a great
impression on the Grand Duchess although most of his
barbs were lost on the card-playing Court which sur-

rounded Elizabeth. The name of the interesting Englishman was Sir Charles Hanbury Williams.

As Ambassador to the Saxon Court, Williams had spent much time in Poland, over which August of Saxony ruled as elective king. In Warsaw, the Chevalier had made friends with the Czartorisky clan and the Poniatovsky family. A strong-minded daughter of the Czartoriskys had married Count Stanislas Poniatovsky and her son was likewise Count Stanislas. The young man was adored by his mother and patronized by her brothers, the powerful Czartoriskys. His career was the subject of earnest family conclaves. When Sir Charles Hanbury Williams offered to take him to Russia as secretary it was decided that Stanislas should go. The Ambassador was almost twenty-five years older than his Polish secretary and called him his son. In Petersburg they lived together in the house of Count Skavronsky on the bank of the Neva.

The Grand Duchess met them both for the first time on St. Peter's day at Oranienbaum. She sat beside Chevalier Williams at supper and conversed with him while she admired the graceful dancing of his secretary. It was the beginning of a political and personal alliance which rapidly developed among the three. Poniatovsky became her lover, while the Chevalier, ever attentive from the background and regularly corresponding with her, was in some curious vicarious fashion also in love with the fascinating and aggressive Catherine. Sitting at supper one evening with Poniatovsky *vis-à-vis*, the Grand Duchess threw out this remark, ostensibly addressed to the French Ambassador, 'There was never a woman bolder than I; I have an unbridled temerity.' There was much recklessness in her at this time.

The British Ambassador had come to Russia with a special mission from George II, who was anxious lest

Frederick the Great should turn covetous eyes on Hanover as he had on Silesia. Williams was empowered to offer an annual subsidy of five hundred thousand livres to Russia in return for which Russia was to stand ready to aid Hanover against any possible depredations on the part of the Prussian King. Such a treaty between England and Russia, Williams actually got signed in September, 1755. But no sooner was this done than the wily Frederick arranged the Treaty of Westminster in which he and the German-English George mutually guaranteed their possessions against both France and Russia. This created a complicated situation for the English diplomat. The Russian Empress loathed Frederick the Great and wanted no allies in common with him. Russia therefore disregarded the treaty begun in the Fall of 1755 and refused to accept the five hundred thousand livres which England had sent. Williams spent his time in Petersburg trying in vain to induce the Russian government to take his money. He also found himself in the curious position of having tŏ represent the interests of Frederick the Great after he had started to work against them. Opposed to him was the whole French party headed by the powerful Ivan Shuvalov, favourite of the Empress. The Chevalier was left to cultivate the Grand Ducal Court and this he did with whole-hearted enthusiasm. He advised Catherine about the government of Holstein which was at that time in her hands and succeeded in buying the Grand Chancellor Bestushev with a pension of twelve thousand roubles a year from the British Government.

Unfortunately for his schemes, Bestushev was no longer a power at Court. Ivan Shuvalov had gathered the reins into his own hands as the health of the Empress declined. But Williams regarded Bestushev as a fine capture. He wrote an enthusiastic account of his success to Catherine and concluded his letter thus: 'These are the scenes written in haste which will make delightful anecdotes for a future century. You alone have my secret; my heart, my life, my soul are yours. I regard you as a creature wholly superior to myself. I adore you and my adoration goes so far I am persuaded that I can have no merit apart from you. . . . Here is my castle in Spain which I have been building for some time and with which I often amuse myself. When you come to your place on the throne, I shall not be here. I shall come here at once. . . . I should wish to come with the credentials of ambassador in my pocket but I should not wish to produce them, because they would oblige me to maintain a rank and etiquette which would disturb me. And I flatter myself that I should live much with you as a faithful servant and humble friend. I should have the entrée to and profit by your hours of leisure, because I always love Catherine better than the Empress. . . .'

Both Poniatovsky and Williams have left extensive records of their experiences in Russia. This is how Catherine looked at the age of twenty-six in the eyes of her Polish lover. 'At this time she had attained that degree of beauty which represents for every woman to whom beauty is given at all the climax of its development. Her hair was black, her skin a dazzling white and vivid red; she had large blue, round, very expressive eyes, very long black lashes, a Grecian nose, a mouth which seemed to ask for kisses. Her arms and shoulders were surpassingly beautiful; she had a tall, graceful figure and her walk was very agile though full of nobility, the sound of her voice was pleasant, and her laugh as joyous as her temperament.' The Grand Duchess found in Count Poniatovsky the romantic lover for whom she had all her life been longing.

Poniatovsky

§ 5

During the summer of 1756, Count Poniatovsky departed for Warsaw to make a brief visit. He failed to return at the expected time and the Grand Duchess bestirred herself to have him recalled to Russia as Polish Ambassador. She enlisted Williams and Bestushev to this end and showered favours upon them until the two elderly diplomats began to be jealous of each other. She had done her work almost too well. At last, however, she succeeded in her purpose and the Grand Chancellor was able to secure the young Pole's return. He imposed as a condition, however, that Poniatovsky should no longer live with Williams on such intimate terms as formerly. The way was now clear for Poniatovsky's return, but still he lingered in Poland. What was the obstacle? A letter which he sent to Catherine explains the cause of his delay.

'And this is how it is. By dint of questioning me with all the tenderness and adroitness possible, my mother understands clearly what it is that makes me so ardently wish to return to you. . . . I pressed her more strongly to consent formally to my return; she said to me with tears in her eyes that she foresaw with grief that this affair was going to cause her to lose my affection on which she depended for all the happiness of her life; that it was hard to refuse some things but in the end she was determined not to consent. Upon which I was beside myself; I threw myself at her feet and begged her to change her sentiments. She said, melting into tears, "This is just what I expected." Nevertheless she went away, pressing my hand, and left me in the most horrible dilemma I have ever experienced in my life. . . . Oh, Poutres [his nickname for Catherine] . . . share with Bonn [Williams] this story about my mother and beg him to write my father and ask him to send me back over there because I am necessary to him. For among other things she disputes with me that I am necessary to him. . . .'

With the assistance and encouragement of one of his Czartorisky uncles, the young Count finally escaped from his mother and arrived in Petersburg in time for the Russian Christmas of 1756. He remained in Russia as the lover of Catherine for another year and a half, and left the country finally in July, 1758. Catherine's daughter, the Grand Duchess Anna, born in December, 1757, was Poniatovsky's child. The infant was taken from the mother by the Empress just as the first one had been and put into the nursery with her three-year-old half-brother. She did not long survive under the Empress's régime and seems to have been soon forgotten by her mother and her father. The life and death of the little Grand Duchess Anna, wafted so carelessly in and out of her mother's career, was the slightest of slight episodes. Catherine was absorbed in political intrigue. Her alliance with Chevalier Williams and Grand Chancellor Bestushev had developed her talents in this direction, and she allowed herself to go far and to take great risks. She saw the death of the Empress approaching and the accession of Grand Duke Peter to the throne. What would then be her position and that of her son by Saltikov?

A midnight encounter which took place between Poniatovsky and the Grand Duke at Oranienbaum caused the Pole to leave Russia and showed Catherine how desperately uncertain her footing had become. The Count was accustomed to come and go in disguise. Wearing a blond peruke he would say, 'Musician of the Grand Duke' and would pass unquestioned. But one midsummer night his ruse failed to save him from embarrassing developments. Poniatovsky tells the story thus: 'On this night I met unluckily in the woods at Oranienbaum the Grand Duke and his whole retinue, all of them half drunk. They asked my *izvostchik* whom he was driving. My page replied, "A tailor." We were allowed to pass. But Elizabeth Vorontsov, lady-in-waiting of the Grand Duchess and mistress of the Grand Duke, who was present, made a few joking remarks about the alleged tailor which put the Grand Duke into a bad humour. As I was leaving the pavilion where I had spent several hours with the Grand Duchess and which she occupied under the pretence of taking a water-cure, I was suddenly stopped, after taking a few steps, by three mounted men, who, sabres in hand, seized me by the collar and dragged me before the Grand Duke.'

According to Catherine's story, Brockdorf the pelican played a prominent part in this scene. The Holsteiner advised the Grand Duke to kill the prisoner. But Peter had no such intention; he only exposed and ventilated the scandal. Poniatovsky was allowed to go free after the episode had become known to the entire Court. With broad patronizing jokes, the Grand Duke invited the Pole to Oranienbaum and facilitated his meetings with the Grand Duchess. The Shuvalovs tried to reassure the Count, but neither Catherine nor her lover was reassured. 'I could not but remark,' says Poniatovsky, 'that all was not clear and that it was time for me to go away.' Catherine says that she perceived through this episode that her lot was finally separated from that of the Grand Duke; that she must either perish with him and through him or save herself and her children and the State from shipwreck. After Poniatovsky's departure for Poland, the Grand Duchess went into strict retirement. Soon after he left, Sir Charles Hanbury Williams left Russia also. The Chevalier was strangely reluctant to go away. He should have gone early in the summer, but he could not decide on his itinerary. At first he planned to journey through Poland but changed his mind and decided to go through Sweden. He got as far as Finland and then came back again saying that his horses had fallen ill. Again he hesitated and it was not until the end of October that he finally took leave of Catherine at Oranienbaum. She was extremely depressed by his leaving and wept the whole day when he came to say farewell. The separation seems to have finally upset the Chevalier's unstable mental condition. After a stormy passage from Kronstadt, he arrived in Hamburg already a sick man, and almost immediately he was declared insane by the physicians and taken to England. A year later he ended his life by suicide and was buried in Westminster Abbey.

Two months after his death, Catherine wrote to the Russian envoy in Warsaw the following confidential message: 'Count Poniatovsky is out of humour with me, but he is wrong if he believes that obstacles or other incidents can detach me from him. I put my profession of faith into your hands, and I desire only the moment of our reunion; I wish he would place himself above all vulgar trifles. There is so much complexity in my present rôle that I have need of that enthusiasm which he pretends I sometimes inspire. Adversity shall not conquer me and if it is necessary to triumph, courage will not be lacking. I esteem and love Poniatovsky above all the rest of the human race. He must be sure of that, and if I have good fortune events will prove it. In the name of God, do not remind your hearer [Poniatovsky] of the scene with the late Williams who, while haranguing me began to sob;

you will picture me inspiring you with courage and all will appear to be smiling. . . .'

These cryptic messages indicate that the relationship between Catherine and Williams was more emotional than the political situation required. The complexity of her rôle in January, 1761, the last year of Empress Elizabeth's life, absorbed all of her attention. During this winter especially she strove to ingratiate herself with the Russian public, possibly because she realized that her recent intimacy with foreigners tended to recall the fact that she herself was not a Russian. Her assurances of affection for Poniatovsky were still sincere at this time for his successor did not arrive in Petersburg until the following March. It was not wholly accidental that her new lover was a Russian.

§ 6

The part which the Grand Duchess Catherine played in the Seven Years' War was devious if not exactly traitorous. In the spring of 1757, the Russian army advanced against Frederick the Great, the 'blasphemous Prince' whom Elizabeth Petrovna so cordially detested. Austria and France breathed a sigh of relief to see their ally at last in motion. But General Apraxin, in charge of the Russian forces, entered the fight with extreme deliberation. He captured Memel and Grossjägerndorf, and then, to the astonishment of all the world, began a most unaccountable and hasty retreat towards the Russian border. Petersburg buzzed with excitement. The French and Austrian Ambassadors demanded an investigation, which the outraged Empress was prompt in ordering. Before the eyes of Europe, her armies had let down her allies. Apraxin's only excuse for his retreat was that he was too far away from provisions.

In the investigation which followed all clues seemed to lead mysteriously to the Grand Duchess, but none of them ever quite reached her. Bestushev was arrested and subjected to a judicial inquiry which lasted intermittently for a year. Nearly all the questions put to him by the commissioners related in some way to Catherine. In the end, but without having incriminated her, he was sent into exile. Adadurov, Catherine's old teacher, and several other subordinates, who had been confidential messengers between Bestushev and herself, were also arrested, investigated, and banished to remote parts of Russia.

Finally Apraxin, the leading culprit in this historical affair, was recalled from the army and arrested on the border as he entered Russia. A court of inquiry was set up then and there and the General was subjected to a trial which lasted some months. On the 1st of August his ordeal was brought to an unexpected close. He suffered a stroke of paralysis and died in twenty-four hours. Like Bestushev, he had not incriminated the Grand Duchess, even though he had in his possession several letters written by her to himself. These letters were taken from him by Count Alexander Shuvalov, the man with the grimace which Catherine had so often ridiculed, and were safely carried back to the Empress Elizabeth. Except for the fact that the Grand Duchess was not allowed to write letters at all, there was nothing incriminating in this correspondence.

No real evidence ever came out against her. Bestushev had found time to destroy all his documents before he was arrested, and Catherine, on hearing of his arrest, destroyed every scrap of written paper in her possession. She made a clean sweep of everything. An innocent sketch of herself, written at the age of fifteen, was sacrificed with the rest, a loss which she always regretted. We must assume

that she felt that there was no time to lose. All her closest
friends and associates were tried and convicted. She alone
survived the crisis without serious consequences.

The historian Bilbassov was able to prove to his own
complete satisfaction by the total absence of documentary
evidence, that the Grand Duchess Catherine, throughout
the whole shady Apraxin business, never once wavered in
her loyalty to Russia. Her correspondence with Chevalier
Williams, however, indicates that she played with fire at
this time and was only saved from the charge of treason
by her amazing instinct for self-preservation. Believing
the Empress to be on the verge of death – and apparently
the infatuated Williams helped her to be over-confident
about the near gratification of this wish – she realized
that the Grand Duke Peter would in that event instantly
reverse any attack on Frederick the Great. Hoping for
the Empress's death and encouraged by a fit that the
unfortunate lady one day had in public, she schemed to
hold Apraxin back from the German campaign. Just
what she did to cause the General to alter his tactics
as he did and when he did is not known to history since
Catherine burned all her papers. But if the Russian
general on this occasion betrayed his Empress and his
country, the Grand Duchess was without doubt one of
the influences which led him into this serious and fatal
mistake.

There came at last a dramatic midnight scene in which
the Grand Duchess faced the Empress and saved herself
once for all. After the arrest of Bestushev, she spent many
weeks in an agony of suspense. At last she wrote a letter
to the Empress asking for an interview, and waited for
an answer six weeks longer. By this time she was actually
and literally walking the floor, a symptom which belies
the good conscience which Bilbassov would have us

believe she enjoyed at this crucial time. By pretending to be sick and calling in her father confessor, who interceded on her behalf, she managed at last to induce the Empress to receive her. Her courage and resourcefulness throughout this crisis prove that her famous boast of intrepidity made to impress Poniatovsky in the presence of the French Ambassador was not an empty one.

The Empress, who habitually turned night into day, summoned her to an audience at half-past one in the morning. Alexander Shuvalov, grimacing, came to call her. Catherine pictures for us with brief strokes the room in which she was received by the Empress: the three windows, the wash-stand with gold utensils, the tall screen, and, behind the screen, the favourite of the Empress and the defender of the political interests of France – Ivan Ivanovich Shuvalov. In the gold washbasin she saw the crumpled letters which she had written to Apraxin, a detail which gives us by the way a picture of how the Empress Elizabeth respected important documents. When Catherine arrived in this room, she found the Grand Duke already there. In his presence, in that of Alexander Shuvalov, and in that of the hidden Ivan Ivanovich – three weighty enemies – she was obliged to defend herself. The manner in which she rose to the occasion shows that the woman loved danger.

She began by throwing herself at the Empress's feet and asking to be sent home to her mother. Elizabeth reminded her that she had children in Russia; Catherine replied that the Empress was a better mother to them than she herself could possibly be. Elizabeth further reminded her that the Princess of Zerbst had fled to Paris; Catherine replied that her mother had been driven out of Germany by the persecutions of Frederick the Great, the enemy whom Elizabeth hated. What chance had a mere emotional Empress against astuteness like this? Elizabeth fell back upon her real grievance.

'You are immoderately proud. Do you remember one day in the summer garden when I came up to you and asked you if you had a crick in your neck because you scarcely greeted me?'

'Ah, my God! How could Your Majesty believe that I could be proud towards you? I swear to you that I had not the least idea that your question of four years ago signified that.'

'You fancy that nobody alive is as clever as yourself.'

'If I really believed this of myself, then my present situation and this conversation seem best designed to cure me of my error: until this very day, I have not understood, out of mere stupidity, what you wished to say to me four years ago. . . .'

At this point the Grand Duke began to talk with Alexander Shuvalov in the background, taking sides against Catherine. For a moment the two women allowed the Grand Duke to enter the quarrel, and then excluded him again. He was not really worthy to close with either of them in combat. The Empress brushed him aside and returned to the attack.

'You take part in all kinds of matters which do not concern you. During the Empress Anna's time, I was not allowed to do that. How could you, for example, have the audacity to issue commands to Field-Marshal Apraxin?'

'I? It never once entered my head to issue commands to him.'

'Can you deny that you have written to him? Your letters lie there in the basin. . . .'

The Grand Duchess knew full well that there was nothing in the letters which Alexander Shuvalov had travelled so far to bring home to the Empress. She rehearsed their contents now.

'Bestushev says,' Elizabeth persisted, 'that there were many more letters.'

'If Bestushev says that, he lies.'

'Good. If he lies, he shall be put to torture.'

It was the Empress's last shot and still the Grand Duchess did not flinch. Elizabeth began to walk up and down the room, while Catherine and the Grand Duke fell to quarrelling with each other. It was apparent from the Grand Duke's remarks that he was under the influence of the Vorontsov family and nursed the idea of putting Elizabeth Vorontsov in the place of Catherine. He was not aware that this project appealed neither to the Empress nor to Ivan Shuvalov behind the screen. 'This went beyond the mental capacity of his Imperial Highness, who believed all that he wished,' says Catherine, 'and pushed aside every other thought which happened to interfere with the one that momentarily governed him.'

At three o'clock in the morning the Empress dismissed them. The Grand Duke left the room first and vanished down the corridor with his usual long flying strides. Catherine returned to her chamber and undressed. It was the middle of April and the white dawn filled the room in which for so many days past she had paced the floor in suspense and sleeplessness. She went to bed and slept soundly.

§ 7

It was true that Catherine's mother, the Princess of Zerbst, had fled to Paris. The redoubtable Johanna Elizabeth had, by a series of political errors, succeeded at last in reaching the city of her dreams, the haven of art and fashion for which she had always longed. To achieve this paradise she had made a stormy pilgrimage; and her joy in her achievement was to be short-lived, for her residence in Paris proved to be her undoing.

In the year 1758 she was living at Zerbst with her son, Friedrich August, the reigning Prince. It cannot be said that she was living altogether quietly there, for Fritz had married a young wife with whom his mother did not get on well. According to the Princess, Fritz also did not get on well with his wife, who had been an obscure Princess of Hesse-Cassel. After five years of marriage, they still had no children. Presumably the domestic atmosphere at Zerbst was anything but pleasant, although the relations of the three with the outside world were peaceable enough. The Princess of Zerbst received a comfortable pension from the Empress of Russia and there was at least a hope that the future Empress, who was Fritz's own sister, would one day succeed in making him a real Kurfürst of Germany. The Zerbst family had only to be good and await events.

Suddenly the French foreign office cast an eye on this little principality. Would it not be possible to use the Princess of Zerbst to influence her daughter, the Grand Duchess of Russia, who was suspected of being pro-English and anti-French? The French ministry decided to take the chance. A dashing French officer, the Marquis de Fraigne, was dispatched on this mission and arrived without difficulty at the castle of Zerbst. Although France and Germany were at war, little Zerbst had declared itself neutral. A French officer might therefore visit the Prince in perfect safety, protected by its neutrality. De Fraigne lingered on at Zerbst, while the weeks passed by in pleasant social converse. The Princess Johanna Elizabeth wrote letters to her daughter, which never reached their

destination but conveyed to Frederick the Great all that
he needed to know.

Suddenly this idyllic scene became a volcano. Frederick the Great was not pleased to have a French officer
tarrying at Zerbst. He sent a detachment of soldiers to
arrest the stranger and remove him to Prussian soil where
he could be properly court-martialled. But the Marquis
presented his side and argued his case so well that the
Prussian soldiers retired without him. The offended
Frenchman, aided by the foolish Prince of Zerbst and
the still more foolish mother of the Prince, sent an
indignant protest to the King of Prussia. After all,
Zerbst was neutral, and the Prussians ought really to
apologize.

Frederick's answer was prompt: a squadron of artillery
appeared before the old grey walls of Zerbst. Either de
Fraigne would come out or the walls would go down.
The Marquis decided to give himself up, and the Prussians took him quietly away. But the Princess of Zerbst
and her son had pushed the issue too far and Frederick
was not going to let them off too easily. He imposed a
penalty of a hundred thousand ducats and the supply
of forage enough for a regiment. It was a devastating
penalty; it ruined them. In desperation the Princess and
her son fled and abandoned the principality to the
Prussian King. In their haste they left behind them the
young wife of the Prince. Or did she perhaps decline to
go with them? Perhaps she thought she had nothing to
lose by remaining with the Prussian occupation. However this may have been, she did not long survive the
flight of the others. Within less than a year, she died of
a stroke of paralysis. It began to look as if the house of
Zerbst was doomed to extinction.

In the meantime, the fleeing mother and son went first

to Hamburg. From Hamburg Fritz departed to enlist in the Austrian army and fight Frederick the Great, while his mother went on to Paris. She believed that the French Government would welcome her with open arms after the great sacrifice that she had made for that country. But the French Government lacked appreciation. They now knew as much about Johanna Elizabeth as Frederick the Great knew when she came back from Russia with Mardefeld's dismissal in her chatelaine. The Princess loved intrigue but she was doomed to fail in it; her projects always turned against her, as if she tried to crack a whip too long for her strength and was caught in the bite of its cruel tapering end.

The French Government made ineffectual attempts to delay the progress of the Princess as she hastened towards Paris. They sent a last desperate message to arrest her in Brussels, but Johanna Elizabeth had reached the last lap of her journey to Paris before the message arrived. There was a certain pathos in the letter which Berni, the foreign minister, wrote to the French resident at Petersburg. 'The Princess of Zerbst hastened so that the letter which explained the necessity of postponing her arrival in France did not reach Brussels until she was already in Valenciennes, from which one could not prevent her from coming on to Paris.' Berni wished the Empress to understand that he had not connived at the Princess's flight to France.

Elizabeth was furious with the Princess of Zerbst. The mother's behaviour coincided with the daughter's meddlesomeness in the Apraxin business. The full wrath of the Empress fell upon the mother's frivolous head; she promptly withdrew the lady's pension. The Princess, who pretended to observe an incognito in Paris as Countess of Oldenburg, had set up an establishment and plunged into

147

literary and Court society. Suddenly she found herself cut
off without a sou. Her letters to the Empress are pitiable.
As her creditors pressed her harder and harder, she
multiplied her petitions. The Empress condescended to
be positively vindictive. She sent a message to the
bankrupt woman that, after first paying her debts, she
ought to leave Paris. This silenced the poor woman at
last.

This was in the autumn of 1759, and the Princess was
already ill of dropsy. She passed the winter in bed
attended by physicians. Her letters to Russia ceased to
petition for money; she seemed to realize that Elizabeth
was inexorable. The Grand Duchess, who did not know
of her mother's financial distress, sent her a present of
some tea and rhubarb. But the Princess died before this
little gift arrived. It was only with the greatest effort
that Catherine and Ivan Shuvalov, whom she finally
persuaded to help her, could induce the Empress to pay
the debts of the deceased Princess. Elizabeth was willing
the Princess's personal effects should be sold at public
auction. It was hard even for the favourite, Ivan Shuvalov, to persuade her to save her kinswoman's memory
from this disgrace. Towards Johanna Elizabeth she had
always been revengeful.

§ 8

The Empress did not long outlive her enemy. For
many years she had really been an invalid. She had
secretly imported a famous French physician who said
that she suffered from 'vapours' and convulsions. Elizabeth's personal physician was a Greek, Kondoidi, who
at first refused to consult with the foreign specialist.
After much diplomatizing on the part of the French and
Russian Governments, the rivals at last consented to meet.

It turned out that they agreed in their diagnosis of melancholia and hysteria, and so they shook hands over the poor Empress who continued to get no better. Nothing more definite than this was the Empress destined to die of. Owing to the convulsions to which she was subject, her death seemed several times imminent; but then she would suddenly pull herself together and death would recede to a respectful distance. Her illness dragged on like the Seven Years' War and the outcome was as unpredictable. From the beginning of the year 1761, however, her condition patently grew worse. During the summer she fell into convulsions which caused her to lose consciousness for several hours at a time. On Christmas Day, 1761, she died, at the age of fifty-two. Her span of life was but slightly less than that of her turbulent father, Peter the Great, who died at fifty-three.

There were three people who had awaited her death with varying degrees of impatience. To Frederick the Great the news was as manna in the wilderness; it made him at last victor in the Seven Years' War. To Grand Duke Peter, it was the release of all his dreams; as Czar of Russia, he could now follow his illusions wherever they led him, even to the last limits of destruction. To Grand Duchess Catherine, it was not altogether opportune. Three years before she had been more eager for Elizabeth's death than she was when the Empress at last made way for her. Catherine was at this time pregnant with her third child and more than ever at odds with the Grand Duke, her husband. Her new lover was Gregory Orlov, a handsome young captain of artillery.

While Peter celebrated his accession to the throne with the usual ceremonies, she withdrew herself discreetly from the public gaze. She draped herself in heavy black and paid her daily homage to the corpse of the Empress, kneeling for hours beside the sarcophagus. According to custom the body lay exposed to public view for six weeks. In the fifth week, with her own hands and without a quiver, she placed a golden crown on the head of this malodorous object. It was her final act of obeisance.

8

Orlov

I n the six weeks which intervened between the death
and the burial of Elizabeth Petrovna, the new Czar
had offended public opinion in numberless ways. While
the Grand Duchess was diligently observing all the rituals
ordained by the Greek Church for the dead Empress,
Peter III was conducting himself as a boy just let out
from school. His sharp strident tones could be heard
down the corridors, conveying the joyous excitement he
was unable to control. He could neither kneel endlessly
beside the coffin, as Catherine did, nor even stand,
but paced restlessly about the church talking and grimacing. On the day of the funeral his grotesque behaviour shocked the people in the street. He was in a good
humour, says Catherine, and allowed himself his little
joke.

As the long procession passed through the Nevsky
Prospect, across the bridge, and into the island fortress
of Saint Peter and Saint Paul, Peter walked immediately
behind the coffin. He wore a mourning robe of state
with a long train, the end of which was borne by Count
Sheremetiev. The Czar's little joke was to stop for a
moment from time to time and then hasten forward with
long strides to overtake the coffin. The unhappy Count
was unable to manage the train of his master, which
flapped wildly in the wind to the great delight of the Czar
who repeated the jest again and again. The procession
was finally so jammed by this trick that a messenger was
sent forward to stop the leaders until they could catch
up. The new Czar, who amused himself so well at the
funeral of his aunt, was nearly thirty-five years old. The
public was scandalized and his courtiers blushed for
him before the gossips of Europe. Still they continued

to kiss the hand of his Imperial Highness and to observe all the forms of supreme respect. Like crows they circled in awe around this feeble image of dignity and power.

The reign of Peter III lasted altogether six months. His ukases were a hotch-potch of foolish and reasonable commands. One day he gave an order that the gentlemen of the Court might hunt ravens and other birds in the streets of Petersburg; also that they might shoot on sight all dogs found in the vicinity of the palace. Another day he freed the nobles from compulsory military service. Although the princes and counts were delighted with this law, they still mistrusted their capricious emancipator and feared his next measure. Petersburg was filled with rumours of what that might be. It was reported that Peter III meant to divorce Catherine and to marry Elizabeth Vorontsov, and that, to cement this innovation, all the other ladies of the Court would be required to divorce their husbands and take new ones. So nervous became the public and so whimsical was their Czar that this nonsense was easily believed.

Wherever Peter III appeared in public his reputation for capriciousness grew. When he went to see the guard changed, which he often did, he would beat the soldiers and even the spectators. Countess Dashkov tells a story of how his negro servant Narcissus was redeemed by a ceremony after having had a fight with the scavenger of the regiment. It was at a military parade. An officer suggested jokingly, 'Let Narcissus pass three times under the banners of the regiment.' Peter, intensely serious, was delighted with the idea; he insisted that the points of the banners should draw blood from the negro's head, which caused Narcissus to set up a loud yell to the immense amusement of the officers and the solemn satisfaction of the Emperor. His beloved Narcissus had been cleansed by a ritual. Numerous stories of his behaviour survive as sufficient evidence that his mind had wholly lost its balance. Bilbassov says of his condition, 'a man of sound sense and clear memory cannot understand the conceited blindness in which the Duke of Holstein, who had become Emperor of Russia, lived. The frequent drunkenness of Peter III does not explain it. . . . It must be traced back to the unfortunate coincidence between the personal qualities of Peter III and the unlimited power which became his by inheritance. . . . He had lost the power to think straight.'

The pathos of his condition was that it inspired in his own private circle so much hatred and so little sympathy. As a rule, only the women, to whom he turned with childish appeal, took pity on him. Even Catherine, his wife, who has gone down in history as his greatest enemy, wrote tolerantly of him in her memoirs, 'He did not have a bad heart; but a weak man usually has not.' And Elizabeth Vorontsov, his mistress, was loyal to him all through the final crash of his fortunes with which his brief reign came to an end. Her behaviour in that crisis shows that her attitude towards Peter all along had had something in it besides the mere ambition which was supposed to have guided her. But Peter had no friend among the men. He was afraid of men and therefore he challenged and insulted them on every occasion. From the period of his early fights with his tutors, it could be foreseen that Peter's greatest safety in the future would consist in keeping as far as possible away from those of his own sex. It would be an ominous day for him if he were ever cut off wholly from the mercy of women and cast entirely on the protection of men.

§ 2

The political acts of Peter III were of a kind which no Czar of Russia could have perpetrated and survived. He prattled about his devotion and allegiance to the King of Prussia with an openness which embarrassed even the Prussian representative. One of his first steps as Czar was to make peace with Prussia. Not satisfied with a mere cessation of hostilities, he signed a treaty of eternal peace with Prussia in April, 1762. It was celebrated with great pomp and ceremony, during which the Czar brought forth his famous toast to the '3 times 3.' On being questioned he said that the three whom he had in mind consisted of himself, Peter III, George III of England, and Frederick III of Prussia. When it was pointed out to him that Frederick was only the Second, it did not disturb him in the least or interfere with the elaborate design of fireworks which he ordered to burn upon the sky above the Neva this historic alliance: '3 X 3.' It was a union over which Elizabeth Petrovna, now sleeping in the Fortress of Saint Peter and Saint Paul, and Sir Charles Hanbury Williams, now sleeping in Westminster Abbey, had once waged a long and bitter controversy. Peter like a mischievous child had suddenly brought it to pass. But it was too much like a harlequinade. What Europe wanted to know was, how long would it last? Peter was playing with big destinies.

His domestic policies were as ill-inspired as his foreign policies. The whole of Russian politics revolved around the two pillars: the Army and the Church. During his seventeen years as Grand Duke in Russia Peter had never made friends with either. Soon after his accession he issued an order confiscating the possessions of the church and allowing the priests an income from the State. This of course was never executed as the six months of his reign were not long enough to accomplish such a revolution. It sufficed however to solidify the antagonism of the people towards a Lutheran Czar who had no respect for icons and priestly robes and who read the German Bible. They believed he wished to change their creed.

Peter's tactlessness with the army was no less damaging than with the church. He made his uncle, Prince George of Holstein, generalissimo of the Russian army. This was a double error, in that he placed a foreigner in command and resigned to him a place which as Czar he should have filled himself. He took away the long, loose Russian coats of the soldiers and put them into tight German uniforms. His next step was to mobilize the army for a campaign against Denmark. He was Czar of all the Russians yet a few square miles of Holstein territory in the possession of Denmark occupied all his attention and filled all his military dreams. 'He had a passionate love,' says Catherine, 'for the little corner of the earth where he was born. He was constantly preoccupied with it. He had left the land of his birth at the age of twelve or thirteen years; his imagination grew heated whenever he spoke of it, and because no one in his entourage, beginning with myself, had ever been in this land, wonderful according to his accounts, he daily told us stories about it which we were supposed to believe, but which put us to sleep. He grew angry when he saw that we did not believe him.' This had been his attitude as Grand Duke; as Czar of Russia he behaved as if he had just come into his own as the ruler of Holstein and seemed to forget entirely his vast Russian domain.

His indifference to being crowned was a part of his

satisfaction with the rôle of mere Duke. It was immemorial custom to crown the Czars of Russia in Moscow,
in the Kremlin, with all the vivid pageantry of the Church
and Army arrayed against that rich Byzantine background.
Peter neglected to make any preparations for this ceremony. His model in all things, Frederick the Great, had
never been crowned; nor had Frederick's father before
him. As a matter of fact, both of these Prussians, father
and son, were too penurious to spend money on coronation spectacles. But the Czar did not question their
reasons; the precedent was sufficient. When Frederick
heard that Peter was dilatory about his coronation ceremony, he was alarmed and wrote to the young Czar
urging him to proceed at once to Moscow and be crowned
there. He reminded Peter III that Ivanushka was still
living in the Schlüsselburg fortress and that he represented a potential rival to the throne. The Czar was
impervious to this good advice. He replied that the
crowns were not ready. The months passed and the campaign against Denmark was his only interest. But even
this he postponed from time to time. Almost ready to
march, he nevertheless decided to delay a few weeks in
order to celebrate his name-day, June 29, with the usual
garden-party gaieties at Peterhof.

§ 3

During the six months of Peter III's reign, Catherine
lived in strict retirement. When obliged to appear in
public, she wore heavy black draperies edged with costly
ermine which served a double purpose: they showed her
respect for the late Empress whom she genuinely mourned
and they concealed her pregnancy. In April the new
Winter Palace of stone overlooking the Neva, which had
been built by Elizabeth, was completed. The Imperial

family moved out of the old wooden palace on the Nevsky Prospect, of whose draughts and other discomforts the Grand Duchess had often and bitterly complained. Here Catherine was assigned rooms at the opposite end of the palace from the Czar, where on April 11 she gave birth to a son. He was called Alexis Gregorevich Bobrinsky. His last name was taken from the beaver-skin in which the new-born babe was wrapped. Bobrinsky went through life as Alexis, son of Gregory. With this child, Catherine finally abandoned the pretence that Peter was the father of her children. Her eldest son, Paul Petrovich, remained as the sole representative of this fiction.

Catherine concealed the birth of her second son and brought him up in a school for cadets. Her position was too insecure to allow her to keep Orlov's child with her. As with the other two, she was again deprived of any maternal satisfaction in the care of him. Ten days after her confinement, on her thirty-third birthday, she appeared in public to receive the customary congratulations. She carried off the occasion as if nothing had happened. Little Bobrinsky's birth had not caused a ripple on the surface of things. Presumably the Czar did not even know of his existence. Catherine subsequently bore two daughters to Orlov who were spirited away even more completely than little 'beaver-skin' had been. They were brought up under fictitious names at Court and properly married in the course of time. There is nothing to tell us whether their lives developed happily or otherwise.

Four months after his accession, Peter III called his wife a 'fool' in public; it was at the great dinner of state given to celebrate the peace with Prussia. To Peter's foggy mind this doubtless seemed only a casual insult, as was the case when he made Count Buturlin into a lifelong enemy by calling him a 'son of a bitch' at a dinner-party. The Czar sat at the head of the table and proposed a toast to the Imperial family. As the pokals clattered down upon the board, Peter observed Catherine sitting in her place. He sent the adjutant who stood behind his chair to inquire why she had not risen and the adjutant returned with the reply that she herself belonged to the Imperial family. The silly inconsequential Czar leaned forward in his place and shouted down the table, in the presence of the assembled Russian nobles and foreign diplomats, 'dura,' which means 'fool.' It is the epithet which one *izvostchik* bawls out to another in a street argument. The Empress's eyes filled with tears and she turned to Count Stroganov who stood behind her chair and begged him to say something amusing to keep her from crying. It was for Catherine the last straw. Two months from that date the reign of Peter III came to an end and the reign of Catherine II began.

The conspiracy which the Grand Duchess had made during her intimacy with Poniatovsky and Williams had been more elaborate than the one in which she now engaged. In those days, three years before the Empress died, Catherine had had plenty of money – English money – at her command. She says herself that on the day of Elizabeth Petrovna's death she was literally bankrupt; she had not sufficient credit to order herself a new dress for Christmas. 'On this day,' she adds, naïvely regretting that she had not ordered it, 'the Empress died, something which I had not been able to foresee.' Ten years afterwards she still regretted the dress she had foregone.

In the year 1762, as Czarina, she found herself in the possession of an income. This time it was Russian money

not English money at her disposal, and she had acquired
other Russian resources as well. Formerly, Catherine's
confederates had been foreigners; this time there was no
suspicion of foreign influence in her friendships. The
five brothers Orlov were the centre and the focus of her
plans and there were enough of them to do most of the
secret work needed in the barracks. Alexis, the eldest,
was a tough-minded person who had some of Catherine's
own strength. Gregory, the second brother and her lover,
famous for his good looks, was softer and more sensitive.
There still remained Ivan, Feodor, and Vladimir, who
moved under Alexis' orders. It was a typical Russian
brotherhood with Alexis as leader. The Orlovs all lived
in the barracks where they quietly suborned the guards
with gossip and money. Count Cyril Razumovsky,
Lieutenant-Colonel of the Ismailov Regiment, had long
been subservient to Catherine's charm. He gave her no
trouble and his military position was useful to her. One
woman, the Countess Catherine Dashkov, who played a
conspicuous though unimportant rôle in the preparations
and their execution, must be included among the inner
circle of conspirators. They were all Russians of ancient
Russian lineage, except Catherine herself, who liked to
forget that she had German blood in her veins.

The Countess Dashkov occupies a prominent place in
the history of Catherine's revolution. Her memoirs were
published as early as 1840 and were the first authoritative
account to be circulated in Europe. In the stories which
multiplied around her name during the nineteenth
century she figures as an Amazon and a leader only
second to Catherine the Great. She was actually not very
important. Her age precluded that, for she was only
nineteen when Catherine deposed Peter and ascended the
throne. The Countess had a strategic value due to the

fact that she was the sister of Elizabeth Vorontsov, Peter's mistress. Her allegiance to Catherine's party divided the Vorontsov family as Catherine wished to divide it. She was a possible source of information concerning the other camp, but she was also a possible channel for leakage in the opposite direction. For this reason, Catherine tells us, she was not fully initiated into the secret plans of the Empress and the wholly devoted Orlovs. The Empress had a rendezvous with her Dashkov at which we may assume the nineteen-year-old Countess told all she knew without being told much in return. Catherine once wrote to her, to reassure her anxiety about a rendezvous, 'As for your reputation, it is better established than that of the whole calendar of saints.' The scorn is a bit transparent. Peter III, with all his stupidity, put the case clearly enough when he said to Countess Dashkov, 'My child, you would do well to recollect that it is much safer to deal with honest blockheads like your sister and myself than with great wits, who squeeze the juice out of the orange and then throw away the rind.' Catherine was not quite so egoistic as Peter made out. She did not throw away the rind; she preserved it carefully. The Countess Dashkov enjoyed the patronage and protection of the great Empress all her life.

Another confederate of the Empress in her conspiracy was Nikita Ivanovich Panin, the governor of her son. Panin had lived fourteen years in Stockholm as Russian Ambassador. There he had imbibed the concepts of liberalism and had formed a vague picture of Russia as a constitutional monarchy. Panin's critics say that he did not sufficiently realize the political differences between a compact little country like Sweden, with its one blood and one faith, and the vast empire of Russia with its

conglomerate races and cultures and religions. To his
delight, Panin found, on his return to Russia when he
was recalled to educate the infant Paul, that the Grand
Duchess Catherine had also imbibed the new ideas from
her diligent reading of French authors. Panin took hope
for the future of his country when a liberal Empress
would be in a position of power. This powerful position
he pictured in a special way. Like other observers about
the Court, he perceived the tragic impossibilities of Peter
as Czar and imagined that in some way he would have
to be supplanted. Panin's solution of the future, however,
was to elevate Paul as actual emperor and Paul's mother
as Regent. He wished to establish a régime like that
which Elizabeth Petrovna had overturned, that of Ivanushka and his surly mother, Anna Leopoldovna. Panin
prepared elaborate schemes to this end, some of which
he put on paper. The Grand Duchess, prior to 1762,
read his plans with interest. After 1762, she declared that
she had never really agreed to them.

§ 4

On the night of the 27th of June, 1762, the Imperial
family was more than usually divided, although the
morrow was to usher in the celebration of the Emperor's
name-day. Peter Feodorovich slept at Oranienbaum;
Catherine Alexeievna slept at Peterhof; and the little
Grand Duke slept in the Summer Palace at Petersburg in
the care of Nikita Panin. It was planned that the Czar
and his retinue would drive over the next morning from
Oranienbaum to Peterhof where the usual name-day celebration would take place. Catherine, unattended except
by a maid, waited at Peterhof for her husband and his
gay party to come over from Oranienbaum and enliven the
place.

She slept that night in the little red brick pavilion known as Monplaisir. Her bedroom opened upon a terrace, lapped by the waves of the blue Finnish Gulf. It was a doll's house built by Peter the Great, whose head almost touched the ceilings, as near the edge of the sea as he could place it. The Empress Elizabeth loved Monplaisir for her father's sake and because she had a kitchen there where she herself might cook. The big Czar and his tall daughter have left their memories about this pavilion at Peterhof. But Catherine the Great, who spent the most dramatic hours of her life there – hours which were to make her the Empress of Russia – never liked the place. As an old woman she used to say that she hated the noise its fountains made and that her dog hated the gurgle of those fountains too. She would never spend any money in developing and beautifying the dwelling after it came into her possession.

On this particular night in June, 1762, the fountains were still awaiting the coming of the Czar on the morrow when they would play. In the pale light, the gilded statues shone on the terraces leading down to the sea. At six o'clock in the morning a man came stealing through the park, skirted the main palace, and made his way down to the pavilion at the water's edge. He wore the uniform of a Captain in the Preobrazhensky Regiment and he seemed to know where he was going. A French window opened into the Empress's bedroom. He stepped inside. Catherine was sleeping in a broad silken bed alone. 'Matushka, little Mother, wake up,' he said. 'The time has come.' The man was Captain Alexis Orlov, the brother of Gregory Orlov, Catherine's lover.

The night before had been a restless one in the city of Petersburg. The army had been mobilized for the campaign against Denmark and the General, Prince George of Holstein, was ready to march as soon as the celebration at Peterhof should release the Emperor to accompany them. The war was unpopular and the soldiers grumbled. They did not like their German commander and they did not like their uniforms. Nevertheless they stood ready to go: it was the Czar's orders. Late in the evening the news went round that Captain Passeck had been arrested: again the Czar's orders. The report was passed indifferently enough from person to person until it reached Alexis Orlov. Immediately the five Orlov brothers were all in action. Captain Passeck was the boon companion of Alexis and was one of the forty officers who had been sworn into the conspiracy. Arrest was likely to be followed by torture and Captain Passeck's secrets were not secrets which could be told to the inquisitors of Peter III. So Alexis evidently thought, for he hired an ordinary carriage from the street, took with him Lieutenant Bibikov, and drove out to Peterhof. It was midnight when they left the city, and it was six o'clock when Captain Orlov entered Catherine's bedroom and awakened her.

Her festival dress was laid out ready for the day; but she did not put it on. She donned instead the black mourning gown which she had taken off the night before. Together with Orlov and her maid she passed out through the park on foot, for the carriage had been left in the road outside the grounds. They were half an hour in reaching it. Catherine and her maid seated themselves in the carriage, Bibikov stood up in the back and Orlov sat on the box with the driver. The hired horses turned their faces towards Petersburg. They had travelled their twenty-nine versts that night, and had now to trace the same distance back again. Nevertheless, urged on by Alexis Orlov, they covered the distance in less than an hour and a half. The white dust from the roadway rose in clouds and settled on the black garments of the Empress, for the carriage was an open *calèche*. About halfway to the city they met Catherine's hairdresser on his way to Peterhof to prepare her for the gala day. The Empress sent him back telling him she would not need him. About five versts from the city, they met Gregory Orlov and Prince Bariatinsky. The Empress changed to Gregory's carriage because his horses were fresher. Escorted by her lover and Bariatinsky she drove up to the Ismailov Regiment. It was the Regiment of Count Cyril Razumovsky, who had long been in love with her as Grand Duchess and had assisted all her projects in Russia.

An old priest was found to administer the oath of allegiance, while the whole regiment headed by Razumovsky hastened to swear fealty to Catherine II of Russia. The Empress got into her hired carriage again and, preceded by the priest and followed by the regiment, went on to the Preobrazhensky Regiment. Here the oath of allegiance was again hastily administered and the augmented procession moved forward to the Nevsky Prospect. The third regiment, the Semionovsky, suffered a moment of indecision, but they too were in line by the time the procession reached the Kazan Cathedral. It was now nine o'clock. Catherine entered the Cathedral and was met by the priests who blessed her with the cross. The nobles crowded around the new Empress, competing with the military to kiss her hand. From the Cathedral the procession went on up the Nevsky Prospect and turned into the Morskaya, proceeding to the new Winter Palace.

At ten o'clock, just after the Empress entered the palace, another hired carriage was seen dashing up to the entrance. A fat man and a little boy in his night clothes were sitting inside. It was Panin and the Grand Duke

Paul, and this was their first appearance on that stirring
June morning. They had slept late. Count Panin had
always been dilatory, unready. It is said of him that the
Empress Elizabeth had once cast her eye upon him as a
likely favourite. She summoned him one day to wait for
her outside the bath; but when she emerged she found
him doubled up on his chair fast asleep. So she decided
to employ him in the diplomatic service. On the morning
of Catherine's accession, after fourteen years of international diplomacy, Count Panin had not changed. When
he entered the Winter Palace with his charge, the Empress came to meet them and carried the boy out on the
balcony to present him as her heir. This was the end of
Panin's scheme to make Paul emperor, Paul's mother the
Regent, and himself Grand Chancellor. He remained
always rather resentful about it and did not fail to hamper
the ambitions of the Orlovs whenever he had a chance.
Catherine said of him, 'Count Panin was naturally indolent, and he had the art of making his indolence pass
for calculating prudence.'

The doors of the Winter Palace were thrown wide open
and anybody from the street could enter and kiss the
hand of the new Empress. The palace was a gorgeous
new building, only just completed, yet all the common
soldiers were free to tramp through it and take the oath
of allegiance to their Little Mother. It was a master
stroke. 'The least soldier of the guards,' Catherine wrote
to Poniatovsky, 'on seeing me said to himself: that is the
work of my hands.' Other master strokes of the Empress
were the fluent manifestoes which she composed from
time to time during the following days, to be set up and
printed in the cellar beneath the Academy of Science and
distributed to a people who could not read them. In 1762,
few of the nobles could read. Fortunately the manifestoes

were carefully preserved in the archives for the enjoyment of a more literate age.

The first one drafted by her facile hand read thus:

'We by the Grace of God, Catherine II, Empress and Autocrat of all the Russias, etc. etc., All true sons of the Russian Fatherland have clearly seen the danger which threatened the Russian Empire. Namely, the law of our Orthodox Greek Church has been shaken by the disregard of ecclesiastical traditions, so that our ancient Orthodox Church in Russia was exposed to the extreme danger of being obliged to adopt another confession. Secondly, our glorious Russia, which has been lifted to a high degree by its conquering weapons, has been placed in complete subjection to its bitterest enemy by the new peace for which so much blood has been spilt, while the inner organization of the country, on which the whole Fatherland depends, lies in ruins. Therefore and because we are convinced of the danger to our faithful subjects, we have seen Ourselves obliged with the help of God and His Justice, but especially in response to the distinct and undissimulated wish of Our faithful subjects, to ascend the throne as Autocrat of all the Russias, whereupon all Our faithful subjects have taken the solemn oath of allegiance to Us.

CATHERINE.'

During the day the Empress and her counsellors decided that a military campaign to Peterhof was necessary. The object was to secure the person of Peter III and obtain his abdication. As Brückner well points out, the so-called army which Catherine II led to Peterhof was partly a spectacular, romantic parade and partly an exhibition of political genius.

At ten o'clock in the clear light of the evening of June

28, 1762, the Colonel of the Guard — Catherine herself —
took her place at the head of her troops. She was mounted
on a white horse and wore oak leaves in her hair. Her
uniform was borrowed from a lieutenant in the Life
Guards. It was doubtless chosen because the lieutenant
and the Empress happened to be of a size, but it scarcely
clothed her new position and title. For Catherine had
not hesitated to assume the title Colonel of the Guards,
the traditional place of the Czars of Russia which Peter
had resigned to his Uncle George of Holstein. Beside her
at the head of the troops, likewise clad in military uniform,
rode the Countess Catherine Dashkov. During the night
she remained beside the Empress, while her sister, Elizabeth Vorontsov, stuck close to the Emperor. There was
deep jealousy between the sisters.

Catherine II left the following note, written in her own
strong free flowing hand:

'Gentlemen and Senators! I go now with the Army to
secure and safeguard the throne, and leave in your care
as my highest representatives with the fullest confidence
the Fatherland, the People, and my Son.

CATHERINE.'

The Senate solemnly responded in a note which overtook the Empress at two o'clock in the morning, resting
on her way to Peterhof: 'His Highness, the Czarevich,
is as well as could be desired. In the house of Your Imperial Majesty, as well as in the city, all goes well and the
measures you have commanded are being carried out.'

Catherine bestrode her horse and rode onward to
Peterhof. She had lived for this triumphant moment:
little Fike riding her pillow in the dark bedroom at
Stettin; Grand Duchess Catherine cantering about the

courtyard in Petersburg while an admiring riding-master kissed her boot — these earlier exhibitions had prepared the way for this spectacular ride at the head of her spectacular army. But it was her last ride of the kind. In the future, she would be too busy and perhaps a shade too serious.

§ 5

Eight hours after Catherine and Alexis Orlov had left Peterhof, Peter and a gay party drove through the park and halted in front of Monplaisir. The ladies and gentlemen sprang from the low *chars-à-bancs* and strolled about the terrace. No one came to welcome them. The red pavilion was empty and silent. Peter went through the rooms searching for Catherine in vain. It is said that he even looked under the bed. Mystified and vaguely alarmed the party wandered down to the pier where three small vessels were moored.

Here they received the first news of events in Petersburg. A man bringing the inevitable fireworks for the Czar's name-day landed from a small boat at three o'clock. He told how the Preobrazhensky Regiment had hailed Catherine as Empress at nine o'clock that morning and how he had nevertheless just gone about his business of the day, which was to bring the fireworks to Peterhof. This seemed definite enough. Catherine had revolted.

Peter was accompanied by Count Münnich, Prince Troubetsky, Chancellor Vorontsov, Count Shuvalov, several other nobles and officers, and about seventeen ladies. His old tutor, Stehlin, tells the story of this day. Throughout the sunny afternoon the party remained on the lower terrace. The ladies and gentlemen withdrew a little to the garden, where they lay stretched out under the open sky through most of the fine summer day and a part of the fine summer night. Peter and his advisers lingered near the canal and wrote one ukase after the other which the Czar signed against the stone balustrade and sent to Petersburg. He paced up and down the walk beside the canal and took everybody's advice in turn. Finally Chancellor Vorontsov volunteered to go to Petersburg and bring the Empress to her senses. Then Shuvalov and Troubetsky departed on similar errands. But like the other less important messengers whom the Czar had already dispatched to the city, these gentlemen did not return.

Peter's fears increased. The Holstein Guards who had been sent over from Oranienbaum to defend Peterhof against attack reported that there was no ammunition in the place. Gradually, as the hours passed, a plan matured by which the whole party would go to Kronstadt in the three vessels which lay at anchor at the foot of the canal. A messenger was sent to the island and returned with the report that the way was clear. It was an error, as Peter learned when he tried to bring his yacht into the Kronstadt harbour at four o'clock in the morning. None of the three vessels was allowed to approach the island and the watchman called back brutally across the water, 'There is no Peter III. There is only Catherine II.'

The Czar's yacht fell away and took the course towards Oranienbaum. The Czar himself lay on the deck in a dead faint.

Early the next morning, forerunners from Catherine's advancing army began to gallop up to Peterhof. First and foremost on the scene, at each stage of the developments, was Alexis Orlov. Quiet, undistinguished, inexorable, he was the Empress's own man. The Colonel herself arrived at Peterhof at eleven o'clock. She sent messengers forward to Oranienbaum, demanding Peter's abdication, which the trembling Czar was by this time in no mood to refuse. General Ismailov brought back to the Empress the official document in which the Czar renounced all claims upon the throne.

It was General Ismailov who lured the ex-Emperor into a carriage with the promise that he would be sent to Holstein with Elizabeth Vorontsov. As soon as they had passed the gates of Oranienbaum, the Czar was separated from his favourite and brought as a prisoner to Peterhof. 'To prevent him from being torn to pieces by the soldiers,' says Catherine, 'he was put in the charge of a reliable guard under the command of Alexis Orlov.' From this time on Peter was at the mercy of his military guards; he never saw his mistress again. But the ghosts of his father, Brümmer and Bergholz, and all the tutors and governors who had tortured his childhood in the name of discipline, now crowded upon him with unspeakable terrors. Only now they bore the names of Alexis Orlov, Feodor Bariatinsky, and other Russian officers.

§ 6

Peter was driven up to Peterhof in a closed carriage, with curtains drawn. He was taken into an empty room, stripped of his uniform, and left in utter solitude. At the other end of the palace, remote and invisible, sat the terrible Empress. From her came messengers from time to time, directing this and commanding that. One of the messengers was Count Panin, amiable, soft Panin. The Empress apparently wished to communicate with him through human agents as well as wolves like Alexis Orlov. But if Peter was a bleating lamb, Panin was a fat old sheep. His interview with the deposed Czar, in which the prisoner kissed his hand, alternately pleading and commanding, left a painful wound on a sensitive personality.

Panin afterwards said that he considered it one of the greatest misfortunes of his life that he was obliged to see Peter III on this day. The memory haunted him and made him fearful on behalf of the little boy he was bringing up, Paul Petrovich, who believed himself to be the son of the martyred Czar.

The Empress allowed the prisoner to choose the place of his confinement. Peter chose Ropsha, a small estate with a large garden and a fishing pond not many miles from Peterhof. What the Empress really intended to do with Peter no one knows or ever knew, probably she herself least of all. But this is what she said she intended, though it was many years afterwards that she wrote it. 'To go with Peter to Ropsha, the Empress named Alexis Orlov, Prince Bariatinsky, and several other officers. They chose a hundred men from the different regiments of the guard. They had orders to make the life of the monarch as agreeable as possible and to provide what he wished for his entertainment. The intention was to send him from there to Schlüsselburg and, according to circumstances, to allow him after some time to go with his favourites to Holstein. So little was his personality regarded as dangerous.'

What actually happened at Ropsha was quite different. Peter's tragedy came swiftly. Shut up in a bedroom and not allowed to leave it even for exercise, his existence was unutterably miserable. After the first night he complained of the bed and asked to have his own bed brought from Oranienbaum. Curiously enough, this whim was promptly gratified by Alexis Orlov who had the great four-poster and all its trappings brought to Ropsha and set up before nightfall. An English traveller who saw this bed several years afterwards describes it for us. 'It had a white satin coverlet, and was on a large four-post bedstead, with curtains of pink and silver brocade, and was ornamented at the top with a plume of red and white feathers.' But even his own bed brought little comfort to the victim. He remained in twilight and solitude, for he was not permitted to open the green curtains which hung at the windows. In desperation, he asked for companions, and again his request was granted. His negro, Narcissus, his dog, and his violin were brought, at the Empress's command, from Oranienbaum. He begged for Elizabeth Vorontsov's presence, but this was refused him. Presently he fell ill with diarrhœa, a disease to which he was always subject in a crisis. His personal physician was brought to Ropsha.

The leniency of the Empress bears out her statement of her intentions. Comforted by Narcissus, his dog, and his violin, Peter might live on at Ropsha indefinitely. But it was a dull life for the guards. Orlov, Bariatinsky, Passeck and the others were accustomed to all the excitement of life in Petersburg. Playing cards all day and all night at Ropsha was monotonous entertainment by comparison. Six days of it gave them a picture of future weeks, future months, stretching possibly into years. The revolution, with all its hectic anticipations, was over, and this was the result of it for them. It was all very well for the Empress and the others, enjoying life in Petersburg, to be magnanimous towards the prisoner, to take measures to mitigate his suffering and prolong his endurance. In the eyes of men like Orlov and Bariatinsky, Peter was not a man at all. He was no better than a worm that lay in their path and asked to be stepped on. They played cards and drank heavily. Saturday came and at midday Peter was invited to come out of his room and dine with the guards. . . .

In the meantime the Empress, established in the

Winter Palace, received daily messages from the ex-Czar and Alexis Orlov about the progress of things at Ropsha. Three chief petitions from the prisoner and three letters from his jailor project for us the scenes of the tragedy which developed so swiftly and inevitably from the circumstances.

'Madame,' wrote Peter, 'I beg Your Majesty to rest assured concerning me, and to have the goodness to order that the guards be removed from the second room, in order that I may move about in there; because, as you know, I always walk about in the room and I shall otherwise get swollen legs. Then I beg you further to command the officers not to remain in the same room when I have necessities; that is unendurable for me. Finally I beseech Your Majesty not to treat me as a great evil-doer. I am not conscious that I have ever wronged you. While I commend myself to your magnanimous thoughts, I beg that you will at least send me with the persons named to Germany. God will certainly reward you. I am, Your very devoted servant, Peter. P.S. Your Majesty can rest assured of me that I shall think and do nothing against your person or your reign.'

The second note is shorter. 'Your Majesty: If you do not wish to destroy utterly a human being who is already unhappy enough, have pity on me and send me my only consolation, that is Elizabeth Romanovna [Vorontsov]. In this you will be doing one of the most merciful deeds of your reign. Also if Your Majesty would but visit me for one instant my highest wishes would be fulfilled. Your very devoted servant, Peter.'

The two preceding messages were written in French but the third and last one was written in Russian, the language which Peter hated and Catherine loved. The drowning man caught even at this straw. 'Your Majesty:

I beg you, since I have fulfilled your will in everything, to allow me to go abroad with those for whom I have already petitioned Your Majesty. And I hope that your magnanimity will not leave me without nourishment. Faithful servant, Peter.'

The letters of Alexis Orlov, brought by the same messenger, picture what was happening meanwhile in the guards' quarters at Ropsha.

On Tuesday he wrote: 'Little Mother, Gracious Empress: Health we all wish you for countless years. We and the whole command are well as this letter leaves us, but our monster has grown very sick and has had an unexpected attack of colic. And I am afraid that in the end he might die to-night and fear still more again that he might live. The first fear I have because he chatters pure nonsense, and that does not amuse us; and the second fear, because he is really dangerous for us all because he often speaks as if he had his former position.

'According to your orders, I have paid the soldiers for half a year, also the under-officers with the exception of Potiomkin, because he serves without salary. Many of the soldiers have spoken with tears of your Graciousness, they had not deserved so much of you, to be rewarded in so short a time. I send you herewith a list of the entire command at present here; but a thousand roubles were lacking, Little Mother, and I have added them in ducats. There was much laughter here among the guardsmen on account of the ducats, when they received them from me. Many asked questions because they had never yet seen any and gave them back to me because they thought them worth nothing. . . . Until death, your devoted slave, Alexis Orlov.'

On Saturday morning, Orlov wrote: 'Our Little Mother, Gracious Empress: I know not what I should do

for I tremble before the anger of Your Majesty, that
you do not believe something awful about us, and that
we are not the cause of the death of your rascal and also
of Russia and our law. But now the lackey Maslov sent
to serve him has fallen ill and he himself is so sick that
I do not believe he will live until evening, and he is
already quite unconscious; which the whole command
knows and begs God that we become rid of him as soon
as possible; and this Maslov and the officer dispatched
can inform Your Majesty in what condition he now is, if
you are pleased to doubt me. This written by Your
Faithful Servant . . .'

On Saturday evening, a messenger from Ropsha galloped up to the Winter Palace with the last letter from
Alexis. 'Little Mother, Merciful Empress. How shall
I explain or describe what has happened? You will not
believe your devoted slave but before God I will speak
the truth. Little Mother! I am ready for death but I
myself do not know how the misfortune happened. We
are lost if you have not mercy upon us. Little Mother,
he lives no longer in this world. But no one had thought
that, and how should we have had the thought to lift
hand against the Czar? But Empress, the misfortune
has happened. It came to a quarrel at table between
him and Prince Feodor: we could not separate them, and
already he was no more. We cannot ourselves remember
what we have done, but we are all to the last man guilty
and deserve death. Have mercy upon me, if only for
my brother's sake! I have made my confession and there
is nothing to investigate. Pardon me or quickly make
an end of me. I hate the light of day: we have angered
you and our souls are hurled to destruction.'

On Sunday morning the Empress informed the public
by an official statement that Peter III had died of a

hæmorrhoidal attack and would be buried in the Alexander Nevsky Cathedral. There is no record that she ever tried to give anyone at any time a confidential explanation of Peter's death. The letters of Alexis Orlov were put away and never came to light until after her death. Her silence remained unbroken. Formerly this woman had worried excessively about what Europe might say about the birth of her first child and her relations with Saltikov. Now Europe had nothing less than murder to talk about, and talk ran high. But Catherine seemed impervious to any curiosity concerning this foreign gossip. As an old woman, however, she one day suddenly asked Diderot, 'What do they say in Paris of the death of my husband?' When Diderot was too embarrassed to answer, she turned the conversation by a jest at his expense.

§ 7

During his brief reign, Peter III had reversed the foreign policy of the Empress Elizabeth. The Austrian and French interests had gone into eclipse, while the Prussian interest had blazed up again. Frederick's envoy lived at the elbow of the Czar whispering good advice to a mental invalid who was unable to profit by it. No sooner was Peter III out of the way than the Austrian and French envoys came out of their retirement and began to plead their cause with Catherine II. They took for granted that Frederick the Great had had his day and that his enemies, Austria and France, would now have theirs. Had not the Empress issued a manifesto in which Prussia was referred to as Russia's 'bitterest enemy'? Had not Field-Marshal Saltikov advanced upon Prussian soil, opening all of a sudden an offensive campaign? For a moment Frederick the Great trembled in his well-worn boots while the hopes of France and Austria ran high.

But the Empress was not occupied with the interests of Prussia, or Austria, or France. She preferred the interests of Russia, which happened to be her own. She recalled the hasty General Saltikov from Prussian territory so adroitly that he scarcely knew he had been recalled. She assured Austria and France of her goodwill and friendship and left them thinking that their temporary estrangement from Russia during Peter's reign had been wiped out. Catherine II wished to have peace with Europe. She had called Frederick the Great the deadly enemy of Russia on the day of her accession; but a few days afterwards she confirmed the peace with Prussia which Peter III had made and which her manifesto had denounced. The Empress made no attempt to justify this inconsistency. She was a woman of action and explanations have a way of taking too much time. From her accession until her death she was one of the busiest monarchs in Europe.

She recalled Bestushev and presented him with a great house furnished with comforts. The old man was nearly seventy now and of no great service to her. But she owed him much and he was a magnificent monument because he had known Peter the Great. She recalled Biron, also aged with exile, and made him the Grand Duke of Courland. He was useful to her there because he kept the House of Saxony from getting a foothold in Courland. Poniatovsky, who had long awaited this day in Poland, now wrote asking to be summoned to Russia, but she did not recall him. She discouraged him from writing to her at all, saying, 'I must walk straight ahead; I must not be suspected.' She had long ago planned with Poniatovsky and Williams that the Count was one day to be made the King of Poland. She now urged the Count to stop at home in Poland and abide the course of events.

One of Catherine's first acts as Empress was to give orders for her coronation. The ceremony which Peter had postponed until he had at last died uncrowned was foremost in her thoughts. Four days after her accession, she ordered the fireworks for her coronation; and seven days afterwards, the day on which the death of the unfortunate Peter became known, she announced the date. It was to take place in September. She gave Prince Troubetsky fifty thousand roubles and sent him to Moscow to get everything in readiness. He carried with him the specifications for a great spectacle, and, with the assistance of a corps of official merry-makers, managed to complete all preparations within the time arranged for. Promptly on the first day of September, the Empress left Petersburg with an enormous train. There was evidently to be no postponement of the date originally set for the ceremony, no repetition of the succession of postponements which had delayed the marriage of the Grand Duke and the Grand Duchess under the late Empress. The new Empress had none of the dilatoriness of Elizabeth; she had respect for time. In this regard, she remained always only half a Russian.

Between Petersburg and Moscow, a slight cloud threatening delay rose above the horizon. It appeared in the direction of the train of Count Panin and his pupil, the Grand Duke Paul. The Empress received a message from Panin that his pupil had fallen ill of a fever and might not be able to enter Moscow on the expected day. Would the Empress travel more slowly? The Empress halted and waited with impatience. She was rewarded by a second message saying that the Grand Duke had another and a worse attack. The Empress no longer wavered; she sent her ultimatum to Panin. It directed that Panin and his train should travel forward when the boy's health permitted; in any case, the Empress would enter Moscow on the following Friday. On the receipt of this message, Paul's health suddenly became better and he was able, under the escort of Panin, to enter Moscow in the company of his mother.

Catherine's coronation took place in the Kremlin on Sunday, September 23, 1762. In the early morning the regiments marched through the towering gates and stationed themselves in front of the four great cathedrals whose pinnacles rise like glittering golden tulips above the city. At ten o'clock the Empress appeared on the Red Staircase leading to the Uspensky Cathedral. Six chamberlains carried her train and Count Sheremetiev bore the end of it. Six months previously he had carried the train of the erratic Peter at the funeral of the Empress. This time his offices were accepted by his sovereign with supreme decorum. The procession advanced slowly, while the great crowds who had gathered without the military cordon and occupied the roofs of the houses gazed in awestruck silence at the ermine-and-silver clad figure of the Empress, their Little Mother. Only the myriad bells of Moscow spoke and the cannon thundered their salute.

From cathedral to cathedral the stately procession advanced. As Catherine placed the crown upon her own head, the cannon fired a salute on the Red Square. Surrounded by Prelates and Archimandrites, she nevertheless chose to give the Holy Communion to herself. As she had on the night of June 28 unhesitatingly placed herself at the head of the army as Colonel, she now placed herself with equal assurance at the head of the Church of

Russia. Now, as then, no one questioned her right to do so.

While the Empress distributed honours in the Granovitaya Palata, the sacred chamber into which women had been first admitted by Peter the Great, the whole city of Moscow was turned into one vast festival. The merry-making was prolonged for weeks. The fountains ran with wine, bread and roast meat were given for the asking, and silver roubles were thrown to the people. No single tradition of grandeur or graciousness was overlooked by the new Russian monarch. An allegorical pageant called the Procession of the Triumphant Minerva brought the coronation festivities to a close, but by this time winter was so far advanced that the performers shivered in the flying snow.

The triumphant Minerva was a happy allegory for Catherine. Not so happy perhaps was the inspiration of the Archimandrite of Troitsky who welcomed her at the gates of the Cloister with an oration comparing her to Judith. Afterwards a group of students, wearing gold-embroidered garments and green wreaths on their flowing locks, sang a cantata composed in her honour. The unmusical Empress could not distinguish one note from another but she bore herself graciously throughout. A few years later, grown more accustomed to power and partly satiated, she was less tolerant. She would sometimes send a page to the orchestra in the theatre and arbitrarily stop the music.

§ 8

Captain Gregory Orlov became Count Orlov on the day of Catherine's coronation. She also named him Adjutant-General and gave him her portrait set with diamonds which he wore on his breast. Gregory Orlov sat many times for portraits which may still be seen in Petersburg showing him to be as handsome as report has made him out. He was indolent and unaspiring, content to be the escort of her Majesty and to eschew all influence in public affairs. In the spring of 1763, after Catherine had been Empress for about a year, a rumour of her marriage to Gregory Orlov was whispered about. Whence arose this rumour? Had the slothful Gregory suddenly become ambitious? It was more likely that the idea came from Alexis, the head of the Orlovs.

Count Gregory occupied an equivocal position. He was a parvenu and the favourite of the Empress. Among the nobles, the Orlovs were not popular. Among the forty officers who had supported Catherine's conspiracy, were many who regarded them with a jealous eye. They had been showered with honours and riches, though the Empress had done much also for a number of her supporters. The intimacy between the Empress and Gregory Orlov aroused distrust. If the favourite were promoted to the position of a consort, the Orlovs would certainly become powerful. Their fellow-conspirators were not pleased to be so far outstripped.

There is a legend that about this time the Empress sent Chancellor Vorontsov to sound Count Alexis Razumovsky on his alleged marriage with Empress Elizabeth. According to the story, the ancient Count, fast falling to decay in his chimney corner, behaved very strangely when questioned. He produced an old yellow satin-covered document which he kissed dramatically and then threw into the open fire. Tradition says this was his certificate of marriage which he sacrificed to prevent its being used as a precedent by Gregory Orlov in his suit with the Empress. He destroyed by this act his last chance to go down to posterity as an honest husband. But he also destroyed whatever hopes of a precedent the Orlovs may have had. The story was first told by a descendant of the Razumovsky family and may well be doubted.

Whatever may have happened in Razumovsky's house, the gossip did not stop. The Empress, attended by Gregory Orlov, left Moscow for Rostov to spend the month of May in a cloister. No sooner had she left the city than old Bestushev produced a petition, suggesting a second marriage for the Empress on the grounds that the Grand Duke Paul had such delicate health. When this paper reached Panin, he asked the Empress outright whether it was issued with her permission or not. The Empress said not, but Panin did not believe her. The town-talk increased, and little groups began to put their heads together behind closed doors. Presently a certain groom of the Bed Chamber, Chitrovo, who had been one of the guards of the late Czar at Ropsha, was arrested and held for a secret investigation. The young man's grandfather was enraged. He met old Bestushev in the street and scolded him. 'Mercy on us, your Highness. What power these Orlovs have, that gentlemen can so completely disappear!'

Chitrovo was accused of having made threats against the life of Alexis Orlov. The Empress, watching everything from her hiding-place in the cloister, saw that matters were growing serious. Messengers galloped back and forth between Rostov and Moscow, while Catherine directed the hearing of Chitrovo to the last detail. The least word from his lips was set down on paper for her. In the end she sent him off to his own country estate. It was a light sentence, for she did not want to increase the talk.

She gave peremptory orders that the investigation was to be kept secret. But it was no longer possible. All Moscow was talking of the affair, and the Empress knew that Moscow was talking. She decided to issue a manifesto which she called the 'Manifesto of Silence' and which she ordered to be read aloud in the streets of Moscow. The President of the Senate summoned the crowds together by the beating of drums and then read aloud to them these commands of the Empress:

'It is Our Will and Wish, that each and all of Our faithful subjects shall attend alone to their office and occupation, and shall refrain from spreading unseemly and bold rumours. But against Our expectations and to Our great distress and dissatisfaction, we hear that there are people with wicked thoughts and manners who think not at all of the common good and peace; but, attacked by singular ideas about things which do not concern them and of which they can have no real knowledge, nevertheless they busy themselves with putting these ideas into other weak heads. ... Although such harmful judgments really deserve punishment, for they damage Our own and the general peace, we shall not in this case proceed with full strictness; but, with Our inborn humanity, maternally admonish all those who have been affected by these restless thoughts to refrain from unnecessary conversation. .... If however Our motherly admonition has no effect upon their wicked hearts and does not lead them back upon the way of the good, then let every one of these bad people know that we shall proceed with the full strength of the law. ....'

With the issue of the Manifesto of Silence, the talk stopped. But the project of marriage with Gregory Orlov also came to an end. When Catherine returned to Moscow the subject had been forgotten. It was the only attempt of her reign to acquire a legal consort and to win back the good name she had lost. Henceforth she was to remain the widow of Peter III and the mistress of many lovers. She made two valiant attempts to attain an honourable position by marriage but both of them failed for wholly different reasons. The first time was when she married the ineffectual Peter. The second time was when she tried to marry Gregory Orlov and was stopped by public opinion in Russia.

9

Catherine the Great

IN 1762, Petersburg was still a wooden city. The Court itself had only just removed from the draughty wooden palace on the Nevsky to the great stone palace on the Neva. The houses were simple or multiple structures of squared logs of the type still seen in Russian villages. Cellars and basements were unknown. To the substantial German mind of the Empress, the superficial grandeur of her capital was an object of secret derision. 'Greifenheim's house,' in which she had been born, had been better built. She wrote a verse about the house that Jack built without any stairs because the stairway had been forgotten.

The composition illustrates what the Empress often said of herself, and very truly, that she was no poet. But it very well expresses what she thought of Russian building in her time. She called her doggerel a *Chanson*.

> 'Jean bâtit une maison,
> Qui n'a ni rime ni raison:
> L'hiver on y gèle tout roide,
> L'été ne la rend point froide;
> Il y oublia l'escalier,
> Puis le bâtit en espalier.'

When a fire broke out in the city, it was a glorious spectacle. During the first winter of her reign, the Empress watched from her window two hundred and forty wooden houses going up in flames. As the sparks ascended from the roaring logs against the blackness of the winter sky, she watched the disaster with mixed feelings, for she yearned to rebuild that quarter of the city. Within three years it was actually rebuilt of brick. Several great fires devastated the city during the early part of her reign and the Empress restored the ravaged sections with brick and stucco washed pink and green by Italian architects. First raised by Peter the Great and developed by Catherine the Great, Petersburg was and remains for all time a wholly un-Russian city, a fitting monument to these two rulers who joined Europe and Russia together.

Though Catherine II prided herself on being a Russian she cherished a private scorn for much that was precious to the Russians. Her honest opinion of Moscow, set down in her journal, shows this. 'At that time [1750], even more than now, it was in general very hard for the nobility to leave Moscow, the city which they all so loved, where laziness and indolence are their chief occupation. They would gladly spend their whole lives there, driving about in a richly gilded carriage behind six spans of horses, a symbol of the false idea of luxury which reigns there and conceals from the eyes of the masses the slovenliness of the master, the complete disorganization of his household and his manner of life. It is no rarity to see a splendidly gowned lady in a wonderful carriage with six lean and shabbily harnessed horses drive out from a great courtyard heaped with dirt and rubbish. Her unkempt lackeys in smart livery disgrace her by their boorish behaviour. Generally speaking, both men and women grow soft in this great city: they see and practice only wretchedness, which leaves the most undoubted genius to perish and decay. Because they follow their humours and their whims, they evade all laws or execute them badly. The consequence is that they never learn to command at all or that they become tyrants. . . . Besides this there was never a people who had more objects of fanaticism before their eyes, such as wonder-working saints at every step; churches, parsons, cloisters, praying brothers, rascals, thieves, useless servants in their houses — and such houses! What dirt in those houses, which occupy whole fields and have mudholes for courtyards! In general every person of fashion in the city occupies not a house but a small farm.' The Empress complained that if she sent for a person in Moscow, she had to wait until the next day for her answer. The Muscovites had time. The Muscovites were Russians.

Although Catherine was free in her criticism of the Moscow nobles, her own Court at Petersburg was just as extravagant and ostentatious though possibly more orderly and cleanly withal. Both gentlemen and ladies wore jewels and diamonds. Gregory Orlov, at the height of his fortunes, had a suit of clothes which cost a million roubles and which was sewed all over with diamonds. Orlov's extravagance was mild compared with that of his successor, Potiomkin, who was clearly obliged to outshine the achievements of his predecessor. Historians have estimated what the Empress spent on the clothes and upkeep of her several favourites and how much she turned over to them in the form of estates and other valuable goods and have found the total immense. In this she seems to have but continued the tradition of Elizabeth who gave the Anitchkov Palace to Razumovsky and a handful of national monopolies to the Shuvalovs. All the nobles about the Court had inherited lavish standards from Peter the Great and the favourites of the Empress could not possibly be outshone by Sheremetiev and Stroganov who were counts and rich men by inheritance. Catherine's favourites were parvenus; they owed every copeck to her. She always saw to that. The Empress herself was an upstart; but the nobles of Moscow were not. In the palaces there with their miry courtyards dwelt the ancient blood of Russia. While the Empress criticized their dirt and ostentation, she knew that in the eyes of Moscow she herself was a parvenu and her favourites were but creatures of yesterday.

§ 2

Up to the time of Catherine II, the Czars of Russia had been addressed by the European Courts as 'Your Majesty.' As soon as the Empress was crowned at Moscow, she notified the sovereigns of Europe that she expected in the future to be addressed as 'Your Imperial Majesty.' Her request was granted except in France, which had the consciousness of being the most civilized country in the world and was bound to regard Russia as a savage interloper. France would gladly have pushed the big, unwieldy, dirty chaos known as Russia back into the arms of Asia. The French maintained that 'Czar' did not mean the same as 'Emperor' at all. But Catherine said the two titles were exactly the same, and insisted that 'His Most Christian Majesty' of France should always address her as 'Her Imperial Majesty' of Russia. At last the French minister, Choiseul, agreed. Then he sent official communications to Russia in which the word 'Imperial' did not appear. Catherine refused to read them or to recognize an envoy who carried papers addressed merely to 'Her Majesty.' Pushed thus into a corner, Choiseul finally declared that 'Imperial Majesty' was impure French, a corruption of the sacred language which the French Academy existed to protect. The argument between Versailles and Petersburg spun itself out for years.

Like a good and faithful wife, Madame de Choiseul joined in the quarrel and went about calling the Empress of Russia a 'monster.' It was this lady who provoked from Voltaire his famous words in defence of Catherine the Great. 'I may boast to you that I stand rather in the good graces of the Empress; I am her knight towards and against all. I know well that she is reproached for several small matters concerning her husband. Those are family

188

affairs in which I do not mix. Moreover it is also well if one has a wrong to repair it. Then it becomes one's first interest to make great efforts to win for oneself the respect and admiration of the public. Certainly her dreadful husband would not have accomplished one of the things which my Catherine accomplishes every day.'

Catherine II was her own foreign minister. The men whom she placed at the head of the College of Foreign Affairs were followers not leaders. When she ascended the throne, she knew more about the international relations of Europe than she did about the internal affairs of Russia. She was to learn about Russia after she became its Empress. In 1762, the relative positions of the European nations had been made prominent by the warlike activities of Frederick the Great. International problems were perfectly familiar to her. Her opinion was formed and she was ready to take action. Catherine had been inspired by Machiavelli's *Prince*, which she had read during the Poniatovsky period when she intrigued for power with Sir Charles Hanbury Williams for an ally.

In his monumental work on Catherine the Great, Bilbassov devotes a chapter to a detailed account of the reading of the Grand Duchess during the years of her virtual imprisonment by the Empress Elizabeth, and emphasizes the influence which her favourite authors had on her subsequent career as Empress. Bilbassov found on her table Voltaire, Montesquieu, Tacitus, Boyle; in short, a collection of the works of free-thinkers who might be expected to form the mind of a future liberal monarch. Catherine read all of these, but she also read Machiavelli, whose name is not mentioned by Bilbassov in his carefully prepared chapter on her reading. In one of her letters to Chevalier Williams, she quotes a maxim of Machiavelli to the effect that a man is rarely as wicked as he ought to be. Williams was a little shocked apparently, for he replied, 'What I say is, thank God, the wicked rarely have the courage which they ought to have to execute their wickedness.' To which Catherine replied coolly, 'So much the better, if le bon Dieu has curtailed the courage of the wicked for the execution of their wickedness.'

The foreign policy of Catherine was uniformly aggressive. In her domestic policies, her intentions were at least liberal, but all her dealings with foreign nations were astute and predatory. The trail of Machiavelli was over all. She worked for the expansion of Russia and boasted as an old woman of the number of square miles which she had added to her territory. Russia was a parvenu and she was a parvenu; their cause was one. Europe should be astonished, and it was astonished. It responded by calling her the Semiramis and Messalina of the North and Catherine the Great. In these high-sounding titles she exulted, and her personality settled into them as her body settled comfortably into its ermine robe.

§ 3

When the squire inherits wide ancestral acres, his first thought is for his boundaries and his fences. So it was with Catherine when she became heir to Russia. Courland was entrusted to Biron, the decrepit old Duke ruled by his daughters and devoted to Catherine. Thus the Empress secured this boundary well and could henceforth dismiss it safely from her mind. She next considered her own border provinces and found them too restless for her taste. Little Russia, Livonia, and Finland needed to be stabilized, and she wrote to Viazemsky recommending treatment to that end. 'These provinces, like that of Smolensk, must be induced in the gentlest manner to Russianize themselves, so that they no longer look around them like wolves in the forest.'

To Poland she gave her own personal attention. Catherine's name plays a great rôle in the history of that country as one of the originators of the historic looting known as the partition of Poland. Three monarchs shared the booty: Catherine of Russia, Frederick of Prussia, and Maria Theresa of Austria. Maria Theresa is the only one of the three who has never been accused of inventing the idea. Since Catherine herself exonerated the Empress of Austria in a letter which she wrote to Grimm in 1770, Maria Theresa's lack of responsibility for the crime in Poland seems sufficiently established. 'As far as the dear worthy Lady Prayerful is concerned,' wrote the Empress Catherine, 'I can say nothing more than that she suffers from severe attacks of covetousness and imperiousness. To weep is a sign of repentance, but since she always holds fast to what she has and quite forgets that not to do a thing again is the best kind of repentance, there must be something stubborn in her bosom. I fear it must be the original sin of Adam which plays this crazy comedy. But what does one ask more from such a woman? If she is faithful to her husband, she has all the virtues and needs nothing more.' Maria Theresa's retaliation was to speak of the Empress of Russia as *cette femme* and talk about her openly as an immoral woman. Notwithstanding this exchange of personal insults, they co-operated willingly in the seizure of Polish territory.

The exact part played by Frederick the Great in the partition of Poland has never been so clearly established. It is an embarrassing episode for the Prussian historian to explain. To assert, as Schlözer does, that Frederick only gradually and reluctantly consented is an attempt to whitewash the hero in a way which makes him slightly unheroic.

To ascribe the initiative to the Russian Empress is to place the great Frederick in a secondary position which is inconsistent with the invincible front he has always presented to history. Nevertheless the actual idea, that is, the execution of the idea seems to have occurred first of all to Catherine. The expectation of the disaster had long existed in Poland, which had been forewarned a century before by one of its Kings, Jan Casimir, who said that one day the thing would happen just as it actually did happen. The dismemberment of Poland had been seen as a possibility by all the international politicians of Europe for more than a century before it became a definite picture in the mind of Catherine II. She alone had the energizing image in her mind that leads to action, and was undoubtedly responsible for the first Partition of Poland, although Frederick the Great shared the guilt for the second and third partitions which logically followed.

The steps by which Catherine came to this decision are not difficult to trace. Soon after her accession to the Russian throne, the King of Poland lay down to die, and he actually did die in September, 1763. The King of Prussia and the Empress of Russia, who had been misled so often by false reports, were both upset by the event when it finally occurred. Frederick sprang up from the table with the remark 'I hate those people who always do things at the wrong time.' Catherine also sprang from her chair when the news came, galvanized for action. She had hoped for it so long. Her long-deferred plans to make Stanislas Poniatovsky King of Poland required instant attention. She had already instructed her Ambassador, Count Kayserling, concerning his duties in the present crisis. He had in fact been selected for the post with this event in view. 'I am sending Count Kayserling without delay as Ambassador to Poland,' she had written to Poniatovsky, 'in order to make you King after the death of August III. If my Ambassador is not successful in making you King, then I desire that Adam Czartorisky shall become King.'

Adam Czartorisky was the uncle of Stanislas, a representative of the same family, and was also devoted to the Empress of Russia. Catherine was willing to allow Poland a second choice from this family. This did not mean, however, that she strove any less efficiently and determinedly to place the handsome Stanislas upon the throne. She told Kayserling that if he could not manage it for less to spend as much as a hundred thousand roubles on the election. Nor did she put her faith in the influence of money alone. Russian regiments were marched into Poland to camp ominously near the electoral convocation. The Empress wished, however, to avoid bloodshed. She preferred to enlist the aid and influence of the Prussian King in order that Poland might feel its eastern and western neighbours closing in upon its existence like a gentle but inevitable vice.

Catherine gave presents quite unblushingly. No sooner was the Polish King dead than couriers with messages and gifts began to enliven the road from Petersburg to Berlin. Knowing Frederick for a *Feinschmecker*, Catherine sent him melons from Astrakhan and grapes from the Crimea. Frederick gallantly replied, 'There is a great disparity between water-melons from Astrakhan and the electoral assembly of the Polish provinces, but you know how to comprehend all in the sphere of your activity. The same hand which presents water-melons distributes crowns and preserves the peace in Europe, for which I and all who are interested in the affairs of Poland shall eternally bless you.' Catherine's gifts continued. Russian caviare and sterlet were followed by Russian furs, black fox and marten. And

finally, when Frederick expressed an interest in the dromedaries so commonly used by the peasants in Russia, the
Empress had two of the best animals to be found in
Ukrainia sent with her compliments to the master of Sans
Souci. As the first water-melons had been heralds of Poniatovsky as King, the dromedaries were harbingers of the
first partition of Poland.

Not wholly unlike the late Czar of Russia, Poniatovsky
was made King against his will. Catherine, the King-
maker, forced this unwelcome distinction upon him. He
believed and many others believed with him that Catherine
intended, after making him ruler of Poland, to marry him
and annex his country to her own. The Porte suspected
this to be the plan of the Russian Empress and accordingly set about to defeat it by opposing the election of
Stanislas on the ground that he was not married. Poniatovsky's family, the Czartoriskys, saw the logic of the
Porte's objection and urged the Count, who had certainly
reached a marriageable age, to choose a suitable consort.
But Poniatovsky stubbornly refused to take the fatal step.
The utmost that he would consent to do, and this
was only after an emphatic message had arrived from
Catherine at Petersburg, was to sign an undertaking
that he would at least never marry any but a Roman
Catholic. This promise quieted the Turkish opposition
and the election was allowed to proceed. It took place by
immemorial custom in the open field by a vote of voices.
It was a fine day and there was no disorder. Poniatovsky
wrote in his journal, 'The election was perfectly unani-
mous and so tranquil that many ladies were out on the
electoral field.' He became, at the age of thirty-two, King
Stanislas August of Poland.

The country had vindicated its cherished republican
system and enthroned an elected King. The courts of

Europe hastened to send acknowledgments and congratulations. The last country to be heard from was Russia. As soon as Catherine had got her King elected with her military pickets and her hundred thousand roubles, she lost all interest in the Polish situation and left the Minister of Foreign Affairs, Count Panin, to conclude matters. 'The thing seems incredible,' wrote the Prussian Ambassador to his master, 'nevertheless I assure your Majesty that this is so. The notification of Poniatovsky lay unanswered for six weeks on Panin's well-known work-table.' This seemed amazing to Frederick the Great to whom promptness and system were fetiches. To Catherine such things were conveniences.

That Poniatovsky, a king in spite of himself, never thoroughly enjoyed his reign was only to be expected. His country was torn by internal dissensions, political and religious. The new King was a man who had been bullied all his life, first by his mother and then by his mistress; in short, a man of charm but no force. There was nothing within him with which to cope with the turbulent conditions of his realm. Catherine had a genius for reconciling what seemed to be opposites; but the Polish King, who had run away from his mother to his mistress and had then run away from his mistress to his mother again, could not hold two antagonistic interests in his mind at the same time. Poland was a cauldron of conflicts: district against district, class against class, religion against religion. Under Poniatovsky, the old familiar feuds blazed higher and higher. His health suffered and he was miserable. After three years of such devastating responsibility, he wrote to his Ambassador in Russia: 'The last orders given by Prince Repnin (the Russian General) to introduce legislation for the dissidents (Greek Catholics) is a real thunderbolt for the country and for me personally. If it is still humanly possible, try to make the Empress see that the crown which she procured me will become for me a shirt of Nessus. I shall be burnt alive and my end will be frightful.'

Thus the King wailed on his comfortless throne, a gentle mouse trembling under three watchful pairs of eyes belonging to three of the most greedy monarchs of the century. Perhaps it would be more accurate to say that the three watchful pairs of eyes were trained upon each other and that they rather overlooked as negligible the victim cowering in the centre of the stage. Maria Theresa, the Austrian widow who never laid aside her weeds; Frederick II, the shabby bachelor who wore patches on his clothes; and Catherine II, the parvenu sovereign who painted her face – the conjunction of these three arch aggressors boded no good for Poland, weakened as she was by incessant domestic tremours. Yet the catastrophe which had been gathering for years and which was inherent in the circumstances, was precipitated at last as if by an accident.

In the autumn of 1770, Catherine entertained a distinguished foreign guest. He was a short man with a stiff pompous carriage and a silent inexpressive demeanour. He had come to Petersburg rather reluctantly at the request of his brother who felt that any invitation from the Empress of Russia should be accepted and exploited. There was no knowing what might be hidden behind the advances of this woman. The stiff, silent guest whom she entertained this autumn was Prince Henry of Prussia, the brother of Frederick the Great. Prince Henry was almost as unsociable as his brother but he had a sharp eye and sensitive perceptions. He was ideally qualified to spy upon the affairs of the Russian monarch.

Catherine, who never lost an opportunity of displaying

all her riches before this family, entertained Prince Henry regally. She installed him and his retinue in a palace facing the Alexander Nevsky monastery, an edifice so huge and magnificent that it was later converted from a residence into a school for imperial pages. The modest, unassuming Henry moved about with considerable discomfort in the rich and gorgeous setting which the hospitable Empress provided for him. His appearances were punctual and meticulous, but it was impossible for anyone to look at him and fancy that he enjoyed the balls and masquerades which were given for his entertainment. The Russians did not like him and made fun of his solemnity and coldness. With the Empress, however, he got on extremely well. Their conversations were carried on at great length and an intellectual sympathy developed between them which led to a long and interesting correspondence. Prince Henry's letters to the Empress do not contain the overstrained flattery with which his brother, Frederick the Great, always addressed her. There is evidence in their letters to show that Prince Henry of Prussia was one of the people of her own generation who understood this woman perfectly. In her old age, she turned against him violently, but he cherished no resentment against her. He respected Catherine sincerely, and was never afraid of her as the great Frederick always was, not because she was an Empress but because she was a woman.

Prince Henry stepped sedately through all the brilliant festivities of a Russian Christmas and New Year in Petersburg. The Winter Palace had never been so gay at this season since Catherine became Empress, for the visit of the Prussian Prince provided an excuse to outdo anything she had ever done before. In January, just about the time when things began to quiet down a bit, a disturbing rumour came over the snows from Moscow. It was said that Maria Theresa had sent Austrian troops across the border to occupy a little piece, a very little piece of Poland The Austrian monarch had ready her excuse but the Russian monarch did not think well of it. Neither of these august ladies ever gave the other the benefit of the doubt in any situation. Catherine dropped this casual remark in the presence of Prince Henry: 'It seems that in this Poland, one has only to stoop and help one's self.' Prince Henry regarded her words as a significant message for his brother to whom he reported them, adding, 'Although this was only a chance pleasantry, it is certain that it was not said for nothing and I do not doubt that it will be very possible for you to profit by it.'

And so began the three famous Partitions of Poland. In the first partition, Poland lost four thousand square miles and the three partitioners felt equally well treated. Twenty years later, the second partition took place in which the Empress of Russia profited immensely more than her partners in the looting. Poland raised up national heroes, chief of whom was the romantic Kosciuszko, who came to her defence. But their exploits only served as an excuse for the third invasion, which reduced Poland to a mere remnant, and finally and utterly deprived Poniatovsky of his throne.

For a time the ex-King lived in Poland under the protection of Russia and later he went back to Petersburg where he found asylum until his death. He outlived by several years the mistress of his youth, who had first given him a throne and then taken it away again. Poniatovsky was no hero but he was a good deal of a philosopher; he accepted his decline and fall without any great gestures of tragedy. He had never wanted to be King. His star went down in peaceful obscurity, while the national hero Kosciuszko impersonated for the world the tragedy of Poland.

Both of them were supported by pensions from the Russian Government. Catherine's estimate of the ex-King of Poland is illustrated by a legend which is believed even to this day. The story goes that she brought his lost throne from Poland and used it for a water-closet in her apartments at Czarskoe Selo.

§ 4

In the eighteenth century, Russia took her census every twenty years. It was an autocratic revision carried on in a slipshod way under military orders. When Catherine ascended the throne it was time for such a census to be taken. The new Empress was impatient for the results; she wanted to know how many 'souls' she had and how much of the earth's surface she owned, for it was in such personal terms as these that she pictured her possessions.

Returning from Moscow in June, 1763, just after the fiasco of her plan to marry Orlov, she turned her attention to the census. The Senate was preparing to go ahead according to precedent. Although Pastor Wagner had been a specialist in geography, his pupil the Empress had nevertheless very vague ideas about Russia. She was obliged to ask the Senators to tell her how many cities there were in her kingdom and discovered to her horror that not one of them knew. Without a moment's hesitation she took five roubles from her pocket and sent a messenger post haste to the Academy of Science which had published an atlas of Russia to be had for this price. The Empress presented the atlas to the Senate with her compliments.

The discussion of the census proceeded. Catherine learned that it was customarily taken by military troops and cost almost a million roubles, and that it invariably sent the peasant population into a panic. They evaded the lists by hiding in swamps and forests and fleeing across the border into Poland. The consequence was that trials, investigations, and punishments followed in the wake of every census in such numbers that the Senators dreaded to undertake it at all. Sadly they shook their bewigged heads and deplored the necessity of causing so much commotion among the terror-stricken people. They made speeches one after the other without offering any suggestion as to how these regrettable consequences could be prevented. The attentive Empress listened until she was tired and the discussion finally came to a dead end. Then she asked a few questions.

'Why have such a number of troops and pile up these heavy costs for the treasury? Is there no other way?' She was told that there was no other way; it had always been done so. 'But this plan seems better to me,' she persisted. 'Publish throughout the Empire that every place shall send a list of its souls to its chancellery, the chancelleries to the governments, and the governments to the Senate.' Four Senators spoke up at once to tell her that it was impossible. The people would not report themselves voluntarily and a show of military force was therefore necessary. The Empress pursued her plan. 'Offer to all those who have not yet registered freedom from punishment and order the local authorities to accept the former evaders upon the present list.' The elderly Prince Shakovsky sprang to his feet. 'That is not justice,' he shouted. 'The guilty shall be handled exactly like the innocent! I have always carefully reported from my district and no one has been omitted. But whoever has enjoyed the advantage of omissions will now stand just where I do!' But one of the younger Senators had got the Empress's idea and came to her support so handsomely that the plan was adopted and carried into execution. Henceforth, the Empress's method was always followed, with the result that migrations to Poland and outlawry in the woods and swamps which once followed every census gradually ceased altogether.

Catherine left a memorandum of the worst internal tangles which she had to undo at the beginning of her reign. The army had been unpaid for many months. The taxes of the Empire had been mortgaged by the senate. There was a scarcity of currency; only a million gold roubles were in circulation in the whole empire. The Empress Elizabeth had handed over nearly every branch of business and all the mines of the country to monopolists, chief of whom were the Shuvalovs. At the time of Catherine's accession, the peasants who worked in the mines were in revolt. The Empress regarded these monopolies with great disfavour and the rebellious peasants with even greater disfavour. Like the German *Hausfrau* that she was, she enjoyed the wielding of a new broom and of giving the country a real spring cleaning. By hook or by crook, she managed to pay the army; she restored the taxing power to the tax officers; she reformed the currency and introduced paper money into common use; she abolished at one stroke all monopolies and followed the example of Peter the Great in encouraging private business enterprise. Finally, she sent her colonels and her cannon down to the mines where strikes had broken out during the reign of the late Czar and bombarded the strikers so thoroughly that they were glad to seek safety in the mines again. Well satisfied with all these 'cleanings,' she wiped her hands on her apron and sat down to her silk embroidery. She was working on a gorgeous robe, with stitches as delicate and perfect as the Chinese can make them, to be presented to the Archimandrite of the Troitsky monastery.

§ 5

Catherine took considerable interest in the status of her sex and questions of morality. She once said that she did not know or understand women. She wrote to Madame Bjelke, 'From my fifteenth to my thirty-third year, I never really had the opportunity to converse with women; I only had handmaidens about me. When I wished to speak with anyone, I had to go into another room where there were only men. So it is due partly to habit and partly to my taste that has been so formed that I really understand only how to carry on a conversation with the latter.' It is true that she had few women friends. The Princess Dashkov who had ridden beside her on the night of the Peterhof campaign was never really in her confidence. She was a lay figure. In old age, the Empress became more and more dependent on the friendship of Countess Bruce and Countess Protassov. But her intimacies, emotional and intellectual, of which there were many, were intimacies with men. She always had a free and jovial way with them.

The Empress initiated some reforms for her sex which foreshadowed typical aspects of the woman problem – a problem which was not really born until the next century. From this point of view, very significant are the steps which she took. Prostitution was a well-developed trade in the Petersburg of those days. In one quarter of the city girls of the town were especially numerous, and venereal disease flourished among them. It was a malady in which the Empress took a vast interest. Whether she herself had had an unfortunate experience or whether she merely remembered that Peter the Great had been prematurely carried off by it, the Empress was horribly afraid of this contagion. She built a fine hospital for the sufferers from this infection, of which Major Masson says: 'One hospital, however, founded by Catherine deserves to be mentioned as a characteristic establishment. It is destined for the reception of fifty ladies infected with a certain disease. No question is asked either as to the name or the quality of those who present themselves, and they are treated with equal care, respect, and discretion. This last word is even marked on the linen appointed for their use.'

Another institution still remaining as a monument to Catherine's reign was the great Foundling Hospital which she built on the banks of the Moskva. Lying against the river, it stands out as one of the most prominent features of the city next to the Kremlin. Its tradition has not faded, as it still houses the maternity welfare work of Moscow. The Empress made it originally a home for foundlings and planned it for the discouragement of infanticide. Her institution has the name of being one of the first of its kind which sprang up in Europe; at any rate, it was the most famous and served as a model for many which came afterwards. Not all of Catherine's subjects were pleased with her innovation. A citizen named Smolin wrote a letter to express his discontent. He reproached her for these foundling homes which only served for the encouragement of immorality. Vice, he said, would show itself more openly and shamelessly as a result; more and more illegitimate children would be born. From this it may be seen that the Puritan ideal of the repression of vice did not lack representation even in Russia in the eighteenth century.

The Empress's efforts to educate her sex met with more approval. A cloister known as the Smolny Convent and founded by Elizabeth Petrovna was taken over by Catherine and converted into a school for young ladies. She gave her personal attention to this experiment which was the pride of her heart. She wrote to Voltaire, 'You know, for nothing escapes you, that five hundred young ladies are being educated in a house which was formerly designed for three hundred brides of heaven. These young ladies I confess far surpass our expectations. They make astonishing progress and every one admits that they are as lovable as they are knowledgeable. Their conduct is justly regarded as blameless without having at the same time the strict and stern manner of the cloister. For the last two winters they have begun to play comedies and tragedies, and they have done better with them than those who make a profession of acting.'

Proud as she is of these five hundred faultless damsels, there is one problem which troubles her. All the French plays, including Voltaire's own, which she can find for the school turn on the theme of love. What is to be done about it? She asks Voltaire's advice. Catherine feels that her girls' attention should not be called so early to the subject. Voltaire agrees and helpfully suggests that as far as his own plays are concerned the matter can be remedied. Ten lines here and twelve lines there, to be obligingly selected by the author, can be struck out without damage to the composition and all the proprieties will be satisfied.

In a gallant sentence, he refers to the Smolny damsels as Amazons. The Empress rejects this title firmly, informing him that they are not intended to become Amazons at all but honest wives and mothers. It appears, however, that this admirable institution had overlooked the problem of dowries. After twelve years of careful cultivation, the young ladies emerged as paragons of virtue but entirely penniless and homeless. Many of them became governesses. Others were snared by the officers of the guards whose barracks adjoined the convent. 'They watched every term of dismissal,' says Major Masson, 'to ensnare the prettiest. It would be more practical to save, out of the

immense cost of their education, a sufficient sum to por-
tion them or at least to keep them till they were provided
for.' The Empress apparently had not foreseen this difficulty. As penniless Princess Fike of Anhalt she had come
to Russia and had got a husband without a dowry. The
Smolny young ladies might do the same.

§ 6

Although Catherine did not hesitate to follow self-interest in foreign relations, she took an idealistic view of her
domestic problems. She turned from Machiavelli to
Montesquieu. When she thought of Courland and Poland she pictured herself as a general on horseback; when
she thought of Russia she pictured herself as the Little
Mother, Matushka. She and Russia were united against
the rest of the world.

The Empress wished to make her people happy without
making herself unhappy. Russia had despotic, conflicting,
chaotic laws. There was a printed code which had been
handed down from Czar Alexis Michaelovich, the father
of Peter the Great. But chiefly the people were ruled by
ukases, of which Catherine's Manifesto of Silence is a good
example. Not always, however, did the Russians obey so
promptly as they had done in this particular instance. It
was commonly said of the peasants when some order had
not been obeyed, 'They are waiting for the third ukase.'
During the reign of Elizabeth Petrovna, the Senate had
discussed the need of codifying the laws but postponements had ensued and nothing had been accomplished.
On the threshold of her reign, Catherine was met by this
need. It was a task made to her hand.

She took the ancient code of Czar Alexis in one hand
and Montesquieu's Spirit of Laws in the other. There
seemed to be no way of reconciling the two; so she decided

that she had better cleave to Montesquieu altogether. She worked three hours every day for more than three years and produced a thick volume. There was but little original thought in it as most of it had been adapted from her philosopher and guide. It was published under the title 'Instruction of Her Imperial Majesty Catherine the Second for the Commission charged with preparing a project of a new code of laws.' It was more briefly known in Russian as the Nakaz.

She worked secretly, showing her book to no one but Panin and Orlov. Count Panin was delighted. The Empress was at last engaged on a plan in which he could whole-heartedly share, that of putting political and social ideals on paper. The Count cried out, while his huge peruke flopped to one side in his excitement, 'These are principles which will cast down walls!' The handsome Gregory thought the literary efforts of his Empress would surely add to her already shining laurels. He wished to take the pages which she read to him and show them to the whole court. But Matushka forbade him to do this.

In the summer of 1767 the work was at last finished. In December Catherine had sent out a ukase ordering the election of delegates for a legislative commission. During the spring, a time of great floods and freshets in Russia, the elections had taken place. There had been much groaning and protesting from districts afflicted by heavy rains, as the swollen streams made travel difficult and dangerous, but the Empress ignored all excuses for delay and somehow or other the streams were forded. In early summer, the delegates began to arrive in Moscow, in kibitkas, on horseback, on foot. They represented cities, districts, social classes, religions, races. There were Russian nobles wearing lace, diamonds, and velvet made up in the latest Paris fashion; there were merchants and military men; there were a few peasants in smocks; there were Tartars and Bashkirs. Over a thousand delegates assembled.

Prior to the convention, the Empress sequestered herself in the Kolomenskoe Palace not far from Moscow. Here she gathered around her various thinking persons, as she called them, and asked them to criticize her manuscript. To meet their conflicting objections, she crossed out so much that only half of the Instruction was left. Collecting the remnant of her labours, she sent it to the printer, and then had it read before the legislative convention. As many of the delegates could not read, it was necessary that the Instruction should be read aloud frequently and fully. At first the delegates rose in a body at the first sound of Her Majesty's words; but the document was too long and was read too often. Finally they remained seated. Some English visitors who attended the convention called it a riot. Whether the meeting was even as tumultuous as the English Parliament can be on occasion is doubtful. But the Russian delegates wore so many gay, primitive colours, it probably seemed to Anglo-Saxon observers as if they expressed excitement and savagery in every way.

The legislative commission dragged on a year and a half. The first sessions took place in the Kremlin but shifted to Petersburg when the Empress returned to her northern residence. The commission like everything else in Russia accommodated easily to a nomadic life. In Catherine's day, the court, which travelled continually back and forth between Petersburg and Moscow, took their furniture with them, for furniture was scarce and precious. To give a man *meuble* from France was one of the best ways of bribing him. This was one of the lessons that Catherine had learned from the Empress Elizabeth.

When the Empress set forth for Petersburg in December, 1767, she had more people and more furniture than usual in her train. One thousand delegates were swept northward in flying sledges and were re-assembled in the Winter Palace after the Christmas festivities had been duly celebrated. In Petersburg as in the Kremlin, the Empress kept herself modestly in the background. She sat in a box behind a drawn curtain and left the commission entirely in the hands of Viazemsky, Bibikov, and Shuvalov. Her Adjutant-General, Gregory Orlov, was prominent on the floor and on one occasion spoke up eloquently in defence of a peasant who had been called 'lazy and stubborn' by a nobleman. The Empress was not officially present. She sent messages from her box to the chairman but did not appear on the floor. This made it possible for the convention to draw up formal addresses to the author of the Instruction and for her to reply in writing to them. In one of these addresses she was designated for the first time as 'Catherine the Great.' She modestly replied that the title was one which she had not yet earned. Still the title clung and she was to enjoy it for many long years as she was not yet forty when the commission on laws bestowed it upon her.

The Instruction abounds in democratic ideas. It goes so far as to advocate the gradual abolition of serfdom in Russia by allowing the serfs to own property and to purchase their own freedom. But the Russian nobles were not in favour of the reform. Most of the plan was struck out by her counsellors before the Instruction ever went to print and the remainder was eliminated by speeches in the convention. The Empress abandoned all propaganda for the abolition of serfdom for the rest of her life and consoled her conscience by abusing the

Russian nobles in her memoirs. 'What had I not to suffer from the voice of an irrational and cruel public opinion when this question was considered in the legislative commission. The mob of nobles, whose number was much greater than I had ever supposed because I had judged them too much by the people who daily surrounded me, began to suspect that these discussions might bring about an improvement in the position of the peasants. . . . I believe that there were not twenty human beings who reflected on the subject at that time with humanity, really like human beings!'

§ 7

Catherine's campaign against smallpox in Russia won great fame for her in Europe. It must be admitted that her step took courage in those days. The prevalence of the disease was such that everybody believed that everybody had to have it. For instance, the court spoke of the Grand Duke's uncertain chance of life because he 'had not yet had the smallpox.' The royal family had no more protection than the poorest peasant. The fiancé of Empress Elizabeth had been carried off by smallpox on the eve of his marriage and Peter II had died in early youth of the same disease. From the time of Catherine's arrival in Russia she was constantly pursued by the fear of the pest and every time she fell ill she thought it had overtaken her.

She had heard of vaccination in England. Her admiration for English institutions had been encouraged by her friendship with Sir Charles Hanbury Williams and the influence of Voltaire. The practical English had imported vaccination from the Orient, and an Englishwoman, Lady Mary Wortley Montagu, had set a brave example by allowing herself and her son to be inoculated.

On the other hand, there were many voices raised against it. The physicians of the Sorbonne discountenanced vaccination and disregarded the experience of England in the practice. Frederick the Great was intensely afraid of it and wrote to Catherine to urge her strongly not to take the risk. She replied that she had always feared the smallpox and wished more than anything else to be freed of her enslavement to this fear. 'I am so struck by a situation so unworthy that I regard it as a weakness not to escape from it.'

She entered into correspondence with an English surgeon, Dr. Thomas Dimsdale, who was adventurous enough to accept her invitation to come to Russia. He had published a work on inoculation and this had attracted the Empress's attention; she had always been a great importer and reader of foreign books. The famous Dr. Dimsdale arrested her attention, preoccupied as she was at all times with her anxiety about smallpox.

He arrived at the court of Petersburg in December, 1768. He was received as all foreign guests were received with social entertainments which the worthy doctor subsequently described in full in his tracts on inoculation in Russia. The Empress had been warned against the experiment and her fears were rife. Although she had sent for Dimsdale to vaccinate her, she still continued to discuss the matter pro and con. At last she put an end to her fears by ordering the physician to vaccinate her secretly one day. The test succeeded capitally. The ghost of this fear was laid, never to walk again.

The Grand Duke Paul was now vaccinated and Gregory Orlov. On the second day after the operation, Orlov had gone hunting. This was news to send to Europe, still trembling at the bare thought of vaccination. The Empress wrote the story to Voltaire, trusting him to spread it in the proper quarters. All at once she was ashamed that she had ever been so timorous as to fear vaccination. After all, every street urchin in England had as much courage as that! She urged inoculation upon court circles in Petersburg and the aristocratic Russians suddenly became very bold. Dr. Dimsdale was kept busy with impatient applicants. 'A few weeks ago,' said Catherine, 'nobody would hear of inoculation; but now nobody can wait to be vaccinated. It has become the fashion.'

The dramatic example of the Empress did not, alas! put an end to smallpox in Russia. It meant only that the heir-apparent of the throne was now immune and the dynasty was to this extent assured. It meant that a few thousand nobles and their families were immune. But the vast population of Russia was no better off than if the celebrated Dimsdale had never visited their country. Perhaps the greatest contribution of his visit had been to diminish superstition among the least superstitious element, the peasants had never heard of Dimsdale or of vaccination. When the smallpox came, they still fled to the Virgin, whose wonder-working portraits hung in every chapel. When the patient was too ill to go and if the family could afford to pay for it, the wonder-working image of Our Lady would be borrowed from the church and carried to the sufferer's bedside. This, however, was rare. Usually the sick one was borne into the church by the members of the family and laid at the feet of the Virgin whose pity they implored.

So it was in the city of Moscow in the autumn of 1771. For months the plague had raged and ravaged the town. The Empress had sent all the physicians she could commandeer, which meant a great many. Though she professed to hate physicians, she always kept a large retinue available. The stricken city was unusually well taken care of during this epidemic. Catherine had opened hospitals for the victims of the plague. All these innovations failed to win the confidence of the terror-shaken population who had somehow got the idea that the physicians and their hospitals had brought the pest to Moscow. They fled from the medical men and gathered at the foot of the icons with their sick. The Virgin at the Varvarsky Gate became more popular than the others, and the victims of the terrible pestilence lay massed at her feet day and night. She became the worst centre of contagion in the entire city, distributing the pest to hundreds of new victims every day.

The physicians were at their wits' end. They dared not take any radical steps to prevent the frightened people from doing what they pleased. The Bishop of Moscow, Father Ambrosius, was an enlightened man who saw that the physicians were helpless. Relying on his authority as a priest, he resolved to adopt a desperate remedy. He had the Varvarsky Virgin removed under cover of night and hidden away. When the pilgrims arrived in the early dawn, Our Lady had vanished. The panacea was gone, and Death glowered in the vacant niche. Father Ambrosius believed that the authority of the Church was enough to make these fear-driven human beings submit. They were his children who had always obeyed. He thought that, as soon as they knew that the good father had done it, they would disperse to their homes and the plague spot would be wiped out. But instead of dispersing, they were suddenly welded into a mob, a growling, threatening, stealthy, bloodthirsty pack. As the menacing thing began to move, Ambrosius fled from his home into the Kremlin, and took refuge in the Donskoy Monastery. On down into the crypt he fled, hiding himself in the darkest corner he could find. The mob came after him and invaded his sacred retreat. They found him in the darkness and tore him limb from limb.

When the Empress received a report of the tragedy, she realized that the population of Moscow was out of hand. The plague raged on. While the victims multiplied, the hospitals stood empty. Riots were added to smallpox until it seemed as if the old Muscovite city must soon perish under its burden of afflictions. The Empress had but one resource left and that was a military occupation. She sent Gregory Orlov with a regiment to take charge of the town. Gregory had been vaccinated by Dimsdale three years before, and the fact that he believed himself immune gave him extraordinary courage and effectiveness on this occasion. It must be admitted that Orlov was not ordinarily distinguished for courage and initiative. His record in putting down the smallpox in Moscow is exceptional. For once he seemed to take a leaf from the book of his brother Alexis. He bullied the populace into complete submission, so that the dying could at least die quietly undisturbed by mobs and riots. He asked the physicians what they wanted to have done and dragooned the people into actual obedience. A certain German doctor is said to have furnished the sanitary ideas which Gregory Orlov put into execution and which finally helped to wipe out the plague. Whatever the scientific man may have contributed, the heroic feat of Gregory Orlov is unquestionable. For once he behaved like a fearless man and deserved his mistress's encomiums.

The Empress was frenzied with delight. She was no longer obliged to invent reasons for praising her favourite in her correspondence. She wrote to Prince Henry, 'The malady at Moscow has been reduced to a fifth of what it was, thanks to the care and intelligence of Count Orlov. He has, besides, understood how to subdue the fanatical spirit to obedience, not only in the matter of miracles, but he did not even permit the people to enter the Church to hear Mass, because our churches are small; and, since everybody remained standing, the pressure that exists could increase the infection. During the service the people were made to remain outside the churches – an order which they followed to the letter. Another salutary regulation carried out despite the bigots, was the prohibition against burying in the churches and the cemeteries of the city. The Count made his own house into a hospital, and took one of mine for his own use; after which every quarter of the city provided one.'

The Empress heaped honours upon her hero when he returned to Petersburg in December. She built a triumphal arch in the park of Czarskoe Selo with the inscription, 'To him who saved Moscow from the plague.' A medal was struck to commemorate his bravery, on which Orlov's portrait and that of Curtius were united. 'Russia also has such sons,' read the inscription.

§ 8

The favourite's star was to set in glory. When he subdued the Moscow plague, he had been living with his Empress for a period of ten years. The end of the cycle had come. What had gone wrong between these two who had been like married people for so long and who had had three children? There are stories of Orlov's infidelities and Catherine says that he tired of her. Apparently she sincerely believed afterwards that Gregory deserted her, although it was only with the greatest difficulty that she drove the handsome guardsman from her side. She did not hesitate to employ force when force became necessary.

In the meantime, before and after Moscow, Orlov had played his part in the Turkish wars though it was by no means as gallant as his Moscow exploits. The Empress credited him with greater achievements in the South than others did. In the summer after the smallpox, she sent him to the Congress of Fokshani as her delegate in the peace negotiations. Here he swaggered about in a diamond-studded costume and offended the Turks by his high-handed attitude so that the negotiations came to nothing. Stories of Orlov's conduct at this time suggest that he was a man of idiosyncrasies. After the battle of Tchesme he told Catherine with a shudder that the water in the harbour was coloured red with the blood of the Turks who had perished. Two years later, his diamonds and his political indiscretions at Fokshani indicate that hallucinations were growing on him. He was sometimes too timid and sometimes too bold.

Presently he was plunged straight from the clouds to the uttermost depths by a disconcerting piece of news. The Empress had taken a new lover in his absence. A young man named Vassilchikov had been installed in Orlov's apartments. Taking French leave of his political and military responsibilities, Gregory Orlov started at once for Petersburg. Not many versts from the city he was stopped by the most ironical circumstance conceivable. The Empress had had him quarantined in his own palace at Gatchina. There was smallpox in the South, she said, and he must not bring it to Petersburg. She had forgotten that Orlov was immune. She shut him up for four weeks, under military guards. She also put double locks and military posts at the doors of the apartments occupied by young Vassilchikov. All the while she wrote reassuring motherly letters to Orlov and sent him clean socks and shirts. She showered him with gifts; another palace, a thousand more serfs, the title of Prince contributed to the process of weaning. At last it was successful. Orlov came to Petersburg and presented himself at the Empress's receptions, looking on while his rival performed the functions which he alone had performed ever since Catherine had become Empress of Russia. He even overacted his part, making a comrade of Vassilchikov and going about with him everywhere.

Gregory Orlov was now past forty years of age. Cut adrift at this age, the exile did not know where to turn. At first he comforted himself with women of the streets, showing himself in their society in the vicinity of the Palace. He went abroad and boasted and squandered like the swashbuckler that he was. He came home again; hung for a short time in suspense and inaction and then married his first cousin, a girl of nineteen far gone in tuberculosis. The Senate issued a ukase commanding them to separate, as first cousins were not allowed to marry by the Russian Church. The Empress knew exactly what such ukases were worth; she had herself married a cousin when she came to Russia. As head of the Church, she issued a dispensation to Gregory Orlov and his bride and gave them her blessing. They went away to Europe where they wandered from specialist to specialist, trying to find some one who could restore the young wife's health. But steadily she faded. Long before she died, Orlov had been declared insane.

Horrible stories are told of his last days: that he was constantly pursued by the apparition of the murdered Peter and that he covered his face with excrement to shut out the vision. Yet it was not Gregory who had struck the blow. His brother Alexis had done that, Alexis

who throve on honours and riches and outlived them
all, even the Empress herself. But Gregory had always
been soft and he could not endure his exile from
Catherine. Yet the Empress always said that he had tired
of her.

10

Potiomkin

THE middle-aged Empress grew enormously stout. Some of the clothes which she wore at fifty and thereabouts were preserved in the Kremlin Museum. A skirt of blue velvet, a favourite garment, testifies to the ungraceful breadth which detracted from her Majesty's appearance and afflicted her pride. She had always been eager to look her best and as she grew older and stouter and more toothless, her cheeks grew brighter and brighter with rouge. She made up every day as if for a dress rehearsal. Her *friseur* came regularly to arrange her really fine rich crop of hair, and the only time, so far as is known, that he was turned away for more important matters was the day when the Empress rode up from Peterhof to Petersburg to seize her husband's throne. She was proud of her hair, and her hair-dressers were persons of considerable importance in her life. Yet none of them approached in this respect old Yevreinov who had been her first barber and paternal adviser when she came to Russia, and who had been banished from Court because of his friendship for her.

She liked to dress well but not to eat well. Her contemporaries say she had no interest in food, that she employed wretched cooks and kept a poor table. Those who enjoyed the distinction of dining daily with the Empress had to put up with bad cooking. When the cook burned the food, the Empress thought it a joke and that was the end of it. She herself had such an indifferent palate that all the dishes set before her were pretty much alike. At supper she ate nothing, and wine she eschewed altogether. A decanter of currant-juice, unfermented, stood beside her plate.

But this does not mean that she avoided stimulants

entirely: she was addicted to both coffee and snuff.
Catherine's morning coffee was a daily feat which has
impressed itself on history. Her cook used one pound of
coffee for the five cups which she drank to the last drop.
She was apparently immune to caffeine. 'Anybody else
would have got heart disease from this concentrated
poison,' says one biographer, 'Catherine however needed
it for her health.' It certainly seems true that the health
of those persons who lived to acquire the surname of
'The Great' was invariably in need of some very peculiar
things. The constitution of Catherine the Great might
be expected to develop unique requirements, and it did.
Besides one pound of coffee daily, it needed vast quanti-
ties of snuff. Like Frederick the Great, also a snuff
addict, Catherine spilled the brown powder in her pockets,
and her clothes reeked of it.

The story goes that her son Paul detested snuff and
could not endure the smell of it. This prejudice is said
to have aided the conspiracy which was formed against
his life. But for his hatred of the smell, the Emperor
might have discovered the conspiracy. A certain official
who was talking with him had in his pocket at the moment
a paper which divulged the plans and the names of the
conspirators. Paul put his hand into the man's pocket
on some jesting pretext, but hastily withdrew his fingers
when they encountered loose snuff, which disgusted him.
And so, according to the story, Paul's fate was sealed
and the conspiracy which was to cost him his life matured
in secrecy.

Perhaps it was Catherine's snuff-taking and coffee-
drinking which had made her palate indifferent to food.
Nevertheless she continued to put on weight in the most
distressing way until her tiny feet ached from carrying
her heavy body. The stout old lady never lost the dignity

of her carriage or the uprightness of her posture, thanks to the hangman's jacket in which she had spent so many years of her youth. Her bearing was extremely impressive. It was one of the things for which her aunt, the Empress, and her husband, the Czar, had hated her. Her blue-grey eyes had a commanding and open gaze. She had a long chin and a firm jaw. In short, she had the features which are supposed to go with a commanding personality and which in her Majesty's case fulfilled the tradition. Withal her eyes were friendly and smiling, and at times roguish. The person on whom they rested had an impulse to obey.

The Empress loved flattery. Her letters from Grimm, from Voltaire, from Frederick the Great, are full of it. Best of all she liked to be praised to her face. Diplomats arriving at the Russian Court were warned by their well-wishers to indulge the Empress in her whim. It was said that there was no limit to either the amount or the crudity of what she could enjoy. This was an exaggeration. She wanted the tributes to sound convincing, the flowers to seem real. Diderot, for instance, was not always happy in his efforts, and the Empress could be cynical if the flatterer allowed her to catch him red-handed.

'I do not like flattery,' she wrote to Prince Viazemsky, 'and I expect none from you.' But the Prince would not have risen to be one of the chief advisers of her reign if he had taken her instructions too literally. 'Sie hatte die Eitelkeit eines parvenu, eines self-made man,' says Brückner, borrowing from both French and English to express her quality. The German Princess, whose native language has no word to express exactly the kind of person that she became as Empress of Russia, was every inch a parvenu, if not literally a self-made man, and she had the psychology of this type. Certainly she loved flattery, an art in which the eighteenth century excelled.

The qualities of this complex Catherine scatter themselves before us like the pictures in a scrap book. She was this and she was that, and in every instance she was also the opposite. Perhaps the simplest way to organize the variegated picture of her complex personality is to say at the start that she was a despot, in private relations and in public life. No temperament more dominating, not even that of Peter the Great, ever held sway over all the Russias, whose throne, by the way, both of them obtained by usurpation. Catherine was a successful tyrant because she knew how to command and also how to yield. She had extraordinary insight into human nature with not many prejudices to block the view. In all directions not so blocked, she was extremely clairvoyant. She was lenient with her servants, allowing them to sleep late while she waited on herself and made her own fire. Petty graft she passed over with a jest. Laughter she adored. One of her scientific essays discussed the different ways of laughing. When Voltaire died it was not his wisdom that she mourned but his gaiety. 'Since Voltaire died,' she wrote, 'it seems to me that honour no longer attaches to good humour; it was he who was the divinity of gaiety. Procure for me an edition, or rather a complete set of his works, to renew within me and confirm my natural love of laughter.' Voltaire once compared her with Saint Catherine, but she repudiated the title of saint. She prided herself on being a child of nature, and one of the rowdier children of that careless mother besides.

History has said of Catherine that she was a woman with a masculine disposition. She had brains, she was ambitious, she kept favourites. All this is comprised in the statement that she was one of the absolute monarchs of her time; she followed a trade to which women were not ordinarily admitted and got herself into it by her own efforts. To out-Herod Herod was her way of staying there. She said of herself that she had a masculine disposition and we know that she loved to play the part of 'Monsieur' in her correspondence and in her horseback riding, and that she named herself Colonel of the Guards. As she grew older and stouter, the rôle of 'Matushka' blotted out that of 'Monsieur' and 'Colonel'; but the change to Little Mother betokened no lessening of the aggressive note in her personality. It was her tendency to dominate, and she could always find a rôle, either masculine or feminine, in which she could play her natural character.

Catherine's estimates of her own character are the best that have been written. It is a great loss to students of human nature that her sketch of herself, written at the age of fifteen, was destroyed. We should like to compare it with one which she wrote at the age of sixty-two, addressed to Senac de Meilhan, as the adolescent portrait had been addressed to Count Gyllenborg. Her pen, it seems, moved best when her thoughts were directed towards some person as if in a conversation *à deux*.

'I have never believed that I had the creative spirit,' she wrote, 'I have come to know many people in whom I have recognized, without envy or jealousy, much more genius than I have. It was always easy to influence me, because in order to do that it was only necessary to have really better and actually worthier ideas than my own. Then I was as teachable as a lamb. . . . I have never tried to force people's views but I have also in certain particular cases held my own opinion. I do not love strife, because I have always found that in the end each remains of the same opinion. Besides I have never learned to lift my voice. I have never been resentful, because providence has given me a position in which I could not be so towards individuals, and because, in order to be just, I could not regard the circumstances as equal. In general I love justice but I am of the opinion that there is no unconditional justice and that moderation alone corresponds to human weakness. . . . When old people preached severity to me, I confessed my weakness to them with tears in my eyes and it sometimes happened that many of them, also with tears in their eyes, came over to my opinion. I am by nature cheerful and open-hearted, but I have lived too long in the world not to know that there are bitter natures which do not love cheerfulness and that it is not everybody who can endure candour and truth.'

§ 2.

The love relationships of Catherine the Great form the most fascinating aspect of her life and character. For nearly two hundred years she has been celebrated as a Northern Semiramis, a Russian Messalina. Myths and romances in countless numbers have been woven around her personality. Posterity knows her as a loose woman.

She loved to picture herself in heaven conversing with Confucius and Cæsar and Alexander the Great. If she could have seen herself as the theme of all the pornographic stories which still exist in Russia about her to-day, or as the heroine, with three hundred lovers, who sparkles so wickedly on so many modern stages, she would, without the least shadow of a doubt, have been extremely happy and delighted. That posterity should think of her as a female Don Juan would be exactly to her taste. She thought of herself as this; or, rather, as a female Henri le Grand whose life was in so many respects the inspiration of her own. It was said of the brilliant

Henri le Grand that but for his fatal prowess as a Don Juan he would have succeeded in driving the Turks out of Europe. Catherine hoped to succeed, though her hero had failed, in both. She was willing to go down to posterity as a light woman, but she hoped also to be remembered as the monarch who had driven the Turks out of Europe.

The number of her lovers was after all only thirteen if we count her husband. They were openly acknowledged and no legitimate consort could have enjoyed a brighter glow of publicity. The Empress did not indulge in secret *rendezvous* or episodic affairs. During the period when she was breaking away from her ten-years' union with Orlov, there were passing episodes, but these were only means to an end. Nothing is more surprising than the formality with which she surrounded her favourites or the curious acquiescence and matter-of-factness with which they were regarded by society in Russia. Most of the romancing and denouncing came afterwards when Catherine and her twelve lovers had gone the way of all flesh.

The Empress was, in this aspect of her life as well as others, a woman of few explanations. But she wrote a sort of apologia for her sex life and left it as a legacy to history, inserting it in the memoirs which she wrote for publication. 'I was very affectionate,' she said, 'and gifted with an appearance which was very attractive. I pleased at the first glance, without employing any arts or pains to that end. I was very sympathetic and possessed rather a masculine than a feminine temperament. As I have already said, I pleased the men. The first half of the temptation was there and the second followed the first according to human nature; for to tempt and be tempted are very close to each other. And if a strong feeling is added to this, however strongly the principles of morality may be imbedded in the mind, one goes farther than one would wish; and even now I do not know how that is to be prevented. In this case, perhaps absence might bring aid; but there are cases, situations in life, and circumstances which make absence impossible. How can one in the midst of Court life flee, remove oneself, turn aside? That would at once attract attention and cause talk. Yes, if one cannot remove oneself, nothing is harder in my opinion than not to yield to that which allures. All that is said to the contrary is hypocrisy and ignorance of the human heart. One does not hold one's heart in one's hand, and it does not obey the commands of reason.'

This was a sincere effort on the part of the sixty-year-old Empress to be truthful and candid about her past. Aside from certain obvious misrepresentations, such as saying that she had an attractive appearance though she did not believe it herself, she thought that she was speaking the truth. But one is struck by the extraordinary weakness of her defence. A woman who has had twelve lovers and has learned no more from life than to defend herself on moral grounds shows that she has remained unteachable to the last. Her explanation of her conduct might suitably be given by a girl of fifteen. Catherine once said of Diderot that in some respects he was a hundred years old and in others he was no more than ten. It was a wise remark and could be equally well applied to herself. When she tries to explain the irregularities of her sex life by saying that temptation has been too strong for her to resist she speaks as the pupil of Pastor Wagner. It shows that her conduct was still just as much of a mystery to herself as it was to anybody else. She had learned however one thing which Pastor Wagner and the rationalists of the eighteenth century had not taught her, and that is that the heart does not obey the commands of reason.

However impulsive the Empress may have been in the initial stage of a love affair, she was shockingly rational in the way that she developed it. Like Frederick the Great, she had a terror of venereal disease, but she had a less ascetic method of protecting herself. She required the hopeful candidate to submit himself to a medical examination at the hands of Dr. Rogerson, her Scottish physician. He was then put through a kind of ordeal or apprenticeship by Countess Bruce or Princess Provtasso who were known for their function as *les éprouveuses*. If these experienced ladies recommended the young man for his office, he was installed in the elegant apartments prepared for his reception. In the drawer of his dressing-table he found the generous salary allotted to the Empress's Adjutant-General, and then began for him a life of the most appalling regularity.

At ten o'clock every morning, he called on the Empress, and at ten every evening he escorted her to her private chambers. When she drove out, he sat beside her, and on all occasions stood ready to offer his arm. He was dedicated to his duties and lived in complete retirement. After Gregory Orlov, none of Catherine's lovers was allowed to make visits or receive them. No Sultan could have been more arbitrary with his harem than Catherine with her favourites. She lavished presents and honours upon them; her extravagance towards them knew no bounds. The English Ambassador Harris, who had a talent for statistics, estimated that she spent 250,000,000 roubles in cash on the men she kept. The amount seems staggering even for our day. Yet it was not enough, with all the other perquisites added, to prolong the bondage of the victim more than two or three years on the average. After Gregory Orlov, they all escaped in one way or another at the end of a period of about this duration.

Vassilchikov, with whom she carried on the most perfunctory affair she ever had, describes his life with the Empress thus: 'I was nothing more than a kept woman and was treated as such. I was not allowed to receive guests or to go out. If I made a request for anyone else, I received no answer. If I spoke for myself, it was the same. When I wished to have the order of Saint Anne, I spoke to the Empress about it. The next day I found a thirty thousand rouble banknote in my pocket. In this way, they always stopped my mouth and sent me to my room.'

It must be said that Vassilchikov's courtship was probably the poorest performance given by any of Catherine's lovers. The only one of them who had royal blood in his veins, for he was supposed to be a descendant of Rurik, he was nevertheless the last and least of all in the eyes of his mistress. Catherine had installed him in Orlov's stead to displace the absent Gregory, and Vassilchikov's office was primarily to help her wean the Count. Not that the Empress was aware that she was pushing Orlov out of his warm nest into a cold hard world. On the contrary, she had got the idea that Orlov intended to desert her and she did not mean to be left in the lurch. She also thought at first that she was in love with Vassilchikov, tall scion of the Ruriks, and was bitterly disappointed when the affair proved cold. Her complaints of their relationship were fully as dismal as his and her disappointment even more pathetic. This appears in a confession which she wrote for Gregory Potiomkin, who in turn displaced Vassilchikov and became Gregory Orlov's first real and genuine successor. It appears that Potiomkin had heard stories about his predecessors, which shows that gossip had already begun to exaggerate the number of the Empress's lovers. To reassure him, the Empress wrote a brief confession in which she told him all the facts about her previous relationships.

The Empress's list begins with Sergei Saltikov and tells how she accepted him on the advice of Madame Choglokov and how Madame Choglokov in her turn had been induced to act by the 'insistence of Sergei's Mamma.' This sudden peeping out of Sergei's mamma from behind the scenes of Catherine's life makes a vivid impression. The lady was already an invalid, it seems, who pulled the strings of history, just once and silently, and died.

The next lover named in Catherine's confession is the King of Poland. 'He was amiable,' says his mistress, 'and was loved from 1755 to 1761. After he had been away three years, that is since 1758, and because Prince Gregory Gregorevich, to whom well-meaning people called my attention, took trouble for me, I changed my way of thinking. He would have stayed for ever if he had not grown tired. I learned this on the very day of his departure from Czarskoe Selo for the Congress and drew from it the simple conclusion that with this knowledge I could no longer have any confidence. The thought tortured me cruelly and led me to make out of desperation a choice by chance (Vassilchikov). During this time, yes until this month, I have fretted more than I can say and never more than when others were satisfied. Every expression of tenderness caused my tears to flow and I believe that never since I was born have I wept so much as in this year and a half. In the beginning I thought I would get used to it, but the longer it lasted the worse it grew. For the other person began to sulk for three months at a time and I must confess that I was never more contented than when he was angry and left me in peace. But his tenderness forced me to weep.'

The confession ends for the time being with Gregory Potiomkin, the lover to whom it is addressed and of whom she begs forgiveness for earlier sins. 'And now, Sir Hero, can I after this confession hope for forgiveness of my sins? You will see that it is not fifteen but only one-third as many. The first, against my will, and the fourth, who was taken out of desperation, cannot be charged to frivolity. Of the other three, only believe the truth. God knows that I took them not out of debauchery, to which I have no tendency. If fate had given me in my youth a husband whom I could love, I should have remained true to him for ever. The trouble is that my heart would not willingly be one hour without love. . . . But I write you that needlessly and accordingly you will love or will not wish to go away to the army, out of fear that I could forget you. But really I do not believe that I could be so foolish. If you would attach me to yourself for ever, then show me as much friendship as love, and beyond everything, love and speak the truth.'

§ 3

Potiomkin must have understood his lady's wish and satisfied it in his way, for Catherine loved him fifteen years. She had loved her first Gregory ten years before she cast him off; her second Gregory held first place in her affections for a longer period. She had a degree of faithfulness with which she has never been credited. Not that Potiomkin lingered in the terem all this time. As official favourite and public escort he lasted only two years. He was too restless for captivity and he could not bear to be stared at, a part which the handsome Orlov had played to perfection. A curious arrangement was reached between the wandering favourite and the Empress. Potiomkin went away to Novgorod, to the Turkish wars, to the Crimea; he was driven hither and thither across the endless plains of Russia by his craving restless spirit. The Empress, left alone, something that she could not bear, took one lover after the other in his place. But always Potiomkin returned and compelled her to dispose of them. At a word from him, she turned them out.

According to the legend, Potiomkin became a sort of panderer to his lady and the gentlemen whom he chose for her survived as long as they remained in his good graces. What really happened was that the Empress chose each new lover for herself and certainly with the hope that he would see her through. But, after a year or two, the unmanageable Potiomkin would suddenly arrive on the scene and turn the rascal out. His appearance would be preceded by threatening letters about what he was going to do. For instance, the big blond Yermalov sat uneasily in his arm-chair one day because Potiomkin had written her that he was coming to Petersburg to send 'that white nigger' away. Potiomkin came and the white nigger went. Catherine turned her attention to dark lovers and chose two of them, Mamonov and Zubov.

Mamonov proved to be one of her few mistakes. He was a normal man who fell in love with one of the ladies of the Court of his own age and married her. It was the only time that Her Majesty was ever actually deserted by one of her lovers, unless Saltikov may be said to have done so, and it was a shattering experience. She chose another dark man, Plato Zubov, and tried to gain for him the approval of the absent Potiomkin. The little black boy, she wrote, was learning fast, sent his love to Papa, and so on. But Potiomkin wrote back that he was returning to Petersburg 'to have a tooth out,' which had

an ominous play on Zubov's name, which means 'tooth.'
The conflict over Zubov's removal brought to an end
the relation between Catherine and Potiomkin which had
lasted for fifteen years. Potiomkin was not able to send
this rival away.

The lovers who followed Potiomkin were Zavadovsky,
Zoritch, Korsakov, Lanskoy, Yermalov, Mamonov, and
finally Zubov. Except for Lanskoy, who died, and Mamonov, who married, Potiomkin had arbitrarily dismissed
all of them or believed that he had so dismissed them.
When he could no longer do that he realized that his lady
had discarded him for good. He became, as Gregory
Orlov had become fifteen years before, an exile from the
warm nest that had sheltered him for so long, and, like
Gregory Orlov, he could not survive his banishment.

Potiomkin had a fascinating personality. He was not
likeable but he seized the imagination and captured the
attention. Legend has pictured him as a great Russian
brute who drank heavily and swore outrageously. Doubtless he swore, as every Russian swears as naturally as
he breathes. But he was not a drunkard and he was not
a brute. He was a frightened, timid hare, with a certain
creative genius which appeared now and then without
ever developing very far in any direction. He could be a
real poet on occasion, although he is known as the author
of only one song, and also a real general on occasion,
although he trembled at the sound of guns. The most
contradictory things have been said about him because
the most contradictory things were true about him.

He had the tall, well-built figure which Catherine required of her lovers, but otherwise his appearance was
not prepossessing. He had lost an eye and it is characteristic of Potiomkin's reticence that nobody knew when
or how the accident had happened. Potiomkin himself

never spoke of it, but his feelings on the subject may be imagined from the fact that when a one-eyed man was sent to him one day with a message, Potiomkin struck him down. Various stories are told about the loss of his eye. Alexis Orlov is said to have put it out in a struggle over a game of billiards. Another story told is that Potiomkin himself destroyed it because it had a blemish, probably a squint. It is doubtful whether Catherine herself knew the true cause of the accident. In writing about Potiomkin, she passed over his handicap as if it did not exist. And yet she made one indirect reference in her memoirs. In speaking of the ignorance of the Russian Court, she remarked that even an ordinarily intelligent person at this Court was like a one-eyed man among the blind. Another peculiarity of Potiomkin's which she passed over in silence was a nervous jerking of his face, a kind of facial *tic* which she had formerly detested in Count Shuvalov. One trait, however, she did refer to sometimes in a jesting tone and that was the way he constantly gnawed his finger-nails. The rest of his peculiarities she passed over in silence.

Potiomkin was cynical, morose, and silent; a wistful, tortured creature who was obliged to make people afraid of him in order to conceal his timidity towards others. They called him 'Cyclops' and his imposing figure did not belie the reference to the one-eyed giant. Legend has made a great deal of the middle syllable of his name, 'tiom,' which means dark, and has served to accentuate the romantic picture of Potiomkin as a villain and a hero.

Like Razumovsky who had been the favourite and the reputed husband of Empress Elizabeth, Potiomkin was a Southerner, a Ukrainian. The men of his family had followed either a military or a cloistered life. His father was an obscure captain, and an uncle, who had risen to the rank of colonel, retired from the army to enter a monastery. Gregory Potiomkin reversed his uncle's course. He first became a monk or almost became one, having spent several years in preparation travelling from one monastery to the other. He was well versed in the theology of the Greek Church and was extremely superstitious. His orthodoxy was another aspect of her lover which Catherine, who prided herself on being a freethinker, did not like to expose. During the first year that she lived with him, they made a pilgrimage through the old Russian cloisters together. It happened that Prince Henry of Prussia was due to pay a visit to Catherine during these months, but she wrote asking him to postpone his visit until the following year. Usually she liked to have foreign guests accompany her on her travels, but this time she did not wish to have the Protestant prince and the Greek theologian together on one pilgrimage.

Up to the age of thirty-five, when he became the favourite of the Empress, Potiomkin seems to have had no love affairs and no idea of marriage. He was deeply attached to his sister, whom, with her five daughters, Catherine kept about the Court. With one of his nieces, Countess Branicky, Potiomkin was especially intimate. After he left the Empress, this niece accompanied him everywhere. It was as if, like Catherine, he was morbidly afraid of being left alone, and Sashinka Branicky was obliged to be always with him. One of the scandals about General Potiomkin was that, instead of galloping over the battlefield on a war horse like General Suvarov, he usually appeared driving along in a kibitka with Sashinka at his side. In this state, nevertheless, he managed to cover a great deal of ground, for few Russians travelled farther or more swiftly than did General Potiomkin. And always his devoted niece was near at hand. How Sashinka found time to marry and have children, as she did, is hard to explain. It has been said that her relations with her uncle were not above reproach. If this was true, there would have been nothing in the circumstances to shock the Russian Empress, who had once contemplated marriage with her Uncle George of Holstein and spoke in later life almost regretfully of the unfulfilled engagement. A marriage of this sort was not unusual.

Potiomkin had been one of the original conspirators who had helped to make Catherine the Empress. He had ridden to Peterhof in her train on that white night in 1762 when she seized the Czar and imprisoned him. He had been one of the guardsmen left in charge of the ex-Czar at Ropsha, and he had been present at Peter's death. Alexis Orlov's letter absolves him from all responsibility for the murder. The worst that can be said of him in this connection is that with many others, who were likewise not blamed, he also was present. The Empress did not forget him during the next ten years, for she furthered his career by sending him with a letter to General Razumovsky, who employed him in the Turkish wars. His picture lay dormant in her mind through all this time until it began to take on an increased vividness by comparison with the actual presence of a Vassilchikov whose caresses made her weep. The stories of Potiomkin's wooing give him credit for an amount of initiative which he did not have. In Catherine's confession, addressed to Potiomkin, she says that she deliberately recalled him to Petersburg, whereas the current story tells how Potiomkin schemed to be sent to the Little Mother with a painting and a message and how when he got there he impetuously wooed her. The second story is the one which the Empress would have much preferred to have us believe had her own statements of what took place not weakened its credibility.

'Then came a certain hero,' she wrote. 'This hero was, through his services and his enduring tenderness, so wonderful that as soon as people heard of his arrival they began to say that he ought to remain here. They did not know of course that we had summoned him secretly by a letter, but with the secret intention after his arrival not to proceed quite blindly but to investigate whether that inclination existed of which Bruce had spoken and which many had long suspected; that is, the kind of inclination which I wished that he should have.'

It is not difficult to picture the impulsive Catherine sitting down to her writing table one fine morning to pen the letter which brought Potiomkin to Petersburg as fast as a kibitka could carry him. The image of the dark, morose man, biting his nails and glowering at the world, which had slept so long at the bottom of the pool, had at last risen to the surface and now floated there with a sharp commanding vividness. Potiomkin's time had arrived. He came to Petersburg and for two years he remained in close attendance on the Empress. He played his part in the Hermitage gatherings in his own peculiar way. He was a ventriloquist and could imitate to perfection the voices of various animals. He could reproduce with uncanny accuracy the voice of Catherine herself uttering some characteristic remark. This trick hugely delighted the Empress who had also a gift for mimicry. In return, she would caterwaul a duet with the Princess Dashkov who, like the Empress, was unable to sing any tune.

Potiomkin was a semi-Tartar in his habits. Slovenly and indolent, he would lie on his couch for days clad only in a khalat. In the same informal habit he would visit the Empress, to the horror of the Europeans and the astonishment even of the Russians. Potiomkin fancied himself in this informal costume, over and beyond the fact that the careless undress suited the inertia of his temperament. The loose khalat was not unlike the monastic robe which he had once intended to wear and which now and then, when things went wrong between himself and his imperial mistress, he thought of putting on again. He was friendly with all priests, with whom he spent much time, not, it appears, so much in theological discussion, though he is said to have excelled in this, as in cardplaying and betting. His devotion to the Church is seen in that he could stand motionless and decorous all day while mass was being said. He was not physically too lazy for this effort although so indolent that the formalities of Russian Court life were too arduous for him.

Many vindictive *outré* portraits of Catherine's lover have been drawn for posterity. Most of them were produced by French writers who could not understand a man who, notwithstanding all the riches that his mistress placed at his disposal, preferred to live as a Byzantine when he might have lived as a Parisian. To the sophisticated French who left most of the written accounts of Russia in the eighteenth century, Potiomkin was scarcely a Russian; he was almost an Asiatic. The big one-eyed man who sprawled on a couch all day in a bright dressing-gown, playing with a handful of unset jewels or listening to Plutarch's Lives which some one read aloud, was a strange creature who had deliberately turned his back on the civilization of Louis XV and France and who yearned only to revive the ancient glories of Alexander the Great and Constantinople.

The mere name of Alexander was an inspiration to Catherine and Potiomkin: it had been the name of

Potiomkin's father and became the name of Catherine's grandson. It symbolized the magnificent dream which united them. Together they would go to Constantinople. One day Potiomkin burst forth, as he sprawled on his couch and listened to Plutarch's Lives, 'If anyone should come to-day and tell me that I should never go thither, I would shoot myself through the head.' In a similar mood, though less violent, the satirical Empress threatened, in case the Swedes bombarded her out of Petersburg, to set up her capital in Constantinople. If she did not revive the Byzantine Empire, she hoped that Monsieur Alexander, her grandson, would one day revive it in her stead. United in their feverish dream, the Empress and her lover drove in perfect unison towards their common hope. Together they would one day enter Constantinople. For many years they passionately believed it; and when they no longer believed it, they died.

§ 4

Potiomkin, a true son of Ukrainia, was a troubadour. He composed a song to his lady which became a popular lyric. 'As soon as I beheld thee, I thought of thee alone; thy lovely eyes captivated me, yet I trembled to say I loved. To thee, love subjects every heart, and enchains them with the same garlands. But, ah heaven, what a torment to love one to whom I dare not declare it! One who can never be mine. Cruel gods, why have you given her such charms? Or, why did you exalt her so high? Why did you destine me to love her and her alone, the one whose sacred name will never pass my lips, whose charming image will never quit my heart?'

Catherine's churlish lover was not poor in fancy. He could offer tributes to his lady showing an imagination of no mean order. As he composed lyrics in her honour, he could also compose pageants and other exhibitions of great beauty and impressiveness. The famous journey to the Crimea was a magnificent procession. Potiomkin's arrangement of this trip was the work of a poet and a dramatist as well as that of a politician and a general. It employed all his talents at once. His contrivance of effects along the way has been misunderstood. Hence the legend of the 'Potiomkin villages,' which according to his detractors were mere painted facades overlooking the Volga and filled with peasants and cattle who had travelled on foot many hundreds of versts in order to complete the picture. That history should have blamed instead of praising Potiomkin for his artistry shows how little his mission in life and his share in Catherine's grandiose schemes have been understood. Both of them believed that the road to Constantinople would one day be lined with prosperous villages and that the temporary settlements thrown up at so much expense along the route would at no great distance in the future become permanent establishments. No one was deceived by the demonstration of prosperity, unless perhaps it was Potiomkin himself, who half-way believed in the spectacular growth of population induced suddenly by his own imagination aided by Catherine's roubles. Prince de Ligne, who accompanied the Empress on her Crimean journey, tried to correct the story at the outset. 'They have already spread a ridiculous report,' he wrote to France, 'that villages of cardboard have been distributed along our route at intervals of a hundred leagues, that paintings of vessels and cannon and Cavalry without horses are displayed.' The Prince persisted in his efforts to send out to Europe a true description of the Crimean journey. People preferred to believe in Potiomkin's cardboard villages and in the perfidy of their contriver who employed in their construction millions of the Empress's own roubles in order to deceive the Empress. The story is still told to show to what nefarious depths Potiomkin was willing to descend. What it really shows is that he was a daring artist who designed and executed grandiose effects.

The Empress's whole Crimean trip was a theatrical enterprise with Potiomkin as author, producer, and actor. It followed soon after the birth of her two grandsons whom she at first planned to take with her though she abandoned the idea before the start was made. The purpose of the journey was ostensibly to inspect the work of General Potiomkin as administrator in the South. Its actual intention was political, to reconnoitre the way to the Orient while hostilities between the Russians and the Turks were in abeyance. No one understood this kind of political game better than did Potiomkin and his mistress. Ostentation was the breath of their nostrils and for once they had their fill of it. The Empress and her entourage proceeded down the Dnieper in a fleet of twenty boats, each of which was named for some tributary of the stream. Catherine's own vessel was called the Dnieper and was fitted out with mirrors and Turkish rugs, while a smooth green carpet like a meadow covered the deck. Behind the gorgeous Dnieper floated the Bog, the vessel in which Potiomkin travelled. Beneath a silken canopy, he lounged among Turkish draperies, while Sashinka Branicky attended him. Behind Potiomkin's Bog came the other eighteen vessels filled with ladies and gentlemen, musicians and dancers, cooks and lackeys, who strolled the decks and counted the peasants along the shores. The whole social life of the palace was transported to the Empress's fleet; receptions and balls and concerts followed each other as smoothly and uninterruptedly as the bends of the flowing river followed each other south-ward. The fleet had halcyon weather.

Most of the boats proceeded to Cherson, passing successfully the rapids which the Russian peasants were afraid to navigate. One of the aims of the trip was to quiet this popular fear by demonstrating a safe passage. The laurels remain with Potiomkin for the Empress left the fleet and proceeded by carriage for the last stretch of the journey. The royal guest who rode in the carriage with her, the son of Maria Theresa and future Emperor of Austria, did not fancy perhaps the idea of threading the Dnieper rapids. It seems unlikely that the Empress herself avoided the adventure or feared the danger after she had faced so blithely and triumphantly the hazards of inoculation.

At the end of the journey, the excitement was intense. All the world had crowded into Cherson to see the Empress and her Prince. A room for the night cost a thousand roubles and an egg for breakfast cost a florin. Potiomkin was beside himself with joy. He ordered the gates of the city to be moved several versts farther out and told the Empress this had to be because the throng of visitors had decided to remain as a permanent addition to the population. He believed it himself and the Empress believed it with him. It was May and their dream was at fever heat. Looking out over the harbour of Cherson towards Constantinople they could believe anything.

They believed that the Empress of Russia was going to drive the Turks out of Europe and the rest of Europe was going to thank her for her services. In a kibitka they drove to the mouth of the Bug and the Empress looked across the narrow water at Turkish land beyond and lusted after it. The next day three new Russian ships were launched in the harbour. Upon the blue expanse of water they floated down gently and safely from their staples. A great triumphal arch had been reared, on which was inscribed, in beautiful clear Greek characters: 'Here lies the way to Constantinople.' The whole performance was dramatic and picturesque to the last degree but not exactly diplomatic. The agents of the French Government in Constantinople, whose business it was to manœuvre there against the designs of Russia, must have thought that Catherine and Potiomkin were mad. And so they were, a little, but their madness was a great driving force with which mere rational diplomacy would have to reckon seriously.

There was method in the madness of this pair. The Empress employed the same Machiavellian technique in the acquisition of the Crimea that she had already used in Courland and in Poland. Her predatory art was chiefly a matter of simple bribery, a method of bargaining in which no monarch has ever excelled her. The credit, or the blame, for Russia's acquisition of the Crimea usually goes to Potiomkin. He was at least the flawless negotiator of his lady's bargain. The Khan was slowly forced into a corner from which he could only escape by running straight into the arms of the Empress. This was where he found himself in April, 1783, just five years after Catherine's visit to Cherson, while Potiomkin in the name of Russia took possession of his peninsula. The Khan, fleeing the wrath of the Turks, went to Petersburg to live on the pension of a hundred thousand roubles which the Little Mother of all the Russias had generously given him. Catherine had at last won possession of the ancient land of Tauris where Iphigenia, snatched away from her father's house, once lived and reigned as a priestess among barbarians.

Was it not something like this which had happened to

the little Fike of Stettin when she became Catherine of
Russia and the priestess of a foreign temple? Catherine
and Potiomkin restored the ancient name of Tauris to
the peninsula and revived the Greek names of the towns
and seaports, hoping to call back the Greeks who had
abandoned their homes to the Tartars. To Potiomkin
himself the Empress gave the title, Prince of Tauris; and
henceforth he shone magnificently through her correspondence as the Taurian. Every mention of his name
was invested with the glamour of his heroic exploits.

§ 5

When the Empress depended upon diplomacy, she
never knew failure. As an open aggressor, she was not a
brilliant success. She avoided war as long as possible
and especially did she avoid war with Western Europe.
The Swedes forced her into a campaign of defence, but
she much preferred to measure her troops against the
Orientals. With all her bluster and threats against the
French Revolution, she failed to come forward with actual
military support of the intervention which she so loudly
urged and applauded. The Turkish wars were another
matter. If they could have been avoided by any possible
exercise of diplomacy and expenditure of roubles, no
matter how great, they would never have filled so many
pages of history. Unfortunately for Catherine's kind of
pacifism, Constantinople could not be bought. The Empress and Potiomkin had gone as far in the conquest of
the South as Machiavelli could carry them. They had
acquired by high bidding and sharp dealing Crimea and
Georgia, the Tauris and Colchis of the ancient Greeks
redolent of memories of Iphigenia and Medea and the
Golden Fleece.

But the Empress had no thought of stopping there.

Crimea and Georgia only fed the flame of her passion for the East. She watched Constantinople as a cat watches a mouse-hole, with a fascinated attention which nothing could divert. But France did not want the Russians in the temple of Sophia and England was fast coming to share this view. If the Empress had been a little less concentrated and had watched her mouse-hole a little less confidently she would have realized earlier than she did the strength of the opposition which was growing up against her in Western Europe and which was carefully preparing to defeat her aims. Behind Mustapha and the Turks, whom she regarded as the enemy, stood a strong wall of diplomacy raised by the western powers. Catherine's fancy overleaped this wall. For her, beyond Constantinople lay only India. She believed the way was still as open as it had been for Peter the Great when he dreamed of taking it.

The dream was now hers, as she was now Peter. She conducted her campaign against the Turks as Peter had conducted his campaign more than half a century before, and her preparations for war, imitating his, were in many respects even worse. There were not enough recruits for the companies; there were not enough tents for the men; the powder was half dust; all the supplies were either defective or deficient and graft and autocracy were everywhere. The Russians lost their first battles, but everybody was gay about it. Voltaire wrote to Catherine: 'I see with joy and surprise that this convulsion has in no way shaken the composure of that great man whose name is Catherine.' He might have added that Peter the Great with all his six feet seven could not have borne the defeat with greater steadfastness and courage.

The Porte, instigated by the French, declared war against the Russians in 1768. The following year Gregory

Potiomkin joined the army under General Rumiantsov, whom he afterwards displaced as leader of the forces against the Turks. After five years of undistinguished service he was summoned to Petersburg by the Empress and stopped there for two years idle in her boudoir. From this time onward Gregory Potiomkin was a changed man. Although he trembled at the sound of guns, he could fight the enemy at times with the fierceness of a tiger and the cunning of a serpent. At court he went about like a savage, barefoot, without breeches, unwashed and uncombed. At the front these simplicities gave him a degree of independence beyond the other officers. He could live for days on onions alone and the ordinary comforts of life meant nothing to him. It was said that Potiomkin was in most ways a creature of the eleventh century and not at all of the eighteenth. When he went forth to war his eleventh century side came uppermost and found there its congenial expression. He was not unhappy at the front except when the guns roared, and as long as Sashinka stood by to comfort him he could endure even that.

The first Turkish War should, according to the general expectation, have ended with the Congress of Fokshani. The Empress, her foreign minister in Petersburg, and especially the Russian minister in Constantinople, who happened to be in a Turkish prison awaiting peace for his release, were all surprised and disappointed at the outcome of the Congress. They had expected a satisfactory treaty. But Gregory Orlov, who represented Russia, suddenly departed for Petersburg, while the negotiations were still in the air. A rumour of disaster in his private affairs had suddenly reached him, and fearing that his relations with the Empress were threatened he dashed away to reassure himself. We know how suddenly his journey ended, in arrest and quarantine at Gatchina. His nerves were never quite the same again, and no wonder. The shock was great, even for a military officer and a stalwart man. His eccentricities of behaviour increased after this experience but they did not begin there. Looking back over Orlov's previous life it is easy to see that his disorganized state of mind would have made the peace congress at Fokshani a failure even if all the other conditions had been favourable.

The Empress was philosophical, as well she might be. She was obliged again to correspond with the Sultan with cannon balls, as she wrote to Voltaire. The war dragged on for two years longer, while the handsome Vassilchikov occupied Orlov's apartments and made the Empress weep whenever he grew tender. In July, 1774, came the Peace of Kutchuk-Kainardi. Potiomkin signed this treaty. He had displaced the unsuccessful Vassilchikov four months before and was now the Empress's envoy to the Turks. She was enchanted with the terms he made. 'Ah! What a good head the man has. He has had a greater share than anyone in this peace, and this sound head of his is as amusing as the devil.' She hung her darling with blazing orders and gathered honours for him from foreign sovereigns. Potiomkin loved his decorations and adored his jewels. There were occasions when he pinned all of them on his velvet coat until his chest was panoplied with gold and silver and diamonds. In the centre hung a portrait of the Empress at which people gazed intently while talking to him for they dared not gaze at the black patch which he wore over his eye. This was General Potiomkin on those rare occasions when he considered a dressing-gown not admissible.

During the Second Turkish War, Catherine wrote to her lover twice every week. In her letters she showered him with pet names as in public she hung him with orders. He was her belovedest, her little love, her golden pheasant, her Papa. So she spurred him on to battle with the Turks. It was not easy. The Ukrainian either stormed ahead or collapsed in moods of desperate discouragement. There were days when he was ready to evacuate the Crimea and to resign his generalship in favour of Rumiantsov, his detested rival. 'You are as impatient as a five-year-old child,' the Empress chided, 'while the business entrusted to you demands unshakable patience.' The General was subject to frequent relapses to his five-year-old emotions and in such moods he was ready to abandon all to the Turks if the Empress's letters had not served to restore his aggressiveness. She had urgent need to write to him twice a week. The Prince of Tauris was ready to give up Tauris itself whenever these pessimistic moods overcame him.

The Empress was distressed by the terrible cost of war. She discovered that it was even more expensive than diplomacy and bribery. Before war with the Turks had broken out, she had managed to get her way by means of money, and lively military display. But it seemed that actual warfare demanded an additional expenditure of treasure. She complained to the sculptor, Falconet, 'To make war three things are necessary: money, money, money.' Yet she was always able to find the wherewithal to carry on and keep her three quarrelsome generals, Potiomkin, Suvarov, and Rumiantsov, active in the field.

She built a fleet and planned to sweep the Black Sea with it. The Russians, in spite of the efforts of Peter the Great, had never become navigators, a deficiency which obliged her to obtain naval officers from England. The scheme was easily carried out. The English were available and adaptable, and all went well until the Empress

had the idea, inspired from Paris by Dr. Benjamin Frank-
lin, of adding the American naval officer, John Paul Jones,
to her forces. The American hero's exploits resounded at
the moment through Europe while he himself was sojourning in Paris, rather lonely, very famous, and extremely
hard-up. The Empress met his terms, which were sufficiently high, for Jones was a good bargainer, and the
American was soon sailing a Russian ship on the Black
Sea. But luck, it seems, had deserted the little man. He
not only played an undistinguished part in the Turkish
wars but left Russia under the shadow of a personal
scandal, invented, his defenders said, by British officers
serving under Catherine who resented the presence of
the American in the same navy with themselves. However that may be, he earned no honourable mention in
Russia and the history of that country gives no credit to
John Paul Jones for helping to win the Turkish Wars.

In June, 1788, Catherine's fleet won the battle of Ot-
chakov. The victory made a great impression on Europe
and even Frederick the Great spoke of it respectfully.
Was the Empress really marching towards India? She
believed that she was marching towards Constantinople
at least and that the Prince of Tauris would enter the
Turkish city within the year. But France and Prussia
and England thought otherwise. English policy was well
clarified by now and was neatly expressed in a book on
Russia published by an English captain in the year 1790.
'The Turks,' he said, 'happily for us, are not a commercial
people; we cannot do without those valuable articles
which their soil produces almost spontaneously; and the
Turks like the easy possessor of a very rich mine, allow
us to enrich ourselves at our pleasure. Three per cent.
duty equally on all exports and imports is, with little
exception, their only restriction to Europeans engaged in

their trade. Would the Empress be equally moderate, if in possession of the fertile region? Believe me, she would not.'

It appeared that Europe did not wish to be cleared of the Turks by Catherine the Great. The easy-going Mussulman with his three per cent. duty had great advantages over a Christian monarch like the Russian Empress. The representatives of Protestant Europe in Constantinople put their heads together and backed up Turkish diplomacy in the south while the King of Sweden prepared to invade Russia on the north. The Swedish invader was Gustavus III, the son of the Princess Ulrica whose gown had once been offered to Princess Fike to make her presentable at the German court. Ulrica's son had a curious relationship with Cousin Catherine of Russia. He paid friendly visits and wrote flattering letters to her and then made war on her. As soon the treaty was signed, he wrote and asked her to forget their differences, 'like a storm that has passed.' The passing storm, however, had shaken the Empress as she had seldom been shaken. She was not prepared to carry on war on two fronts and the Swedish invasion had made the Turkish Wars no longer endurable. 'If you wish to roll a stone from my heart,' she wrote to Potiomkin on the Turkish front, 'if you wish to free me from a heavy nightmare, then send a courier at once to the army with instructions to begin operations immediately by sea and by land; otherwise you will drag out this war still longer and that you can wish just as little as I.'

Potiomkin was unable to make an attack or to conclude a treaty. He had reached the same state of mind which had rendered Gregory Orlov incompetent to negotiate terms with the Turks at Fokshani in 1772. Orlov's inertia on that occasion had caused the first Turkish War to drag on two years longer. The history of Orlov was repeated by Potiomkin in 1791. Potiomkin's relations with the Empress were threatened in that year as Orlov's had been threatened in 1772. Potiomkin felt that it was time for him to go to Petersburg and dismiss 'the little black boy' who seemed to be settling into his place there with an air of permanence.

As soon as Potiomkin departed from the field, Prince Repnin took command and brought the second Turkish War to a speedy close. The treaty of Jassy was signed at the end of 1791. But Potiomkin was already dead.

§ 6

The myth about Catherine the Great relates that she had three hundred lovers. The same legend is attached to the Empress Elizabeth and the mother of Sergei Saltikov. It belongs to the Russian fable.

There is no need to speculate on the number of lovers that Catherine had; she has herself told us the facts. Besides her husband, there were twelve. After she became Empress she made no secret of her love affairs, but rather the contrary. The only time when any vagueness exists is in the early days before the birth of Paul. Her German biographer, Gertrude Kircheisen, as well as Bilbassov, thinks that her early intimacy with Andrei Chernichev must have gone further than she admits in her memoirs. Chernichev was banished from the Court on her account and Catherine's letters to him, discovered in later years, suggest that their relations were not merely platonic. But Catherine's memoirs are not the only evidence we have concerning her lovers. Her confession to Potiomkin leaves him out. In this document, which has all the marks of a genuine confession, she tells Potiomkin that he is the fifth. The favourites of Catherine as Empress were known to everyone and their number was certainly no secret. After Potiomkin there were seven.

They were: Zavadovsky, her secretary, who was one of the most intellectual of her lovers and minister of public instruction under her grandson, Alexander I; Zoritch, the Serbian, who afterwards founded a school for boys in the country; Rimsky-Korsakov, a sergeant of the guards, the most beautiful and the most stupid of them all, who ordered a library to fit the shelves of his house; Lanskoy, with whom she is said to have had only platonic relations and who died in her arms; Yermalov, the 'white nigger' whom Potiomkin dismissed from the palace at a day's notice; Mamonov, a man of some ability, who married one of her court ladies and eliminated himself from office; and Plato Zubov, the young man of twenty-four who became her lover when she was sixty and lived with her until her death.

Altogether there were thirteen men with whom the Empress made, so to speak, twelve unhappy marriages. The Russians accepted her arrangements without much comment; the irregularity of her relationships did not trouble them. What did scandalize them, however, was the frequency with which she changed the incumbent of the office. She would dismiss her Adjutant-General one day and install another the next day, and her fickleness seemed to increase with her years.

There were a few things which all her lovers had in common. They were tall, well-built men and graced a military uniform to perfection. It is true that so long as they remained in office as favourites they were obliged to lead an idle life and forgo all active service; only sedentary occupations were possible for them. But with two or three exceptions, the men were not intellectual. The Adjutant-General's main duty was to wear his clothes

well and give his arm to the Empress. He was an officer
on leave. At the age of fifty, the restless woman was
capable of falling in love with a military uniform at first
sight, as she did when she espied Rimsky-Korsakov among
the guards at the palace gates. She was as susceptible to
an imposing military figure as any German *backfisch* was
in the day before the great war abolished the temptation. The Empress was herself once a German *backfisch*
in a military garrison where her father, the Prince of
Anhalt-Zerbst, was commandant. He was a tall man
and a handsome one, rather silent and stupid presumably but every inch a military officer who graced
his uniform. Old memories of that impressive Prince,
her father, sometimes rose within her, when she beheld
her favourite in all the glory of his uniform and the
decorations which she had pinned upon him. No doubt
the stiff old Prince had been rather splendid in his
time.

Among the seven successors of Potiomkin, Sasha Lanskoy especially stands out. He was a young man of taste
if not of intellect. In all the enterprises of the Empress
which required artistic judgment Lanskoy had a contribution to make and made it. He was capable of enjoying her correspondence with Grimm and of being a real
companion to his mistress. She was fifty-one and Lanskoy was twenty-two when he became her lover. He was
a poor officer of the horse guards. Like all her favourites,
he had nothing and she gave him all. For four years he
flourished under her maternal care, a sensitive youth much
liked and respected by those about the court. Then in
June, 1784, he fell desperately ill. The physician who
hastened from the city to attend him at Czarskoe Selo
said that he had angina and would die. This was ten days
before his death occurred. Catherine nursed him day and

night, passionately fighting for his life until at last the young man died in her arms.

The Empress resolved to remain a widow. She would live without a lover and comfort herself with her little grandson Alexander. For a whole year, she moped in solitude, shutting herself up in her chamber and valiantly trying to endure her loneliness. She strove to fortify her resolution by poring over a book by a famous German hypochondriac entitled 'Über die Einsamkeit.' To Zimmermann, the author, she sent a ring and a portrait of herself, in grateful acknowledgment of his words on the solitary life. But neither the book nor her correspondence with Zimmermann was able to keep her always faithful to her vows. Her struggles to get on without a lover became more and more pathetic, until after a year of sacrifice she installed Yermalov in the apartments of the favourite.

Her experiment after Lanskoy's death is often brought forward to show that Catherine at last experienced love in the true meaning of the word. But the English Ambassador who wrote after her death that she had died 'a stranger to love' perhaps came nearer to the truth. The woman who had had twelve lovers never learned to love. Death overtook her while she was still trying to learn.

§ 7

When Potiomkin came up to Petersburg in the spring to 'have a tooth out,' as he said, meaning thereby to dispossess Zubov, he growled his usual thunders in advance. But the elderly Empress was infatuated with her young lover and refused to drive him forth at Potiomkin's bidding. It was the first time that Potiomkin had felt himself wholly powerless in this situation and the disturbance within him was acute. Since bluster and threats were of no avail, though with all previous rivals they had sufficed, he fell back upon his prowess as a wooer. The Prince of Tauris would win back his lady as he had won her fifteen years before. He would turn poet and troubadour as he had been in the springtime of their love. At that time Potiomkin had been an impecunious officer who could only afford to write verses to lay at his mistress's feet. Now he was a Prince with princely riches at his command. The Empress loved gaiety and merry-making on a grand scale. Potiomkin decided to give her such an entertainment as Petersburg had never seen, and to stake all on the outcome.

The Prince had built a magnificent palace near the court of his Empress. He had adorned it with the richest materials of the South. His oriental furnishings and treasures would have inspired the great Alexander himself with envy. In a vast room strewn with Persian rugs, his guests dined from Persian glass and golden dishes of Russian workmanship. Potiomkin's cook was a person wholly different from the servants whom the Empress employed in her kitchen. His cook was famous for making the best sterlet soup in Russia, and his master had been known to send a military officer two thousand versts to fetch him a tureen of it. In short, the Prince's table was such a table as had never before been spread in Russia and probably never since. He used his military officers to fetch and carry for his cook. They brought oysters from Riga, melons from Astrakhan, and grapes from the Crimea. The first oranges ever eaten in Russia were served on Potiomkin's table. Even Frederick the Great, who was one of the great epicures of his age, envied the dinners of the Prince of Tauris.

The festival of the despairing lover surpassed anything he had ever done before. His resources were strained to the uttermost. He gave a series of dinners, balls, pageants, arranged around the Empress as the central figure, whose grandeur astonished the court. His food and fireworks were an experience for the most blasé of the Russian nobility. The magnificence of his effects increased from day to day, as the strain of his effort also increased. He was fighting for his life.

For the Empress also the strain was frightful. She endured it as long as she could and then mercifully swung the axe which was to end his struggles. One morning she sent for her host and thanked him expressly for his entertainment of the evening before. She referred to it as a farewell feast and spoke regretfully of his departure for the front which she assumed was immediately necessary. Potiomkin understood. He had lost his last throw.

He left for the South in a mood of the blackest depression. He told his friends that he would never return. As soon as he arrived in camp at Jassy, he fell ill with a fever. His niece, the faithful Sashinka Branicky, was with him and nursed him. What the doctors prescribed Potiomkin would not do; all that they forbade, he instantly demanded. He insisted on eating like a gourmand. In every way he acted like a man determined not to live. His last meal was like the repast of a condemned man on the morning of his execution. He ate a quantity of salt pork, raw beets, a goose and another fowl, all of which he washed down with Crimean wine and Russian *kwass*. He is said to have died from over-eating while in a fever; but he had really died before he left Petersburg. He was scarcely a living man when he arrived at Jassy.

After this orgiastic meal, his bed became intolerable to him. He demanded to be taken from Jassy to Nikolaev, as he said, for a change of air. With his niece in the kibitka beside him, the dying man drove westward.

Potiomkin

Gradually his strength faded and his raging temperature subsided. The attendants were obliged to take him from the carriage and lay him on a rug at the roadside. There beside the dusty chaussée, in the arms of Sashinka, he expired. He had gone the way of Gregory Orlov, but had gone more directly. His Little Mother, his Matushka, had killed her last man.

When the Empress heard of Potiomkin's death, she fainted three times. Once upon a time she had written to Potiomkin, 'Without thee, I am without hands.' This proved to be true. With Plato Zubov's hands, she could never work the same, for Plato's hands worked only for their master. The last years of Catherine's reign were years of disappointment, lack of wisdom and failure. Her glory had passed when Potiomkin died by the roadside. In destroying him, she had struck a fatal blow at herself.

11

Catherine Becomes a Grandmother

OVER a mantelpiece in the palace of Gatchina hangs a portrait of Paul I as a boy of ten. It is the only one of his portraits which bears a resemblance to his mother. Of all the artists who painted him, this one alone seems to have caught an expression of the Grand Duke which suggests the Empress. Fleeting it must have been, for Paul grew up to be strikingly unlike Catherine. He was destined to advertise by his face and figure to all the world the anonymous paternity which had produced him.

Catherine was annoyed by Paul's appearance and disposition, inherited as they were from his father's family. It offended her that he should turn out to be so completely a Saltikov. That her son derived so little from herself seemed a perversity of fortune. She reflected a great deal on the subject. 'My God,' she burst out in one of her letters to Grimm, 'why do children so often resemble their fathers when it would be better to resemble their mothers? That is not common sense; Dame Nature is often a blockhead. One day I shall write a dissertation on that, which I shall dedicate to you.' She did not write the dissertation for Grimm, although dissertations in general were much in her line. She dipped into scientific research from time to time with impressive results. Her contributions to comparative philology won recognition from scholars in that field; but her contemplated study of inheritance of characteristics was never carried out. She never got beyond posing the question, to which, however, she repeatedly returned without ever pushing onward to any kind of theory. She bred dogs and observed that they showed the same tendency as human beings in this respect. 'Witness Sir Tom Anderson,' she said of her favourite hound, 'all his family resembles him.

The same spirit, the same taste, the same figure, the same physiognomy, the same tendency.' She was puzzled and resentful.

Catherine was estranged from her son Paul from the day of his birth. Deprived of all opportunity to express her maternal feelings by the Empress's theft, she had no actual experience of motherhood. Painful associations clustered around the infancy of this over-precious child. Catherine had been deserted by her first lover who openly replaced her by unworthy rivals. She hated Saltikov as she afterwards learned not to hate any of her favourites after their affair had run its course. The child whom she saw once a week in his fox-fur cradle reminded her of bitter disillusionment. As he grew older, his querulous disposition, his under-sized stature, his wizened skin, his baldness, and his ugly nose all helped to make him seem alien to his mother. He was a cringing, sickly boy of whom it was difficult to be proud. She had produced him at such a cost and he represented such an inferior triumph after all. As human material he was in the same class as Peter III, from which many historians have argued that Paul was Peter's son and a genuine descendant of the Romanovs.

Catherine's second son and her first child by Orlov, Prince Bobrinsky, also failed to inherit the genius of his mother. He was brought up under the Empress's supervision by an Italian tutor, Admiral Ribas, and as a young man was a ne'er-do-well and a waster. His mother sent him on a tour through Europe and the gay young Prince of the Beaver-skin left a trail of debts behind him in city after city. Finally the exasperated Empress had him arrested and interned in Riga, after which history knows him no more. He was a spendthrift, like both his parents, but he had none of the mental and moral handicaps of

Grand Duke Paul. After his public disgrace in Riga, he returned to Russia and led an unambitious and uneventful life. He married and left descendants in whom history takes no interest.

The chief part which Bobrinsky played in the drama of his mother's life was to heighten the conflict which always existed between Catherine and her first-born. There was a moment in the Empress's life when she thought of marrying Gregory Orlov, but was suddenly checked in her intentions by the enemies of the Orlovs and the opposition of Panin. Count Panin, who wanted from the first to make Paul emperor, became suddenly energetic when he suspected that the Empress wished to legitimatize Bobrinsky. Even after the danger of the marriage had been averted, his bastard Prince still hovered threateningly in the background, well cared for by the Empress, his mother, a permanent object of suspicion to Count Panin, and of fear to the Grand Duke Paul. This boy who trembled for his life could find no reassurance in the existence of a rival half-brother as long as he kept his health and his mother's favour. The young Bobrinsky, like everything else in their environment, contributed to the estrangement between Catherine and her heir.

When Catherine became Empress, one of her first concerns was to provide for the education of the Grand Duke Paul. She selected no less a person for the post than d'Alembert. But the French scholar declined her invitation. The Empress would not take no for an answer; she stooped to conquer. 'I know you too well for a good man,' she wrote, 'to ascribe your refusal to vanity. I know that the sole motive of it is the desire for peace and leisure to cultivate letters and the friendship of those whom you esteem. But what is there in this objection? Come with all your friends. I promise both them and you every convenience and advantage that depends upon me; and perhaps you will find more liberty and ease here than in your native country. You refused the invitation of the King of Prussia, notwithstanding your obligations to him. But that Prince has no son. I admit to you that I have the education of my son so much at heart, and I think you so necessary to it, that perhaps I press you with too much earnestness. Excuse my indiscretion for the sake of its occasion; and be assured that it is my esteem for you that makes me so urgent.'

This petitioning of d'Alembert brought one of the sharpest humiliations of her life. D'Alembert steadfastly refused. Privately he uttered a sarcastic remark which travelled far. In Russia, he said, people died too easily of colic, it was better to remain in France. The Empress never forgave him this sly reference to her manifesto concerning Peter's untimely end. A decade or more afterwards, when she was engaged in the invasion of Poland, a group of French professors living there fell into her hands and were interned at Kiev. D'Alembert, remembering his old prestige with the Empress, attempted to secure their release by sending a personal petition to the Russian Empress, but she turned a deaf ear to his intercession. The distressed scholar at last appealed to Voltaire who succeeded in getting only a cold reply from the Empress. She said that the French professors were doing very well in Russia and would stay there for the present. She implied that d'Alembert, who had thought that people died too easily of colic in this barbarous land, might now see for himself how well people could live there. The professors were being cared for and would remain interned until the Empress found leisure to release them. Their period of internment was probably not greatly prolonged by d'Alembert's appeal.

When the Empress's efforts to procure higher education for her son shattered on this embarrassing passage
between herself and the French encyclopædist, she gave
up all further attempts to improve on Panin's pedagogy.
Her opinion of the lazy Count as an educator was not
high but it was probably as high as he deserved. Nevertheless she left him in possession of the field. 'At that
time,' she commented, 'everybody believed that if Panin
did not educate him, the Grand Duke would be lost.'
Panin remained in exclusive charge as governor until
Paul's marriage took place. He continued his watchful-
ness even after that from his post as head of the College
of Foreign Affairs until Prince Orlov died in 1783. For
twenty years Panin's chief interest in life had been to
watch and circumvent this man whom he regarded as the
dangerous enemy of his Grand Duke. Panin had failed
to save the Czar when he had piteously kissed his hand
and pleaded, and he could never forgive himself for that
failure. He felt to blame for Peter's death and was therefore obliged to hate, suspect, and persecute Gregory Orlov.
After Orlov's death he no longer had an incentive to live.
The sensitive old man soon followed his arch-enemy to
the grave. The Empress was thus bereaved of two of
her oldest and nearest friends.

§ 2

Compelled to leave Paul's education alone, she waited
impatiently for the time to marry him. She resolved to
be less hasty than the Empress Elizabeth, who had married her nephew at sixteen against the doctor's advice.
Catherine waited until her son had reached the age of
eighteen before she sought a wife for him. Relations between the mother and son improved considerably during
Paul's eighteenth summer. They spent the warm season

together in Czarskoe Selo and the Empress for the first time made a companion of her son. A new sympathy grew up between them; the long estrangement seemed to be over at last. It is easy to account for Catherine's new interest in Paul. Presumably she had been told that it would be safe to carry forward her plans and marry him. The young man found himself taken to his mother's bosom with unexpected warmth. Those who looked on thought this was the beginning of a friendliness at last between the mother and son, but the happy condition was not destined to last long. For once their interests coincided. Paul wanted a wife and his mother wanted him to marry. In all other situations of life which preceded and followed this halcyon interlude the two were ever in conflict.

The Empress surveyed with a critical eye the supply of German Princesses. Some not too powerful Prince's daughter after her own image was the object of her search. At last she selected a mother with three daughters and invited all three sisters to Russia that the Grand Duke might choose among them. In the old days when the Russian Czarevich wished to marry a Russian princess, it was customary for the eligible damsels to seat themselves in two long rows in the Kremlin palace while the young heir passed between them, looking to right and left, until he chose his bride. This ancient custom was in the Empress's thoughts when she invited the Landgravine of Hesse-Darmstadt to bring her three daughters to Petersburg.

Catherine was proud to be able to write to Prince Henry of Prussia, who had also planned to visit her, that his visit would have to be postponed because his apartments would be needed for the young Princesses and their mother. 'I may say to you in confidence, with the indiscretion that is natural to ladies, that these apartments are destined this summer for Madame the Landgravine of Hesse-Darmstadt.' If Prince Henry then so far betrayed her confidence as to inform his royal brother, Frederick the Great, that the Empress of Russia was about to marry her son and heir, the indiscretion of the Empress would be justified. That the King of Prussia had no son was a fact she liked to dwell upon. She was always in one way or another the rival of the Prussian monarch and in becoming a parent she had outstripped him. Paul was about to continue the Romanov dynasty as his mother had done before him, while the childless old King of Potsdam, ageing in solitude, could point to no such happy line of succession. Like the late Empress of Russia, he was obliged to make the best of a nephew as an heir.

The Landgravine of Hesse-Darmstadt came to Petersburg with her three daughters and went away again with two of them. The betrothal and marriage were rather hasty and not particularly gay. The new Grand Duchess, re-baptized as Natalie Alexeievna, was not a vivid personality and her short life in Russia left no legends. It was an unhappy marriage from the beginning and lasted but three years, at the end of which Natalie died in childbirth. Just what happened to the young wife during these years is a story that no one has told. Paul's complaints of Natalie show that he must have behaved very badly towards her. While this marriage lasted, his disposition took on a fixed habit of depression. Scarcely twenty years old, he succumbed to pessimistic moods from which he looked in vain to his wife to extricate him. As Natalie had not the gift of lighting up his *papillons noirs*, his favourite name for them, he settled more and more stubbornly in the black depths of miserable self-pity. Frequently he wept.

No doubt his mother had her moments of anxiety because the marriage did not produce a grandchild at once. In the third year, however, the Grand Duchess became pregnant; the hopes of the Empress were at last to be realized. Catherine made preparations for the lying-in to take place in Petersburg, where Czars might be born although they might not be crowned. In the spring-time of 1776, she expected the son of her son. The fatal outcome of Natalie's lying-in was described by the Empress in one of her most characteristic letters. The swiftness and vividness of her narrative reflect the sure movement of her spirit. In this letter we see her moving through a crisis as she moved through every crisis of a life that was so extraordinarily rich in danger and risks. It mirrors that acceptance of facts which enabled her to pass through murder at Peterhof and to emerge almost unscathed by comparison with temperaments like Orlov and Panin. In Catherine's make-up was some of that tough fibre which enabled Alexis, the head of the Orlov clan, to profit by his crimes while others far less guilty than himself did morbid penance on his behalf.

'On the 10th of April,' wrote Catherine to Grimm, 'at four o'clock in the morning, my son came to find me because his wife perceived the pains of confinement. I leaped out of bed and ran to her. I found her much tormented but nothing beyond the ordinary. Time and patience would end the affair. A midwife and a skilful surgeon aided her. . . . Monday passed in waiting and in a similar condition, very disturbing. . . . The doctors' conference produced no new expedients or assuagement. On Tuesday they demanded my physician and an old *accoucheur* to renew their consultation. . . . They decided to save the mother, as the infant was probably dead; instruments were employed; a combination of unfortunate circumstances, occasioned by malformation and divers accidents, made all that human science could do on Wednesday useless. On Thursday the Grand Duchess received the sacrament. Prince Henry suggested his physician; he was admitted but he agreed with his confrères. On Thursday the Princess gave up the ghost at five o'clock in the evening. To-day she has been cut open in the presence of thirteen physicians and surgeons who found that it was a unique and irremediable case. . . .

'Twenty-four hours before the death of the Grand Duchess, I sent to ask Prince Henry, for my own relief, to take charge of the Grand Duke. He came and has not left him since. He endures his profound chagrin with composure but to-day he has taken a fever. Since the death of his wife, I have picked him up and brought him here [Czarskoe Selo].

'Imagine me, who am tearful by temperament; I have seen some one die without shedding a tear. I said to myself: If you cry the others will sob, if you sob, the others will swoon; and everybody will lose their heads and be at their wits' end; all of whom will be irresponsible. . . .'

While the widowed Grand Duke remained overwhelmed, his mother set about finding a new wife for him. She has been reproached for her unseemly haste in the matter. Brückner says critically that even while Natalie was dying, the Empress's thoughts were occupied with a second marriage for her son. Of this there is not the least doubt. Three years of marriage had ended in a stillbirth; much time had been lost already and the business-like Empress saw no reason for losing more. She had maternal and imperial interests at stake, and match-making was an urgent matter, something to be done with as little delay as possible. It was apparent that the Grand Duke, who had completely collapsed in the crisis and who deve-

Catherine Becomes a Grandmother

·loped a fever afterwards, was unable to do anything on his own behalf. He had no more initiative to bring to the making of a second marriage than he had brought to the first. He would have to be inducted into matrimony once again.

Catherine took counsel with Prince Henry of Prussia, who happened to be in Petersburg at this dismal time. The death of Natalie made it impossible for the Empress to entertain her guest with the same elaborate festivities with which his former sojourn had been celebrated. Prince Henry protested that he was not at all bored, which the apologetic hostess refused to believe. But the melancholy and oppressed younger brother of Frederick the Great was more at home in the midst of tragedy and misfortune than in the gaiety and abandon of a Russian masquerade. In a Court that mourned for the dead Natalie, he was at ease. He had a contribution to make. A second wife for Paul was to be brought from Germany and the Prince was asked to arrange the match. It seems that he approved of the Empress's choice.

One reason that Catherine was already occupied with the thought of marrying her son while his wife lay dying was that she had long wished she had chosen another Princess instead. Three years before, when making her first survey of the field, she had considered the Princess Sophie von Württemberg and had passed her over because she was too young. Time had remedied this difficulty but had substituted another. Sophie had recently become betrothed and was shortly to be married to the hereditary Prince of Hesse-Darmstadt. This young man was well known in Russia and disliked by the Empress. He was a brother of Paul's first wife and had come to Russia to make his career there in Catherine's army. But after a couple of years she sent him home to his father.

'God help him,' she wrote; 'he is better off there than in Moscow.' This annoying young man had then engaged himself to Sophie of Württemberg and the betrothal presented a serious obstacle to Catherine's plans. There was nothing for the Empress to do but to buy him off. Apparently he was able to drive a pretty sharp bargain for he received, as a compensation for his disappointment, a pension for life. 'On condition,' the Empress wrote peevishly, 'that I shall never see or hear from him again.'

This delicate matter was arranged through the agency of Prince Henry, on whom Catherine at this time leaned heavily. She trusted all the details to the solemn silent Prussian. She even consented that her son should leave home under Henry's tutelage to court his bride in a foreign land. So far as the Grand Duke was concerned, the opportunity to visit Prussia gave him the greatest thrill of his courtship and furnished a strong incentive to marriage. He was already in love with Prussia and the Prussian King, in imitation of the ex-Czar, Peter III.

Accompanied by Prince Henry, he was allowed to make a pilgrimage to the land of his ideals and to sue in person for the hand of his bride. Whatever Sophie's feelings may have been when she first saw this ugly little man, she dutifully accepted him and made no fuss about it. The Princess was a tall blonde girl, in stature not unlike the late Empress Elizabeth, but German and *spiessbürgerlich* to her finger-tips. She was and remained all her days an incurable Philistine.

As soon as Paul returned from Germany, the Empress began to expedite the marriage. 'The Princess is yet to come,' she wrote to Grimm, 'and we shall have her here within ten days. As soon as we have her, we shall proceed with her conversion. To convince her, it ought to take about fifteen days I think. I do not know how long will be necessary to teach her to read intelligibly and correctly the confession of faith in Russian. But the faster this can be hurried through, the better it will be. To accelerate all that, M. Pastukov has gone to Memel to teach her the alphabet and the confession *en route*; conviction will follow afterwards. You see by this we are foresighted and cautious and this conversion and confession of faith travels by post. Eight days from this act, I fix the wedding. If you wish to dance at it, you will have to hasten.' The tall Princess Sophie was converted according to Catherine's schedule and became the Grand Duchess Marie Feodorovna.

Within five months after the death of his first wife, Paul was married again. His second wife was a healthy, phlegmatic woman. He was almost happy. 'Wherever *my wife* goes,' he wrote to Prince Henry, 'she has the gift of spreading gaiety and ease, and she has the art not only of dissipating my black moods but of giving me back again the disposition I had almost lost during the last three unhappy years.'

Paul's second marriage was probably the best marriage that could possibly have been made for him. The fair tall wife called up pleasant memories of the devoted nurse who had run to the fox-fur cradle every time the baby in it cried. Marie Feodorovna was complacent and domestic; she loved her flower garden and she loved the proprieties. Paul lived many pious uneventful years with her and the Philistine pair often sat in judgment on the life of the Empress. Nowhere in Europe was the light woman on the Russian throne so severely condemned as she was by her son and his virtuous wife. Marie Feodorovna was like the heroine of a Gartenlaube story and a long and stormy life in Russia never succeeded in making her anything else. She was a sentimental German to the last.

Catherine gave them the village of Pavlovsk for a residence. Here Paul built a little palace and Marie laid out her flower garden. After the death of Prince Orlov, Catherine purchased Gatchina for them. It was a place of evil memories for Paul, the scene of Orlov's final insanity and death. The ghost of Peter III had walked there and had carried off to judgment the guilty soul of Gregory Orlov. These uncanny memories meant nothing to the Empress but they had an unhealthy influence on her son. He shut himself up in Gatchina away from all the world and expressed himself in the development of the place. To this day it reflects his personality as Czarskoe Selo reflects the personality of his mother. In Gatchina he played with his military passions and his mysticism. He tried to make himself as much as possible like Peter III, whose ghost walked with him through the endless corridors.

§ 3

Catherine was forty-eight when her first grandson was born. She called him Alexander, as she said, a 'pompous name.' In 1777, her ambitious imagination ranged over the southern part of her dominions wherever Alexander the Great had passed and where he first met the Scythians. Catherine was just then entering upon her great dream of empire, the dream which dominated the rest of her life. She needed children and children's children to carry on the vast work she had planned. The dutiful Marie responded by producing two sons within a short space of time. Alexander was followed by Constantine, for the Empress loved resounding names. Catherine's joy in these infants was unbounded. She had borne five children but had never nursed one of them. At last her time had come. She took possession of the little new-born creatures and sent the mother back to Pavlovsk, childless. She re-enacted to the last detail the crime of Empress Elizabeth against herself.

In a lyrical letter to Grimm, she announced the birth of her first grandson. But when she spoke of Alexander's future her rapturous tone fell to a pensive strain. 'Aber, mein Gott, was wird aus dem Jungen werden?' She fell back as she rarely did into her native German. 'I console myself with Boyle and the father of Tristram Shandy, who was of the opinion that a name is an influence that matters. . . . Do you think his examples from the family prove anything? His choice of them embarrasses sometimes. His examples only show, to speak the gospel according to the venerable Pastor Wagner, that it is the *naturel* which counts. But where to find that? Is it at the bottom of the pack of a good constitution? . . . It is a pity that fairies have gone out of fashion; they would give an infant all that one wished. I should have made them beautiful presents and I should have whispered in their ears: Mesdames, *naturel*, just a little bit of *naturel* and experience will then do all the rest.'

The interests of a grandmother did not distract her attention from the events of the fast spinning world. As its happenings sped past, like a flying factory belt, she invariably registered the passage of episodes which concerned her. Even the christening of Alexander did not obscure the defeat of General Burgoyne in America. 'Monsieur Alexander was baptized the day before yesterday,' she wrote, 'and every one is doing well, except the English, who hang their heads to their stomachs since the deplorable adventure of General Burgoyne. He should gnaw his fingers after the fashion of Prince Potiomkin;

that sets the blood in circulation. If that of the Parliament of Great Britain remains calm now I call them plodding nags. . . .' She was scornful of George III who was evidently going to allow the American colonies to slip through his fingers. His grandchildren might lose America at the same time that her own might enter Constantinople. That is, they would if *naturel* led them in that direction. Her magnificent dreams for Alexander alternated with an uncertain mood which usually brought on an attack of the German language. 'Aber, mein Gott, was wird aus dem Jungen werden?'

Having appropriated her two grandsons in this unceremonious fashion, Catherine's cupidity seemed for the time satisfied. Marie Feodorovna came up to the Petersburg palace at regular intervals and bore her children there. It turned out that granddaughters were not wanted in Catherine's nursery and the young mother was allowed to take her girl-babies back to Pavlovsk and educate them herself. Catherine thought the little Princesses beautiful and charming, but she was content to give them lovely Greek names and send them home with Mamma. Alexander and Constantine, however, were ardently studied, ardently educated, and ardently sewed for.

The Empress designed a garment for Alexander of which she was extremely proud. She boasted that the King of Sweden and the Prince of Prussia had heard of it and had borrowed the pattern for their own little boys. The picture which she drew and sent abroad vindicated her boast of its simplicity. 'Nowhere,' she explains, 'is there any ligature and the child scarcely knows that he is being dressed. The arms and legs go into the garment at the same time and lo! all is finished. It is a stroke of genius on my part, this garment.' Her letters were filled with the sayings and doings of her darling. She gave a catalogue of his achievements at the age of four. He could write, spell, draw, use a spade, shoulder arms, and mount a horse; he could make twenty playthings out of one and ask endless questions. The other day he had asked whether there were human beings in the moon and whether he had been born in the moon or on the earth. 'I do not know,' said Grandmamma fervently, 'but there is a kind of profundity which springs up in the head of this little monkey.'

In the shadow of this wonderful brother, Constantine was obliged to make such headway as he could. There was less than eighteen months' difference in age between the two boys and in many respects they were treated as twins. They had two low chairs exactly alike in Grandmamma's boudoir and the model garment of her invention was always made up in pairs. In their education, however, certain distinctions were observed. Alexander, the future Czar, was brought up on the English plan as far as possible. This, to the Empress, meant fresh air and liberal ideals and she saw to it that Alexander was nourished on these things from his earliest infancy. Constantine showed from the beginning a strong repugnance to fresh air. The unregenerate infant annoyed his grandmother greatly by 'burying his nose in the linen and shutting out the air.' She gave him a Greek nurse and surrounded him with Greek attendants in order that he should begin life speaking this language only. Constantine was brought up to be King of Greece, where a salubrious climate would enable him to hold his head up and breathe the fresh air like a man. This younger brother of Alexander was destined never to be King of Greece or King of anything, least of all himself. The intensity of his secondary part deprived him of all aggressiveness in infancy, saddled him with an irascible temper, and cast him for an utterly passive rôle in life.

Alexander idolized his grandmother while Constantine hated her. 'Do you know,' Constantine said to the Swedish Prince when he met him in the palace of his grandmother, 'that you are in the house of the greatest whore in Europe?'

Catherine had been obliged by circumstances to refrain from interfering in the education of her own son. Her attempt to import D'Alembert from France had failed and she had allowed matters to proceed as they had started under the guidance of Panin. But she was not satisfied with the results and hoped to do much better for her two grandsons. She wrote an extensive Instruction for the guidance of their teachers, producing this time a far more original piece of work that her famous message to the commission on a code of laws. It contained common sense and insight only occasionally darkened by the author's well-known prejudices. She counselled those in charge of young children to avoid scolding them and to cultivate a gentle attitude in order that they should learn not to fear people. The spirit of Babet Cardel, the spirit of common sense, expressed itself repeatedly in Catherine's pedagogy. Her prejudice appeared in a flat prohibition against the arts for which she herself had no understanding. 'The Grand Dukes are to be taught neither poetry nor music; because it would occupy too much of their time to attain excellence in either. . . .'

Whatever latent talent the two boys may have had in the creative arts was never encouraged to express itself. Grandmother's repressions were too strong. Alexander might have learned to sing like a bird if he had had another Babet Cardel to teach him and if his devoted but jealous grandmother had not cut him off from every opportunity to learn. She succeeded in transmitting her own tone-deafness to him in an aggravated form.

Alexander was as his name indicated destined for a military career; Catherine pictured him as the conqueror of Constantinople at least. But she loathed the idea of what she called Prussian corporalism. The imitation battles of Peter III and her son Paul, their drilling and dragooning, their manœuvring and parading struck her as unwarlike. She preferred the freer methods of her Russian generals, Suvarov, Rumiantsov, Potiomkin. Her grandson was to be a conquerer of the Russian school. In any case, however, he must operate with big guns and tolerate the noise they made. A worry had grown up in her mind around this matter of big guns. General Potiomkin, leader of her forces against the Turks, had a terrible handicap. When the sound of firing came to him in his encampment behind the lines, he trembled in his Russian boots. The Empress knew this well; indeed far too many people knew it well and the idiosyncrasy ill became the chief of the Russian army. If Potiomkin failed to take Constantinople, it would probably be due to this mysterious weakness of his. Mysterious it was, for Potiomkin was really no coward.

If Constantinople held out against Potiomkin, the conquest would remain for Alexander. It was imperative that the young Grand Duke should have no fear of guns. His grandmother decided to prevent the possibility of such a disaster by habituating the child in early life to the sound. She had him systematically exposed to the noise of cannon in the hope that the early experience would inoculate him against this unmanly fear as vaccination had made him immune from the terror of smallpox. Her experiment with the cannon did not work as well as her experiment with vaccination. The boy, it is true, grew up without fear of the noise of guns firing; but that was partly because his deafness prevented him from hearing them. Alexander I was merely hard of hearing. The explanation usually given is that his disability was acquired from being forced by his grandmother to listen to gun-practice in his childhood.

Another feature in Catherine's pedagogy which throws a light on her character concerns the subject of sex and reproduction. She was as rigid with her grandsons as she had been with the young ladies at Smolny. She thought it was better not to call their attention to such things too early. Just as the Smolny pupils had produced Voltaire's plays with the passages about love cut out, so her grandsons were expected to study science and omit the subject of reproduction. Their tutors were instructed to keep them in strict ignorance about all that concerned the relation of the sexes. 'Her great modesty in this respect,' says Masson, 'appears strikingly contrasted with other parts of her character. . . . The celebrated Pallas was giving the Princes a short course of botany in their garden near Pavlovsk; but the explanation of Linnæus's system of the sexes gave them the first ideas of those of human nature and led them to put a number of very amusing questions with great *naïveté*. This alarmed their governors; Pallas was requested to avoid entering into further particulars; and the course of botany was even broken off.'

The Empress, who was devoted to science, who loved the study of comets and philology, who strove industriously to wipe out superstition with knowledge, went so far as to interrupt a course of botany for prudish reasons. The modesty for which she was so often admired but which would be more accurately called prudery was doubtless present in her character. Her efforts to preserve the innocence of her grandsons did not have the happy result which she hoped for. As she had been eager to have grandchildren, she was also eager to have great-grandchildren. Her hopes were destined to disappointment. She married both of her grandsons at an early age but neither of them had descendants. Their marriages were not happy. The outcome was not according to their grandmother's scheme. Not for this did she bring them up in ignorance of sex and sacrifice the course in botany to preserve their innocence. Their sterility was a bitter disappointment to her. Paul's youngest son, the only one she had left to be educated by his mother, carried on the dynasty that she had founded. From the Empress's own point of view, Nicholas, who was brought up by her Philistine daughter-in-law, was a greater success in life than his two elder brothers whom she had so carefully reared. Perhaps she had worked too hard on the training of her precious young. A more casual upbringing might have had happier results for her own purposes, which included first of all the production of offspring.

§ 4

While the Empress was educating Paul's children at the Court, Paul was living in strict retirement at Pavlovsk and Gatchina. He complained bitterly of his exclusion from active life. 'You tax me with my hypochondria and black moods,' he wrote to Prince Henry. 'It may be so. . . . But the inaction to which I am condemned makes the part excusable.' Two years after his second marriage, which had lifted his spirits temporarily, he was again writing to Prince Henry, 'Permit me to write you often, my heart has need to unburden itself, especially in the sad life that I lead.' After abruptly closing his letter, he adds, 'My tears prevent me from continuing.'

Paul was not yet twenty-five years of age when he was writing in this despondent strain. He was already the victim of pessimism and melancholy, any intensification of which might lead him beyond the bounds of mental health. Brückner says that Paul was eccentric in his behaviour, his moods, and his ideas from the very cradle. In middle age he was called insane. Paul's wife, Marie Feodorovna, considered him so. 'There is no one,' she wrote, 'who does not every day remark the disorder of his faculties.' For years before the Empress died, it was reported throughout Europe that her son was mad.

Here was an extraordinary coincidence. If Paul was not the son of Peter III, as had been whispered at the time of Paul's birth, whence came the similarity in their morbid tendencies? The unfortunate Grand Duke seemed to be following in the footsteps of the late Czar. Peter certainly had a severe mental twist with passionate preferences and prejudices which the Grand Duke imitated. In his sequestered life at Gatchina he cultivated the personal habits and tastes of the murdered Peter. He professed, for instance, the same partiality for Frederick the Great and accomplished what Peter had longed for but had never attained: he saw the Prussian idol in the flesh. When Paul and his wife made the grand tour of Europe in 1781, they visited Frederick in Berlin. It was a memorable meeting for several reasons. Frederick the Great for the first time in many years had a new suit made – new throughout. It was a great concession from the Potsdam recluse and miser, an eloquent testimonial of respect for the painted lady of Petersburg who was, incidentally, not so friendly towards Prussia as she once had been. The King's new clothes were the talk of Berlin.

As a topic of conversation, they were only superseded by the Hamlet story. A special production of Hamlet had been announced in the Grand Duke's honour but the director of the theatre withdrew the piece at the last moment as inappropriate for the occasion. The public was agog with curiosity and the sensitive self-pitying Paul became the focus of an over-wrought and over-acted romance of public sympathy. For several days Paul's picture of his own tragedy hung before the German public; Berlin saw him as a Russian Hamlet whose father had been made a martyr partly for his love of Prussia. All this was extremely bad for the melancholy Grand Duke, for whom any picturesque enhancement of his misfortunes added an element of danger to that already inherent in his habitual brooding. The comparison with Hamlet was grateful to him for every reason, but most of all for the reason that Hamlet was his father's own son. If the public identified Paul with Hamlet, it meant that they accepted him as the son of Peter III. This aspect of the drama represented something that Paul was obliged to believe. To doubt it meant for him unendurable suffering, to be escaped at every cost.

As a baby in the cradle, Paul was a sensitive creature, starting and trembling at every sound. He was devotedly nursed by the Empress Elizabeth and oppressed by her hysteria. After her death he was dependent on Panin, a man who dreamed dreams but made no effort to realize them. Panin's tutelage was not a training in courage and Paul's situation especially required it. He was constantly in fear of being poisoned, in fear of being found out to be a bastard, in fear of losing his claim to the throne of the Romanovs. His relations with his mother were always unsympathetic and after his second marriage they became unfriendly. Paul had no interest in politics and ascribed his indifference to the selfishness of the Empress who jealously excluded him from any participation in affairs of state. But he was far too shy and unpractical by temperament to engage in politics in any form; to organize, to compromise, to adjust means to ends were not within his capacity.

He was, on the other hand, profoundly attracted by the mystical movements of his age. By this method he became connected with the protestant religions of Europe, an alliance which was not consistent with his future position as head of the Greek Church. It will be remembered that Peter III could never wholly abandon the religion of his native Holstein and remained to the end hostile to Russian orthodoxy. Paul developed the same tendency to ally himself with strange and rebellious faiths. He became a Freemason, a Martinist, and a Knight of Malta. The Eighteenth Century was prolific in mystic cults at the same time that it took its place in history as the age of enlightenment. As Catherine the Great was identified with all the movements for enlightenment, her son was identified with all the forms of obscurantism which flourished side by side with the new rationalism. Catherine was displeased with Paul's alliance with black magic and prided herself on being free from any leanings toward superstition. When she was a very old woman, her latent credulity burst out; but her lapse at the eleventh hour need not deprive her of her position as one of the shining leaders of the age of reason. Paul always belonged in the other camp, the camp of the credulous, by virtue of his temperament. He might have found a kind of peace there if destiny had not called him to play an active part in life.

After he became Czar his morbid ideas waxed and led him into many grotesque and extreme acts. Like Hamlet, he thought his first duty was to avenge his father. Although Peter had been dead for more than thirty years, he had the grave opened, the corpse exposed to public view, and an impressive funeral enacted. The Czar had been buried in the Alexander Nevsky monastery, while all the other Czars of Russia after Peter the Great had been buried in the Fortress of Saint Peter and Saint Paul. An elaborate funeral procession transported the dead Peter from his old to his new resting-place. As the sarcophagus was borne along the Nevsky Prospect, Alexis Orlov followed immediately after as chief mourner. This was the crown of Paul's revenge, to expose the murderer to the condemnation of the world.

Gregory Orlov was dead but fortunately for Paul's mad drama his brother remained to play the sinister rôle which Paul had invented for him. What the aged Orlov thought of as he trudged along behind the corpse of the man he had struck down thirty-four years ago is matter for speculation. From what we know of Alexis' character, he was probably not occupied with remorseful thoughts. Perhaps he was thinking of the strong fish-soup with which he was going to revive his weak old legs when the Czar's fine funeral was over. Perhaps he was thinking that Paul was as mad as Peter had been, and wondering at the coincidence.

The resemblance between the fate of Catherine's husband and her son was carried out to the end. As Emperor, Paul's morbid suspicions increased and his reprisals against those whom he suspected aroused fear and hatred on every hand. His dread of persecution called forth actual persecution where none had formerly existed. Soon a conspiracy began to take shape among his enemies, headed by the Zubov brothers, Plato and Valerian. The last chapter of Peter's history was repeated. After a brief reign of only four years, Paul was murdered one night by a band of conspirators who said that he was a dangerous lunatic and had to be put out of the way. There is every reason to suppose that his son and successor, Alexander the First, was aware of the conspiracy against his father's life, and more definitely aware than Catherine had been when Peter had been assassinated at Ropsha. One of the things which Alexander had learned from his extraordinary grandmother was to overlook a murder which could not be prevented and make the best of the consequences. In both cases the consequences entitled them to ascend the throne over the dead bodies of their predecessors.

§ 5

Catherine the Great loved to write. She rose at six o'clock every morning and occupied herself with literary work during the three hours or so which intervened before her Russian servants began to rub their sleepy eyes. She had Spartan methods of awakening herself. First she washed her face and ears with ice; then she drank five cups of the strongest coffee ever brewed. She sat down beside her candle with her pen and wrote in a large free flowing hand, instructions, correspondence, memoirs, fables, histories, comedies. Her output was voluminous. She did not wait to finish one piece before she began another, and the first remained for ever unfinished. Every thing she wrote is a fragment. She wrote her memoirs in the 70's, and then wrote them all over again in the 90's. She set down a fragment of autobiography for Sir Charles Hanbury Williams, another for Poniatovsky, and another for Potiomkin. She was careless as to the kind of paper and such things, as may be seen from her notes in the Russian archives which are scribbled literally on scraps of paper, anything which came to hand. Her mind shook itself out freely in the track of a swiftly moving pen.

Catherine Becomes a Grandmother

Whatever she wrote was closely related to the affairs of the day. It was addressed to some particular person or based on some concrete experience. The evolution of her literary expression can be roughly traced like this: during her thirties, she wrote on political subjects and matters of State; during her forties, she wrote her memoirs and corresponded with Voltaire and Grimm; during her fifties, she wrote allegories, chronicles, and comedies; and in her sixties, she turned to reminiscences again, producing the version of her life which she wanted posterity to read. She grew less and less abstract as the years went by.

After the birth of her two grandsons, the Empress had an outburst of imaginative writing. For several years she addressed all her writings to the little Grand Dukes. *The Legend of the Czarevich Chlor* was written for Alexander when he was five years old. Her Russian history, which fills two volumes, pictures a primitive age with appropriate simplicity. She moralizes scarcely at all, for the lives of the Knazia Veliki do not point the right kind of moral.

Catherine's little histories are a narrative of constant wars between the Russians and the Greeks; swift and vivid sketches of nomadic princes and large families of brothers warring against each other for a heritage. The story of Princess Olga who went to Constantinople and was there baptized is told enthusiastically and at length. Olga tried to convert her son but he would not be converted because he said the other men would not like it. She had to wait until her grandson, whom she reared, grew to manhood before she could make her influence felt. It was her grandson who Christianized Russia.

This legend was very popular with Catherine and her grandson Alexander. With her globes, the Empress showed the little boy how the hordes of Genghis Khan had passed across the lands of Russia and where the Scythians had met the Greeks. These lessons made her intimacy with little Alexander the happiest of her life. She collected her writings into a so-called Library for the Grand Dukes. To be sure, the projected Library was never completed; nor was the history of Russia brought down beyond the thirteenth century. So far as her Russian history was concerned, it was a pity that the author left only a fragment. She had a gift for lively compact narrative and the reader feels a distinct disappointment when the story breaks off suddenly before the arrival of the Tartars.

Her faithlessness to history is easy to explain. The artist had found a new love. She had suddenly discovered comedy. The Empress had taken to writing plays in the manner of Molière. An anecdote often told to show the affection existing between Alexander and his grandmother tells how the boy, at the age of eight, gave a performance of a five-act comedy composed by Catherine. In the deeper layers of her memory the works of Molière had been lying long unnoticed. Suddenly the latent memories so long bedded there in forgetfulness and silence began to germinate. At about the same age which Monsieur Alexander had now grown to be, Catherine had once fed upon the plays of Molière because her governess, Babet Cardel, had known them all by heart. As she sat teaching her eight-year-old grandson, the tastes and interests of that age in her own life began to stir and assert themselves within her. Catherine was not content as Babet had been to give her pupil ready-made comedies however masterly. She preferred to compose comedies herself for Alexander. Promptly she fell to work and swiftly were her plays completed. This time there were no fragments; the brevity of the product was exactly suited to her temperament.

She wrote seven pieces in one year, and then abandoned the field altogether, perhaps because the Turkish Wars became too engrossing.

Her comedies all deal with one subject in the same manner. They are satires on the sentimental and superstitious traits of human nature. Her titles show how faithfully she adhered to her theme. The Charlatan, The Dupe, The Siberian Shaman, Family Discord Through False Suspicions, No Good Without Evil were the most popular. Their plots and characters show that the author is something of a psychologist and a good deal of a satirist. It is noticeable that the weaknesses which she especially satirizes are characteristic of the behaviour of her son Paul.

At the time when Catherine wrote her comedies there was no longer any pretence of sympathy between the mother and son. The disintegration of Paul's character had progressed so far that he had withdrawn himself from all the world except those whom his mother called charlatans and quacks. The Empress identified her son with all superstitious folk and castigated the whole tribe in her comedies. She rarely mentioned Paul directly in her memoirs and her correspondence. In the intimate family history which fills her letters to Grimm, his name never occurs. Her hatred found an outlet in her satirical comedies. Here she indirectly exposed his notorious weaknesses and held them up to ridicule. She despised his character as she despised his looks. Paul resembled the Calmuck type in physique and countenance. Short of stature and snub-nosed as he was, his mother could not look at him without being reminded of the Saltikov side of his nature. Anyone who reads through her literary works will be struck by the number of times the Empress refers to the ghastly ugliness of the Calmuck type. She could not get away from it.

The comedies of Catherine the Great were regarded as a great contribution to the campaign against obscurantism. She stepped forth as the Saint George of enlightenment striking down the dragon of superstition. Her satire was levelled against the Martinists, the Freemasons, and the Alchemists; she battered at all groups and organizations that had a secret understanding and talked mysteriously about the problems of life and death. Fortunately for her interest, which had no great tolerance for abstractions, a flesh-and-blood antagonist was raised up to stimulate and increase her energies. The famous Cagliostro decided to make a visit to Petersburg, believing that Catherine the Great would favour his cult. But he had reckoned without his Empress. Catherine was never tired of abusing him, both during and after his sojourn in Russia. When he was imprisoned in France in connection with the affair of the diamond necklace, she exulted in the most unbecoming manner. Some of her strongest and least elegant language was poured out on the head of the talented magician, whom, by the way, she had never even seen. To Grimm, she wrote, 'I have read the memoir of Cagliostro which you have sent me and if I had not been already persuaded that he was a French charlatan, his memoir would have convinced me. He is a rogue and blackguard and he ought to be hanged.'

She was so greatly interested in this man that it must have cost her a great effort to deny him an audience during his stay in Russia. 'M. Cagliostro,' she wrote, 'arrived here at a very favourable moment for him, at a time when many lodges of Freemasons, infatuated with the principles of Swedenborg, desired with all their power to see spirits. They therefore ran to Cagliostro who said that he was in possession of all the secrets of Doctor Falk, intimate friend of Duke Richelieu, who had once sacrificed to him in the

very midst of Vienna a black goat. . . . M. Cagliostro
then produced his marvellous secrets of healing. He pretended to draw quick-silver from a gouty foot and was
caught in the act of pouring a teaspoonful of mercury
into the water into which he was going to put the gouty
member. . . .

'Later on, racked by debts, he took refuge in the cellar
of Monsieur Yelagin . . . where he drank all the wine,
champagne, and English beer that he could get. . . .
Monsieur Yelagin, annoyed by his brother rat in the cellar
and by the thought of all the wine, and beer . . . gave him
an old *invalide* to accompany him as far as Milan. This is
the history of Cagliostro in which there is nothing excep-
tionally marvellous. I have never seen him near or far, —
nor have I had any temptation to do so, for I do not love
charlatans. I assure you that Rogerson thinks of Cagliostro as much or less than Noah's Ark. Prince Orlov, contrary to his custom, has not made much of Cagliostro. He
makes fun of him as of those who from mere curiosity run
to see him, and he has contributed but little to change into
wine the water of the shameless partisans of this poor devil.
But since the more stupid and ignorant the charlatans are
the more impression they create in the great cities, it is to
be supposed that Cagliostro will be in his element in
Paris. . . .'

From the vehemence of the Empress's condemnation,
one suspects that she did not state a fact when she declared that she had no temptation to see him. And she
was far from having finished with the subject. Two of her
comedies, The Liar and The Dupe, were based on Cagliostro's visit, and The Siberian Shaman was inspired,
though not avowedly, by the same theme. Several of her
plays were a great success when produced in Petersburg,
and The Liar and The Dupe took in more than twenty

thousand roubles. The public appreciated the Empress's satire and was intrigued by the timeliness of her literary attack on the most notorious character in Europe.

No one asked the Grand Duke Paul and his consort, the Gartenlaube lady of Pavlovsk, what they thought of the Empress's dramatic efforts. No one asked Paul and Marie about anything. The Empress overlooked them completely. Whenever she referred to her successor, the reference was to her grandson. 'Monsieur Alexander will finish this and that,' she would write. 'Not in my time, but in that of Monsieur Alexander.' She tried to forget the existence of the Grand Duke Paul.

12

She Grows Old

Up to the death of Potiomkin, the Empress had been associated with old friends, who had shared with her the experiences of 1762. Orlov and Potiomkin had both stood over the warm body of Peter, stabbed to death by Alexis and Bariatinsky. Although neither of them had lifted a hand against the Czar, they shared with her the memory of a crime which had to be made good. This was not such a bad thing, said Voltaire, since it made the Empress one of the best monarchs of the century. To redeem herself in the eyes of Europe, she was obliged to accomplish marvels. In a lesser degree the same obligation rested on Orlov and Potiomkin. Although they were both selfish and extravagant, they were good patriots and did their utmost for the glory of Russia. A mysterious force sustained Gregory Orlov, a very ordinary man, through a very remarkable career. Potiomkin, a man of greater ability than Orlov, was correspondingly more effective and more distinguished. The moody Ukrainian must have been surprised to find himself regarded as a great General and a great statesman and to realize that at times he actually was all that he was supposed to be.

For nearly thirty years, the Empress had had the companionship of these two men. After the death of Potiomkin, she was for the first time alone. All at once she became uncertain, inadequate, unsuccessful, and the inglorious years of her reign began. Her claim to the title of Catherine the Great would have been stronger had she died with Potiomkin. The last decade of her life diminished that claim considerably, which has often been construed as showing the strength of Potiomkin's influence and the importance of his ideas. But Potiomkin was merely the staff on which she leaned and which she had broken without foreseeing the consequences to herself.

Young Plato Zubov had no realization of the crime at Ropsha. His conscience was virgin and his youth made him irresponsible and selfish. He was a man without a past, he had nothing to atone. Fortune had suddenly rained treasure upon him out of a clear sky and he accepted her bounty as a child who forgets to say 'thank you.' He was arrogant, arbitrary, and grasping, and he became ruthless after his triumph over the redoubtable Potiomkin. The death of his rival left him invincible and he knew it.

Zubov was not simply youthful; he was youth. The two brothers, Plato and Valerian, were just emerging from the adolescent period which the Empress's grandsons, Alexander and Constantine, were just entering. The difference in age and maturity between the two pairs of brothers was not great. The Empress was in love with Alexander but she adopted Plato Zubov instead and began casting about for a wife for Alexander who had reached the age at which she had come to Russia to be married. 'Monsieur Alexander' she had spoken of from infancy as if he were a man and Zubov she now referred to always as 'the child.' At the age of sixty, the Empress had no eyes for anything but youth. Her lovers had been younger and younger men until all the world expected her to end her life in the arms of a boy.

It was assumed by those about the Court that only striplings need apply for the post of favourite. There was a moment when it seemed as if the seventeen-year-old son of Princess Dashkov might seriously compete. His mother, who had ridden beside the Empress as a sister Amazon on the night of the Peterhof campaign, says in her memoirs that the young Prince had been advised by Gregory Orlov to become a suitor. The Princess was shocked when she heard her son thus tempted by Catherine's ex-favourite. 'As soon as he was gone,' – she tactfully sent young Dashkov on an impromptu errand, – 'I expressed my astonishment to Prince Orlov that he could speak in such a manner to a young man not seventeen years of age, and compromise the honour and dignity of Her Majesty in such a manner. As to favourites, I bade him recollect that I neither knew nor acknowledged such persons, and that this was a subject which I would not suffer to be renewed in my presence, much less in the presence of my son, whom I had brought up with sentiments of the utmost veneration for the Empress as his sovereign and godmother, never, as I trusted, to know any other.'

The Princess nevertheless set off at once for Petersburg, where she soon was sure to be dangerously exposed to the charms of the aged siren on the Russian throne. As soon as the Dashkovs arrived, the mother's fears increased. 'The absurd rumours that my son would be the favourite began to be renewed.' One day the nephew of Prince Potiomkin called at her house and asked to speak with the young Prince, who was out. 'All that you are doing me the honour to say,' the Princess burst forth vehemently, although the messenger had said no more than that Prince Potiomkin wished to see her son, 'could never be meant for my ears. Perhaps it might be your commission to speak with Prince Dashkov. As for myself, while I love the Empress and dare not oppose her will, I have too much self-respect and self-esteem to take part in any affair of such a nature. And if what you are pleased to intimate should ever occur, the only use I shall make of my son's influence will be to obtain leave of absence for some years and a passport to visit foreign countries.'

There is no evidence except his mother's memoirs that the Empress ever really considered young Dashkov.

Soon after his arrival in Petersburg, he was ordered away
to his regiment, a fate which never overtook young men
whom the Empress wished to see about her. The hopes
of his mother collapsed. The Prince went away under a
cloud of failure, like a student who had tried for college
entrance and failed in his examinations. Within a few
weeks he met a peasant girl and married her during a
short leave from his regiment. The rest of his story relates
how his mother never recognized his wife, how he lived
apart from her, and how he died early. He had never been
happy.

Young Dashkov's tragedy throws a light on the Empress's passion for young men. There were mothers in
Russia who were willing to offer up their sons and profit
by an unsuitable love-relationship which could be glossed
over as romantic. There were older men like Orlov who
were ready to advise a fine young soldier to try his fortunes with the Empress. All of these counsellors expected
to receive in some form, whether in passports and funds
for foreign travel or otherwise, pay for their services.
For the lucky young man it meant riches, honours, titles,
consideration. The Empress's generosity was notorious
— and she could not possibly live long. But a long and
princely future awaited the youthful lover who survived
her.

Plato Zubov was a choice after her own heart. The
'child' was not as tall as he might have been but he was
dark like her first lover, Saltikov, who had looked 'like a
fly in the milk-pan' and who had wooed her at first so
ardently. Plato was not diffident. He had taken pains to
put himself in the Empress's way. His uncle, one of
Catherine's field-marshals, had been induced to make him
commander of the horse guards at Czarskoe Selo and the
young officer lost no opportunity of placing himself in the

foreground whenever the Empress passed. Zubov had been on the ground for some time before Mamonov's infidelity was discovered. The dismissal of Mamonov was followed immediately by the selection of Zubov. The Empress spent only one night alone. The next day Plato Zubov was promoted to the post of Adjutant-General and appeared at the Empress's right hand at dinner, as handsome a military figure as had ever adorned the place. There was truculence in the set of the young man's head, though his dark eyes wore that dreamy look which his predecessors all the way back to Prince Christian August of Anhalt-Zerbst had always worn.

There is a tradition, not well established, that her relationship with Zubov was Platonic. If this was true, the ageing Empress took good care that it should not be known. She hated growing old and resisted to the last the infirmities of her advancing years. She detested glasses though she was obliged to use them. This was not, she told her secretary, due to any ordinary process of physical decay but 'because she had worn her eyes out in the service of the State. The loss of her teeth did not worry her nearly so much, because the infirmity was so universal and so irremediable. In spite of powder, wigs, and patches, the teeth of the eighteenth century lady were at the mercy of her years, and the Empress with her millions of roubles was no better off than any peasant grandmother of her realm.

Worst of all, she lost the use of her legs. They became so swollen that she could not move about on them, and was obliged to sit in a wheeled chair while she took her airing in the colonnade of her Czarskoe Selo palace. To reach her beloved English garden which lay directly below, she built of stone and sod an inclined way down which her chair could be gently propelled until it reached the grove of live oaks. Those members of the nobility whose invitations she accepted built similar approaches to their palaces in order that the Empress need climb no stairs. Leaning on the arm of her beplumed, beribboned and bestarred escort, the handsome Plato, she would toil slowly up the incline while her host stood bowing to await her successful arrival. In this fashion Catherine the Great made her last public appearances, tottering before the eyes of all beholders like a child learning to take its first steps.

In spite of her physical handicaps, she persisted in acting as if they did not exist and her prowess was amazing. Her love of society remained as strong as ever and she was always the gayest in any company. Her infirmities were greater than those which had imprisoned Frederick the Great in his arm-chair during his last years, and had shut him off from the world. But unlike the Prussian King, whom she derided as being as 'old as Herod,' she never fell into the mental rigidity which comes from loss of contact with the world. Her reactionary acts, which were plentiful enough in the last decade of her reign, were due to something other than the hardening of the social arteries which sometimes sets in with the advent of old age.

She took to card-playing more assiduously than ever, and her passion for conversation grew rather less than in the old days when she would talk with Grimm and Diderot for seven hours at a stretch. The change may have been due to the fact that she no longer had men like Grimm and Diderot about her to tempt her to these conversational orgies. Madame Vigée Lebrun was in Petersburg during the last years of the Empress, but Catherine never spent seven hours at a time conversing with any woman. Even after sixty, she was not reduced to that. Her energy sufficed to the very last to defend her dominant likes and dislikes. She had suffered great physical losses. The use of her legs, all of her teeth, and half of her eyesight were gone, yet the vigour and virility of her personality remained unimpaired. On the arm of a handsome young lover, she would brazen it out to the end. She wore him as a decoration.

There is no doubt that Catherine was afraid of Zubov; that is, afraid of losing him, and that she spoiled him dreadfully. She spoiled all the Zubov brothers, Plato, Valerian, and Nicholas. It was a repetition of her situation with the Orlov brothers, only the Zubov family was more grasping. Gregory Orlov had stumbled into his good luck, so to speak, but Plato Zubov had worked for his; besides he was younger and times had changed. He lost no opportunity to garner the rewards of his enterprise for himself and his brothers. In a short time, they had acquired all the honours and riches for which the Orlovs had waited ten years and Potiomkin and his protegés fifteen. Needless to say, the Zubovs were extremely unpopular. Nicholas was married and was rather less prominent about the court than Plato and Valerian, who were the centre of its social and political life. They enjoyed the constant society of the Empress.

From the point of view of the elder nobility, Plato and Valerian were upstarts. The ministers and foreign diplomats, who had not achieved at a single bound, were obliged to stand hat in hand as these youngsters passed. Catherine's favourites had always been parvenus and the nobles had grown accustomed to bare their heads to Adjutants-General who had no ancestry. But the Zubovs were not merely unknown; they were reckless youths without experience or any other measure of the power which was theirs. There was not even a Potiomkin to trim their claws, since the Prince of Tauris had been laid away in a nameless grave in the south because Zubov would not allow the Empress to build a worthy tomb for him. No survivor of the Empress's own generation had any influence with her.

The character of the Little Hermitage, in which Catherine had always received her intimates, had changed. In the days when Gregory Orlov had strutted about like an apple-cheeked Adonis with his illiterate conversation, the Hermitage had all been more or less of an age and had frolicked like children together. Later, when Gregory Potiomkin had sulked in a corner while the Empress played cards with tear-marks on her cheeks or had performed his ventriloquist tricks until her sides ached with laughter, there had still been a kind of harmony among them. But the group now threatened to break into two parts along a line of social cleavage which separated the old from the young. As the Empress had grown older, the most prominent men in the Hermitage had grown younger. The two Zubovs and her grandsons now occupied the foreground while all the middle-aged and elderly cavaliers were relegated to the background. Only Leo Narishkin was as old as herself, Leo who had once meowed like a cat to call her forth to a rendezvous with Poniatovsky and whom she had whipped with nettles on the one occasion in all his life when his allegiance had wandered. Narishkin had no influence with her. He was her oldest friend in Russia, now grown as fat as she and caring no longer to play blind-man's-buff which had once been their favourite game. She played cards with him and quarrelled with him and lampooned him in verse. When the evening was over, the Empress got upon her feet with difficulty, and leaning on the arm of her dark-eyed Plato retired to her bed-chamber adjoining. The Princess Alexandrina, who was now fourteen and a member of the Hermitage, was a witness of this unconventional exit of her grandmother.

Gradually the Empress's suite began to feel that the lioness was growing weaker. They now no longer feared her claws. When they saw her looking anxiously to the arrogant Plato for approval, their courage to criticize awoke. Her dependence gave her away. For the first time in her reign rumours of disrespect and ridicule were heard. Long ago when she had thought of marrying Gregory Orlov, the gossips in Moscow had put their heads together and whispered. But they had stopped suddenly enough when the Empress had sent out with a roll of drums her famous Manifesto of Silence. The tongues of Moscow had ceased to wag when Little Mother spoke on that occasion. Nowadays she loosed no thunders and the gossips now realized their freedom.

Her severest critics, as usual, were found in the French colony. These foreigners indulged themselves in vulgar jests at the expense of the Empress and her Court and went so far as to set down their Rabelaisian efforts on paper. At a Twelfth Night party they lampooned the Little Hermitage with a freedom which one might suppose to be Russian if one did not know that the composers of the document were Parisian. One by one they satirized the courtiers, beginning with Zubov.

'Zubov has never rendered any service to the State and is no longer of service to the Empress, since the Sapphics, Branicky and Protassov execute the functions of his office. Let a few emetics be given him, to make him bring up what he has swallowed.

'Prince Bariatinsky, Marshal of the Court, shall be appointed Jack Ketch. A more gentle mode of putting to death than that by the knout is to be introduced; and he shall have the office of smothering and strangling in secret those that are to be dispatched, whether it be an emperor or his son; it is expected, however, that he do not let them cry out, as he did about thirty years ago.

'Marshal Suvarov shall have a patent for dealing as a butcher in human flesh; and the army shall be allowed to feed on it in Poland, where nothing but carcasses are left.

'A committee of *uchiteli* shall be appointed to examine whether Prince Yussupov be able to read; if he can, he shall be appointed prompter to the theatres, of which he is now manager.

'Madame von Lieven, governess to the Princesses, shall retain her place, though she has somewhat the air of an Amazon; but she shall be enjoined not to let beasts only have permission to speak at the table of the young Princess, unless they speak with sense as they did in Æsop's days.

'Prince Repnin, having opened the door one day when Prince Potiomkin called for a glass of water that he might himself repeat this important order to the lackeys, shall receive a patent for the place of first valet de chambre to the favourites; a post which to him will be worth that of field-marshal. However, the crown of laurel which covered his grey hair shall be taken from him, because he suffered a buffoon to tread on him without saying a word; and because the gift of a small house appeared suited to him, and to console him for the insult.

'M. Zavadovsky, director and plunderer of the bank, shall be sent into Siberia to catch sables, to replenish her Majesty's stock of furs, which it will not be in her power to keep up by any other means. She is already unable to furnish her family with them, and Zavadovsky is well known to be a better huntsman than financier.'

Such vulgar ridicule had long been rife in Paris. Since the Empress had welcomed French émigrés to Petersburg, it could now he heard in Russia.

§ 2

Like Peter the Great, Catherine had always hated the French. She envied them their art and culture and resented the French attitude towards the Russians as barbarians. She had adopted Peter's political policy which placed France always on the side of the enemy. There had always been misunderstanding and coolness between the Courts of Versailles and Petersburg, and when the daughter of the detested Maria Theresa became the Queen of France it did not help to make their relations more friendly. If Catherine had any fellow-feeling, as she might very well have had, for Marie Antoinette's ill-judged extravagance, she never expressed it before the revolution. Long ago, she had taken her cue towards French royalty from Voltaire and the Encyclopædists, and for thirty years she had tacitly adhered to it. The outbreak of the French Revolution suddenly changed all that and made her suddenly into a rabid protagonist of the French king. It was the greatest inconsistency of her life, a betrayal of her position as the most liberal monarch of her century.

The Empress had fought pretenders and rebels within her own kingdom. As a usurper herself, she was especially suspicious of conspiracy and rebellion, but she had been cool and wary in dealing with the cases which arose. The Churchman, Arsenii of Rostov, had felt her heavy hand when he tried to defend the lands of the Church against confiscation and had found himself put down from bishop to simple monk and banished to a cloister in a lonely forest. This was at the very beginning of her reign. Soon afterwards came the conspiracy of Mirovich and the death of Ivan VI, the Emperor whom Elizabeth had deposed twenty-three years before and who had gone straight from his cradle to prison. Ivanushka, for he was always remembered as a baby and spoken of as if he were one, had grown into a tall, stammering, red-haired man who occupied as a nameless prisoner a cell in the Schüsselburg fortress. The effort of young Mirovich to rescue him resulted in the death of Ivan and the execution of the conspirator. Although the removal of Ivanushka was convenient for the Empress, or, as she called it, providential, she could not have planned it, for Mirovich was a fantastic and quixotic individual who could not carry out the schemes of others.

For almost ten years afterwards, the Empress encountered no further alarms until the smallpox riots broke out in Moscow. While her attention was fixed on these, Pugachev's rebellion began to roll up in the East and to take on the aspect of a civil war. Pugachev was a genuine revolutionist, an agitator, a leader of the masses. He was, after Stenka Rasin, the second great socialist hero of Russian history, and his rebellion, however complicated by other elements, was essentially a social uprising. The condition of the peasants had not improved under Catherine's régime although there had been a definite hope among the serfs that the liberal Empress was going to do something for them. The Cossack rebel, Pugachev, came along at just the right time to garner the resentment which grew out of these disappointed hopes. He said that he came to give satisfaction to the injured people. They brought the wild man with his blue-black beard to Moscow in a cage and executed him there.

Pugachev had gone the way of Peter III and Ivanushka and the Empress was left in undisputed possession of the throne. She had at last put her house in order, for no other insurrection of any consequence broke out during her reign. She could now pursue her operations against the Turks, uninterrupted by domestic disturb-

ances. Her Russians, the patient 'dark' people, were
quiescent. After Pugachev's blue-black head had fallen
and his blood had stained the January snow of the Red
Square, no other leader appeared to arouse the people
against their Empress.

When the news of the French Revolution reached Russia, Potiomkin and the Empress were marching towards
Constantinople. For fifteen years the peasants of Russia
had been submissive and the Empress had not been aware
of the restlessness in France. The French uprising astonished and alarmed her profoundly and filled Potiomkin
with a paralyzing terror. They had all the reactions that
might be expected of parvenus under the circumstances.
The outraged Empress gave vent to her indignation in the
language of a fish-wife. She did not admit her awful fears.
She boasted loudly to Count Ségur, the French envoy who
favoured the republic, 'Je suis aristocrate, c'est mon
métier.' Of all her Court, only Leo Narishkin could remember her as an awkward country girl who arrived in Russia
without even a bridal chest, and Leo would have been the
last to remind her of her humble origin. He had not forgotten the sting of nettles applied by the Empress when
she was a young and vigorous Grand Duchess.

Catherine followed the fortunes of the French royal
family hour by hour with intense sympathy. She was at
Peterhof when she heard of their flight from Paris and she
was still rejoicing over it when she heard that they had
been arrested and taken back. Something similar had
happened to Peter thirty years before in the Peterhof
palace, but Catherine had called herself at that time a revolutionist and had been in the opponents' camp. This time
she railed loudly and violently against the regicides of
France. She shuddered to think of what might happen to
Catherine the Great if another Pugachev should presently

appear. After the death of Louis and Marie Antoinette, she said that her only hope for France was that a Cæsar or a Genghis Khan might rise up and overwhelm them. She supported the idea of intervention with enthusiasm but beyond her eloquent encouragement she gave no actual aid; all Europe echoed with her tirades and abuse. Her virile language surpassed that of any other monarch. She could denounce the friends of the republic as no one else and praise the old régime with matchless fervour. Her old friend, Prince Henry of Prussia, came in for the most extreme abuse because he would not join the hue and cry against the Jacobins; and Edmund Burke, who denounced the French Revolutionists, although he had favoured the American rebels, was heaped with undiscriminating praise.

The Empress's whole attitude towards the French ·Revolution was one of bluster and ineffectiveness. Even her own camp found it ineffectual and inconsistent. She invited the émigrés to Petersburg, for which the republican side naturally detested her. Her reputation with her contemporaries declined for they felt that this emotional defence was something less than might have been expected from Catherine the Great of former days. In earlier days she had understood the art of pulling the strings in silence and had known how to accomplish her will without threats. She had negotiated the partition of Poland and established the policy of armed neutrality with statesman-like effectiveness. Now she had degenerated into vituperation and inaction. Not only the Russian Court but all the Courts of Europe began to feel that the lioness of Petersburg was growing old.

§ 3

Catherine had married her two grandsons young, much too young their governors thought. It was now time, she

She Grows Old

considered, to marry Alexandrina, her granddaughter, although the Princess was but fourteen. The Empress had been scarcely older than this when she received a proposal of marriage and accepted it, although her father had feared to send so young a daughter to Russia. Catherine remembered that young girl with a great deal of affection and sympathy. 'Tell me truly,' she once burst out in a letter to Grimm, 'wouldn't it be charming if an Empress could remain all her life long only fifteen years old?' It remained always the most vivid year of her life, the year in which she had bidden her dear Papa good-bye and had set out to seek her fortunes in Russia. And now the charming young Alexandrina had reached that ideal age. Her grandmother had already selected a husband for her.

To say that the Empress had selected a husband for her is to put it too mildly. Catherine had once said of herself with absolute truth that whenever she wanted a thing she was obliged to want it most terribly. She now wanted to marry her granddaughter to the grandson of Ulrica, the sister of Frederick the Great. A few days after Catherine's betrothal in Petersburg, Frederick had married his sister Ulrica to the Crown Prince of Sweden. Ulrica's marriage had had one advantage which Catherine's had lacked; the Queen of Sweden had not been obliged to abandon the religion of her fathers. Ulrica had remained a devout Lutheran all her life.

Her son, Gustav III of Sweden, was a man of fashion, an exiled Parisian obliged to live in Stockholm. Gustav was a fop in his habits and a weathercock in his politics. The skeleton in his closet was that his son and heir was not his son. Gustav was an unhappy, complaining man, devoted to his mother yet at odds with her. He was finally assassinated when his son, Gustav IV, was only sixteen. It was this son, said to be a bastard, whom Catherine the

301

Great chose to be the husband of her granddaughter Alexandrina. Her heart was set on the marriage.

Gustav IV was seventeen when he came to the Russian Court at the Empress's invitation as a suitor for the hand of the Russian Princess. He was a serious young man who had reverted to the piety of his grandmother, Ulrica. The young King was accompanied by his uncle, the Duke of Sudermania, an inexplicable man who concealed his hand so well during the ensuing drama that his part in the development of events remains for ever hidden. He was, like his nephew, an ardent Protestant; but he was also a Freemason and a Martinist, a believer in all the mystical cults of the eighteenth century which the Empress disliked but which her son embraced. Sudermania could not have been as indifferent to his nephew's actions as his outward demeanour indicated. But it is doubtful whether he had any real responsibility for the fiasco of the Empress's plans. Gustav's course was so consistent with his character that no other explanation than native bent seems to be necessary.

Catherine's entertainment of her Swedish guests was regal past all precedent. The Court flowered in a succession of balls and festivities the like of which had not been seen since the first visit of Prince Henry to Russia. Gustav was impeccable as to form. The late King of Sweden, his putative father, had been the glass of fashion, and the son, in spite of his ingrowing piety, bore the mark of Paris. The Grand Dukes Alexander and Constantine seemed uncouth by comparison with this solemn young man whose manners were so meticulously perfect. Gustav was an assiduous reader of the Bible, to which he was accustomed to turn for counsel whenever he found himself in any difficulty. If the Empress had had the advantage of understanding modern psychology, she would have known her

Swedish Prince at once for a repressed youth and an elusive bridegroom. But not having this advantage, she pressed onward to the goal on which she had set her heart and plunged headlong and unprepared into the greatest failure of her life. As she said, she was more than half in love with the young man herself.

The marriage contract was all but signed. Only one point of difference remained to be settled: the future religion of the Princess. Catherine had stipulated that the girl should be allowed to keep her faith, and should be permitted to have her Russian confessor and her Russian chapel in the Swedish palace. The young King demurred. On the surface, all went well. Zubov and Markov, who drew up the contract for the Empress, presented an amiable exterior and the Swedish Prince appeared noncommittal.

It is at this point that Zubov is said to have advised the Empress badly. He is supposed to have induced her to stand out for impossible terms and to be responsible for the bad diplomacy she exhibited on this occasion. It is extremely unlikely that this was true. Zubov was as little responsible for the Empress's attitude as Sudermania was accountable for the King's. In the crisis which developed before the eyes of all the Court, the actual contestants were the seventeen-year-old King and the sixty-seven-year-old Empress. It was a life and death contest. They had joined battle over an issue supremely precious to both of them and neither could endure to lose.

The Empress was extremely romantic about the whole affair. She commanded the young couple to kiss each other in her presence and made airy remarks about wishing to capture the handsome bridegroom for herself. In fancy she re-lived her own betrothal, hoping in Alexandrina's marriage to redeem all the undesirable features of her own. Her granddaughter should have not merely half a dozen chemises but every luxury that a bride could wish, and above all she should be saved the ordeal of changing her religion. No doubt Alexandrina would just as soon have changed her creed as not, but Catherine could not picture this indifference. She had forgotten for the time being that she and her fifteen-year-old granddaughter were not one.

On the evening when the marriage contract was to be signed, the Empress shone like a sun on her throne. She had assembled for the occasion the whole grand world of Petersburg. Church and State surrounded her in her full regalia. The bishops stood at attention, in their embroidered robes covered with pearl and smaragd, while military messengers in bright velvet breeches flashed back and forth and Princesses in wide satin skirts curtsied before the smiling Grandmother on her throne. Thousands of candles shone upon the scene. The hall had been prepared for the bedazzlement of Europe, for the Empress in her imagination faced not merely the eyes of her own courtiers but the eyes of all the Courts of Europe. Whatever happened here was not intended to happen privately.

Slowly there crept into the atmosphere of the room a suggestion of suspense. At moments conversation ceased and the company looked around expectantly. But a glance at the imperturbable figure in the purple mantle and the smiling, confident eyes beneath the diamond crown was sufficient to reassure the company and to restore the atmosphere of ease. The Princess Alexandrina had appeared, but Gustav of Sweden for some unaccountable reason did not. The Russian Court had been accustomed to mysterious delays under the Empress Elizabeth, but Catherine's régime had taught them to expect more promptness and dispatch. But even the Empress Elizabeth expected a bridegroom to be prompt. The time dragged slowly along until at last the tall English clocks showed ten. Still the Empress betrayed no anxiety as she faced the question now apparent in all eyes.

At last Zubov appeared and whispered something in her ear. With difficulty she rose, took his arm, and passed through the room to her own chamber. As the door closed behind her, she fell to the floor unconscious. It is said that she had fainted but it is more probable that she succumbed to a slight stroke of paralysis. Zubov had brought the ultimatum of the King. Gustav would not sign the marriage contract as long as it contained the clause which permitted Alexandrina to retain the Russian religion.

The Empress would not admit herself defeated. To be beaten by a seventeen-year-old boy was unthinkable. She needed a little time to bring the youth round and to overcome a stubbornness which she had underestimated. She arranged a ball, and commanded Alexandrina, who had cried until her eyes were red, to don her finery and go on as if nothing had happened. 'Why do you weep?' she wrote on a scrap of paper. 'What is put off is not lost. Wash your eyes with ice and your ears too, and take Bestushev's drops. Nothing is lost. It is I who was ill yesterday. You are vexed about the delay. That is all.'

Alexandrina obeyed her grandmother. The King also attended the ball. But the two young things no longer met as formerly; the King was punctilious and the Princess was self-conscious, and even Grandmamma was not so gay and airy as she had been. She insisted on keeping the recalcitrant young man two weeks longer and refused to consider the negotiations closed even after he had departed for Stockholm with his uncle. Her hopes died hard.

To the Empress, the shock of defeat was dreadful. She was accustomed to success, and failure of any kind was

unendurable. Almost apologetically she wrote to her son
Paul: 'The fact is the King pretended that Alexandrina
had promised him to change her religion and take the sacrament in the Lutheran way, and that she had given him her
hand on it. . . . She told me with the candour and *naïveté*
natural to her how he had told her that on the coronation
day she would have to take the sacrament with him, and
that she had replied, "Certainly, if I can, and if Grandmamma consents." And after that he spoke to her about
it again, and she always referred him to me. I asked her if
she had given her hand to the King by way of promise on
this point. At that she cried with a sort of instinctive
fright, "Never in my life." '

The Princess Alexandrina wilted like the proverbial
jilted maiden of the village. After her grandmother's
death she was married by her father to a Prince of Austria,
where after a brief unhappy married life she died in childbirth. She was always morbid, spiritless, and complaining.
The instinctive fright of which her grandmother spoke
never left her. All of the Empress's family were lacking in
normal aggressiveness. Her lovers, her son, her grandchildren whom she brought up, were all in some degree
afflicted by the same instinctive fear which the Princess
Alexandrina showed. Catherine the Great, like others of
her kind, did not succeed in imparting greatness to her
descendants.

§ 4

After the Swedish King's departure, the Empress's
health grew worse. There were days when her poor
swollen legs would not support her at all and she suffered
tortures with them. The summer at Czarskoe Selo, where
she was always at her best and happiest, did not help her.
When she walked to the little audience chamber where

she received her ministers, she no longer leaned on Plato
Zubov alone but required an attendant on the other side as
well. She took the air in her wheeled chair along the blue-
walled arcade as far as the agate pavilion and then back
again, not an easy journey for a woman, who, had she not
been the Empress, would have been bedridden. In the
month of August she saw a shooting star and said that it
foretold her death. She had grown suddenly and darkly
superstitious.

Returning to Petersburg in the autumn, she put herself
in the hands of a notorious quack named Lambro-Cazzi-
oni. Her doctors were more astonished than offended.
The Empress who had searched Europe for scientific
physicians, who had brought men like Rogerson, Weik-
ard, and Dimsdale to Russia, and who had introduced
vaccination by offering herself as a subject, had suddenly
gone back to quackery. She closed her doors on all the
reputable doctors and admitted the magician only. Lam-
bro-Cazzioni was a lesser kind of Cagliostro, the charlatan,
whom she had satirized in her comedies and abused in her
correspondence, a breeder of the kind of superstition which
she and other enlightened spirits of her age had lived to
exterminate. Pathetically she submitted to all the drastic
remedies that her healer recommended. A daily foot-bath
of ice-cold sea-water was a part of his régime and he went
himself daily to fetch the water for the patient's use. At
first, the Empress seemed to improve. She appeared at the
little Hermitage again and joined in the gaiety, laughing
until her sides ached.

On the morning of November 6, she rose as usual at six
o'clock, drank her customary five cups of coffee, and set
forth cheerfully on the routine of the day. She saw her
lover and her secretaries, and gave her usual orders. Then
she asked to be left alone for a moment and retired to her

dressing-room. The attendants in the antechamber waited more than the usual length of time for their summons, but it never came. When her private secretary finally entered the apartment, he found her lying unconscious before the door of her water-closet. She had had a stroke of paralysis. They dragged the mattress from the bed and laid the dying woman upon it, for she was too heavy to be lifted. This gasping creature, who had been the Empress, lay on her mattress and struggled with death while the hands of the clock went around three times. The following evening she died.

After Peter the Great, the Romanovs had all been buried in the fortress of Saint Peter and Saint Paul. Catherine had deviated from this custom when she ordered the body of the late Czar, Peter III, to be laid in the Alexander Nevsky monastery at the opposite end of the city. Although it seems strangely out of keeping with her ambitious temperament, she herself did not wish to be buried beside Peter the Great. Four years before her death, she wrote these instructions concerning her burial-place: 'In case I should die in Czarskoe Selo, lay my body in the churchyard of Sofia. If in the city of Petersburg, in the cathedral or the burial church of the Nevsky Cloister. If in Pella, bring me along the waterways to the Nevsky Cloister. If in Moscow, bring me to the Donsky Cloister or to the town churchyard near by. If in Peterhof, to the Sergei Cloister. If in some other place, to a churchyard near by.

'The coffin shall be borne by horse guards only and no one else. My body shall be clad in a white dress, with a golden crown on the head on which my name shall be written. Mourning shall be worn for six months but not longer; a little is best. After the first six weeks, the people's amusements shall be resumed. After the burial betrothals, weddings, and music shall be allowed.

'My library with all my manuscripts and all my papers, I bequeath to my dear grandson, Alexander Pavlovich; likewise my jewels; and I bless him from my heart and from my soul. A copy of this shall be put away in a safe place to insure its fulfilment, so that sooner or later shame and disgrace shall overtake those who do not carry out my will.

'It is my intention to place Constantine on the throne of the Greek Oriental Empire. For the welfare of the Russian and Greek Empires, I recommend that the Princes of Württemberg be removed from the counsels of these empires which should have as little to do with them as possible; also that the two half-Germans shall be removed.'

The Empress was buried in the Cathedral of Saint Peter and Saint Paul beneath a white marble slab like that which covers each Czar of Russia who followed Peter the Great. Beside her lies the body of Peter III, brought there by her son a short time after her burial.

She had prepared an inscription for her gravestone and this is what she wished to have said:

Here lies

CATHERINE THE SECOND

born in Stettin on April 21/May 2, 1729.

In the year 1744 she went to Russia to marry Peter III. At the age of fourteen, she made the threefold resolution, to please her consort, Elizabeth, and the Nation.

She neglected nothing in order to succeed in this.

Eighteen years of boredom and solitude caused her to read many books.

When she ascended the throne of Russia, she wished to do good and tried to bring happiness, freedom and prosperity to her subjects.

She forgave easily and hated no one.

She was good-natured, easy-going; was of a cheerful temperament, republican sentiments, and a kind heart.

She had friends.

Work came easy to her; she loved sociability and the arts.

The instructions of the Empress were not followed; her wishes not obeyed. The cold white slab which covers her conveys no word of her last message to posterity.

Adadurov, 140

Adolph Friedrich of Holstein, 58

Alembert, J. R. d', 259

Alexander, Grand Duke, later Alexander I, 250, 268, 272–274, 281–282

Alexandrina, Princess, 294, 301–306

Alexis Michaelovich, 46, 205

Alexis Petrovich, 44, 54

Anna Ivanovna, Empress of Russia, 50, 52, 98

Anna Leopoldovna, 51, 52, 104, 161

Anna Petrovna, 20, 51

Anthony Ulrich of Brunswick, 51, 57

Apraxin, General, 139–144

Arsenii of Rostov, 297

August the Strong, 131

Babet, nickname of Elizabeth Cardel, 31

Bariatinsky, Prince Feodor, 164, 170, 171, 172, 295

Bergholz, 170

Bestushev, 60, 77, 93, 112, 133, 140, 177

Bibikov, 163, 208

Bilbassov, 57, 141, 142, 153, 189, 249

Bjelke, Madame, 202

Bobrinsky, Alexis Gregorevich, 157, 257

Bolhagen, 29

Branicky, Countess, 233, 239, 254

Brockdorf, Herr, 126, 128

Bruce, Countess, 202, 226

Brückner, 166, 220, 264

Brümmer, 61, 67, 69, 170

Burgoyne, General, 269

Cagliostro, 284

Cardel, Elizabeth, 31–35, 40, 272

Catherine I, 46, 50, 52, 55

Catherine II, the Great,
Baptized SophieAuguste Friedrike [F i k e], Princess of Zerbst, 18

Birth, 17

Education, 29 ff

Childhood, 38 ff

Meeting with Frederick the Great, 71

Journey to Russia, 70–76

Arrival in Russia, 76

Conversion to Greek faith, 84–85

Enters the Greek Church, 87–89

Index

Catherine the Great (*contd.*)

Sophie Auguste Friedrike becomes Catherine Alexeievna, 87

Marriage, 98–102

Relation to Saltikov, 118

Gives birth to an heir, 120

Relations with Peter III, 126, 129

Birth of Grand Duchess Anna, 136

Complicity in the Apraxin affair, 139–144

Birth of Bobrinsky, 157

Manifesto of 1762, 166

Revolution of 1762, 158–176

Coronation, 179–180

Foreign Policy, 176, 188, 190, 205

Manifesto of Silence, 183

Partition of Poland, 191–199

Census of Russia, 199–201

Reign, 201

Reforms affecting women, 202–205

Foundling Hospital, 203

Domestic Policy, 205–209

Instruction for a Code of Laws, 205–208

Catherine the Great (*contd.*)

Attitude towards serfdom, 208

Campaign against smallpox, 209–214

Crimean journey, 239–241

Acquisition of Crimea, 241–243

The French Revolution, 242, 297–300

Pugachev's Rebellion, 298

Turkish Wars, 242–249

Favourites, 223–229, 249–252

Relation with Poniatovsky, 132–138

Attempted marriage with Orlov, 180–184

Relation with Potiomkin, 229–242

Relation with Zubov, 288–295

Birth of Grandsons, 268

Education of Grandsons, 269–287

Writings, 280–286

Comedies, 282–283

Failure of the Swedish Marriage, 300–306

Death, 307–309

Charles XII of Sweden, 15

Chernichev, Andrei, 249

Index

Chétardie, 94

Chitrovo, 182

Choglokov, Maria, 107, 116, 118, 228

Choiseul, 188

Christian August, Prince of Anhalt-Zerbst, 12–14, 27, 36, 73, 80–83, 91, 113

Constantine, Grand Duke, 270, 272

Courland, 28, 190

Crimean journey, 239–242

Czarskoe Selo, 103, 214, 261; 291

Czartorisky, Adam, 193

Dashkov, Countess Catherine, 152, 159, 167, 202, 235

Dashkov, Prince, 288, 290

Diderot, 176, 225, 292

Dimsdale, Dr. Thomas, 210, 307

Elizabeth Petrovna, Empress of Russia, 52 ff
    Birth, 52
    Revolution of 1741, 56–60
    Relations with Princess of Zerbst, 63, 91–93, 148

Appearance, 79

Death, 149–150

Eudoxia, First Wife of Peter the Great, 46

Fike, nickname of Sophie Auguste Friedrike, later Catherine the Great, 18

Fokshani, Congress of, 215, 244

Fraigne, Marquis de, 145

Frederick the Great, 21, 36, 65, 69, 71, 82, 95, 96, 128, 131, 146, 191–199, 210, 219, 262

Frederick William I, 11, 38

Friedrich August, Prince of Anhalt-Zerbst, 18, 145

Gatchina, 215, 268

George of Holstein, 68, 155, 162, 167, 234

Godunov, Boris, 44

Granovitaya Palata, 180

Grimm, 220, 256, 263, 281, 292

Gustav III of Sweden, 248, 301

Gustav IV of Sweden, 301

Gyllenborg, Count, 30

Hedwig Sophie, Provost of Quedlinburg, 22
Henri IV, 87, 223
Henry, Prince, of Prussia, 21, 196, 197, 198, 233, 261, 264–266, 300
Hermitage, The Little, 294
Homburg, 19

Ivan the Terrible, 44
Ivan VI, Ivanushka, 20, 156, 161, 297, 298

Jan Casimir, King of Poland, 192
Johann Ludwig, Prince of Anhalt-Zerbst, 12
Johanna Elizabeth,Princess of Anhalt-Zerbst, 63
Johanna Elizabeth, Princess of Holstein-Gottorp, 14–17, 25, 26, 70, 73, 78, 92, 144–148
Jones, John Paul, 247

Karl Peter Ulrich, Duke of Holstein, later Grand Duke Peter Feodorovich, *see* Peter III
Kayserling, Count, 192
Khayn, Fräulein, Lady-in-Waiting to the Princess of Zerbst, 24, 67

Kiev, 90
Kolmogory, 104
Kolomenskoe Palace, 53, 207
Kosciuszko, 198
Krasnoe Selo, 104
Kremlin, 46, 156, 179, 212, 218
Kruse, Madame, 101, 109, 114
Kutchuk-Kainardi, Peace of, 245

Lanskoy, 231, 251, 252
Lebrun, Madame Vigée, 292
Lestocq, 55, 57, 66, 92, 95, 114
Lieven, Madame von, 296
Ligne, Prince de, 238
Luther, Martin, 11, 21, 36

Machiavelli, 190
Mamonov, 230, 231, 250
Mardefeld, 63, 85, 93
Maria Theresa, Empress of Austria, 55, 120, 191, 196, 198
Marie Feodorovna, Grand Duchess, 267–268, 270
Masson, Major, 49, 202, 204, 274

Index

Mengden, Julie von, 52, 104

Menshikov, 44, 46, 47

Mirovich, 298

Molière, 40, 282

Monplaisir, 162, 168

Montesquieu, 205

Morals in Russia, 47–50

Moscow, 186, 211

Narishkin, Leo, 294, 299

Narishkin, Natalie, 46

Natalie Alexeievna, Grand Duchess, 263

Nicholas, Grand Duke, later Nicholas I, 275

Oranienbaum, 111, 132, 170

Orlov, Alexis, 162, 163, 170, 171–174, 181, 216, 279

Orlov, Gregory, 149, 159, 163, 164, 180, 187, 206, 208, 210, 213–217, 231, 287

Panin, Nikita, 60, 160, 165, 170, 178, 182, 206, 258, 260

Partition of Poland, 190–199

Passeck, 163, 172

Paul I,
Birth, 118–119
Appearance, 122, 256, 283
Infancy, 124
Health, 178
Baptized Peter Feodoro-vich, 118
First Marriage, 261–264
Second Marriage, 267–268
Melancholia, 275–280
Journey through Europe, 276–277
Mysticism, 278
Conspiracy against his life, 219
Death, 279

Pavlovsk, 268, 270

Peter Feodorovich, Grand Duke, see Peter III

Peter I, the Great, 11, 15, 44, 45, 46, 50, 53, 84, 186, 201, 243

Peter II, 52

Peter III,
Birth, 16
Baptized Karl Peter Ul-rich, Duke of Hol-stein, 20, 58
Education, 60–62
Karl Peter Ulrich, Duke of Holstein becomes

Peter III (*contd.*)

    Peter Feodorovich, Grand Duke of Russia, 58

    Marriage, 100–102

    Relations with Catherine the Great, 97, 126, 129, 151, 157

    Folie militaire, 127, 154

    Government of Holstein, 130

    Accession, 151

    Reign, 154–156, 176

    Deposition, 168–175

    Death, 176

Petersburg, 185

Poniatovsky, Stanislas, King of Poland, 128, 132–143, 177, 192–199, 228

Potiomkin, Gregory, Prince of Tauris, 187, 227, 229–249, 252–255, 289

Potiomkin Villages, 238

Prascovia Feodorovna, 155

Prascovia Nikitichna Vladislav, 114

Prinzen, Baroness von, 70

Protassov, Countess, 202, 226

Pugachev, 298–299

Rasin, Stenka, 298

Razumovsky, Alexis, 92, 117, 125, 181

Razumovsky, Cyril, 125, 159, 164

Reformation, The, 21, 35

Religion in Russia, 48, 90

Repnin, Prince, 249, 296

Ribas, Admiral, 257

Rimsky-Korsakov, 250

Rogerson, Dr. John, 226, 307

Romanov, House of, 44

Ropsha, 171

Rumiantsov, General, 244, 246

Rurik, House of, 44

Saltikov, Sergei, 118–122, 124, 125, 176, 228

Schlözer, 191

Seven Years' War, 95, 139

Sheremetiev, Count, 151, 179, 187

Shuvalov, Alexander, 140

Shuvalov, Ivan Ivanovich, 118, 119, 133, 148

Smolny, 203

Sophie Alexeievna, 46

Sophie Auguste Friedrike, *see* Catherine the Great

Sophie Christine, Canoness of Gandersheim, 13, 22, 23

Stehlin, 61, 66, 127, 168
Stettin, 11, 26
Streltsi, The, 46
Stroganov, Count, 158,187
Suvarov, General, 233, 246, 296
Sylvester, the Monk, 44

Tchesme, Battle of, 215
Todorsky, Simon, 85, 87
Treaty of Westminster,133
Troitsky Monastery, 89, 94, 180
Troubetsky, Prince, 168, 178
Turkish Wars, 242–249

Ulrica, Princess of Prussia, later Queen of Sweden, 65, 248, 301, 302
Uspensky Cathedral, 179

Vassilchikov, 215, 227,245

Viazemsky, 208, 220
Voltaire, 188, 189, 203–204, 209, 210, 221, 243, 259, 281, 287
Vorontsov, Elizabeth, 137, 144, 152, 153, 160, 167

Wagner, Pastor, 19, 31, 32, 36–38, 85, 90
Williams, Sir Charles Hanbury, 131–138, 177, 189

Yermalov, 231, 250, 252

Zavadovsky, 231, 296
Zoritch, 231, 250
Zubov, Plato, 231, 250, 255, 279, 288, 290, 292, 293, 294, 295, 303, 305
Zubov, Valerian, 279, 293

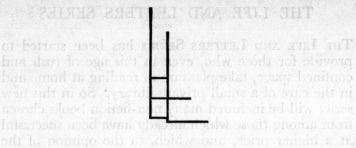

THE LIFE AND LETTERS
SERIES

A series of memorable
books in General
Literature now re-
issued in a uniform
format and at the
price of
**FOUR SHILLINGS
& SIXPENCE** *net,*

THE LIFE AND LETTERS SERIES

THE LIFE AND LETTERS SERIES has been started to provide for those who, even in this age of rush and confined space, take pleasure in reading at home and in the care of a small private library. So in this new series will be included many non-fiction books chosen from among those which already have been successful at a higher price, and which, in the opinion of the publishers, may continue to be of interest to the public for many years to come.

With the idea of the private library in view, the publishers have been careful to keep these books slim, and yet to give them that extra height and breadth which lends elegance to the appearance of a book, and makes for the comfort of the reader by permitting the use of more generous and ample margins. A special colour and quality of cloth has been manufactured for the series. The paper is thin, yet opaque. The binding carries gold lettering with a design on the back, and also on the front. Most of the books contain illustrations; many are very fully illustrated.

As for the price, a series designed for the modest library must be inexpensive, for those with fastidious tastes frequently have short purses. By manufacturing the books in very large editions, possible because of their proved merit and permanent value, the publishers have been able to issue them at the very modest price of 4s. 6d. net.

JONATHAN CAPE
30 BEDFORD SQUARE
LONDON

Anthony, Katherine

CATHERINE THE GREAT   *No.* 13

With a Frontispiece.

This lively and well-written study is a judicious treatment of a temperament and a reputation, and the whole book is a 'contribution to the study, not only of Catherine the Great, but of a significant period in Russian history.' *Time and Tide.*

Bercovici, Konrad

THE STORY OF THE GYPSIES   *No.* 11

Illustrations from photographs by E. O. Hoppé.

'The mystery of the origin of the race (of gypsies) and their language, their achievement of happiness without civilisation, the wild romanticism of their complete denial of our ethical and social values, act like a mixture of opium and the "Hungarian Rhapsodies" upon civilised brains and entice them into wild extravagances.' *Statesman.*

Cummings, E. E.

THE ENORMOUS ROOM   *No.* 2

With a frontispiece portrait of the author.

With an introduction by Robert Graves.

'Colonel Lawrence' wrote to the introducer: 'I call it (*The Enormous Room*) one of the very best of war books.'

'He reveals himself as a man of sensibility and fortitude, and he writes always with such good taste that I do not think anyone reading his book, could feel otherwise than that it is the work of a rare, fine spirit.' *Sunday Times.*

Davies, W. H.

THE AUTOBIOGRAPHY OF A SUPER-TRAMP
No. 6

With 4 portraits of the Author, and an Introduction by George Bernard Shaw.

'I recommend this most remarkable Autobiography of a Super-Tramp to your special attention.' GEORGE BERNARD SHAW.

Printed as it was written, it is worth reading for its literary style alone. The author tells us with inimitable quiet modesty of how he begged and stole his way across America and through England and Wales.

De Kruif, Paul

MICROBE HUNTERS
No. 3

Illustrated by 4 portraits.

This book captures for the reader something of the intellectual excitement and romance associated with the works of the greater scientists. In the words of *The Times*, 'Mr. De Kruif is an ardent and vivid writer . . . with a marked gift of dramatic presentation.' . . .

Horn, Alfred Aloysius

TRADER HORN (The Ivory Coast in the Earlies)
No. 4

Edited by Ethelreda Lewis.

Illustrated by half tones.

'This is a gorgeous book, more full of sheer stingo than any you are likely to come across in a day's march among the bookshops of wherever you may be. Nothing more racy and full of original wisdom than the conversations at the end of each chapter has come my way for an age.' From Mr. John Galsworthy's Introduction.

Lubbock, Percy

EARLHAM   *No.* 7

With a Frontispiece of the Hall.

'The book seems too intimate to be reviewed. We
want to be allowed to read it, and to dream over it,
and keep silence about it. His judgment is perfect,
his humour is true and ready; his touch light and
prim; his prose is exact and clean and full of music.'
Times.

Ludwig, Emil

GENIUS AND CHARACTER   *No.* 9

Illustrated by sixteen half tones.

'As in his longer biographies, it is the dramatic
values of motive and action he seeks, the flashes of
illumination in the chiaroscuro investing a lonely
figure. This is not a ponderous book; it is a series
of vivacious and sometimes very moving studies. It
reminds us of much that we had forgotten, and intro-
duces us to some people who were but hearsay before.'
The Spectator.

Mayo, Katherine

MOTHER INDIA   *No.* 5

Illustrated by half tones.

'It is certainly the most fascinating, the most depress-
ing, and at the same time the most important and
truthful book that has been written about India for a
good deal more than a generation. To say that is,
no doubt, to say a great deal, but it is not to say too
much. Miss Mayo can observe accurately, can understand without prejudice, and can write; a combination of faculties that is unfortunately very rare. Her
book is very heavily documented, almost every statement is a quotation from an authority, yet it remains
continually readable. Her book may have very
important consequences.' *New Statesman.*

Muir, Edwin

JOHN KNOX

No. 12

Illustrated by 4 portraits.

The Times says of this book that it is 'a fascinating piece of writing,' while the *Glasgow Herald* says that 'this study of Knox is an important contribution to the work of revaluing Scottish life and letters now under way.'

The study is not concerned with the truth or the falsehood of Calvinism, but rather presents the Calvinist in all his multifarious activities from the greatest to the most trifling, and shows his creed working out, here in heroic and there in ridiculous form. We would remind the reader that this historical study inevitably deals with Mary Queen of Scots.

Niles, Blair

CONDEMNED TO DEVIL'S ISLAND

No. 10

Illustrated from drawings by Beth Krebs Morris.

An account of one of the most wretched and unhappy places on the globe. Mrs. Blair Niles is the first woman to have been allowed to visit the most notorious Devil's Island since it became a penal colony. She describes this penal settlement in the person of a young French burglar, and tells an almost unbearable tale of thousands of men starved of hope and leisure.

Shand, P. Morton

A BOOK OF FOOD

No. 8

Dr. Johnson said: 'Most people have a foolish way of not minding or not pretending to mind, what they eat. For my own part I mind my belly most studiously and very carefully; for I look upon it that he who does not mind his belly will hardly mind anything else.'

'But, when one takes this book as a whole, one may fairly say of it what bar-tenders sometimes say of their own special (generally their most expensive) cocktails, that it would create an appetite for a brass monkey. It contains admirable things. . . . This is the book for everyone who loves the art, whether as a creator or merely as a connoisseur. . . .' *Saturday Review.*

Siegfried, André

AMERICA COMES OF AGE

No. 1

A French Analysis.

Illustrated by 8 maps and diagrams.

Translated from the French by H. H. Hemming and Doris Hemming.

A study of the United States at the present day in its economic and psychological aspects.

'Every intelligent person ought to read André Siegfried's *America Comes of Age*. It is a brilliant study of the most important, and in some ways the most interesting, though certainly not the loveliest, nation on earth.' W. R. Inge.

M. Siegfried has devoted himself for over thirty years to the study and teaching of political science. The development of the British Empire has been a subject on which he has specialised, and to obtain first-hand information he has not only lived in Great Britain from time to time, but he has also visited most of the Dominions. He has also travelled widely in America, visiting the United States on five or six different occasions.

Sullivan, J. W. N.

BEETHOVEN, His spiritual development.   *No.* 15

Illustrated.

'Few men are better qualified to write a study of Beethoven than Mr. J. W. N. Sullivan. He is a curious blend of scientist and musician; . . .' *The Spectator.*

'It is a striking merit of Mr. Sullivan's book that it explains Beethoven to the unmusical philosopher.' *The New Statesman.*

'. . . the courage of its opening chapters, in which he re-asserts the claim of music . . . to have a bearing upon the nature of reality.' Mary Agnes Hamilton in *Time and Tide.*

Williams-Ellis, C. & A.

THE PLEASURES OF ARCHITECTURE *No.* 14

Profusely illustrated.

The distinguished authors of this standard work have for some time been very valiant champions of England's green and pleasant land, and this book, illustrated by many line blocks in the text and sixteen pages of half-tone, will bring enlightenment and entertainment to those who like a well-built house or office block when they see it, but are not quite sure as to the reasons why they like it.

'For instance, there is a good chapter on plans, comparing a modern house with a French château (where the joint came in smoking through a series of state bedrooms); and the account of living English architects (letters A, B, and so on) is quite brilliant.' *Manchester Guardian.*